Praise for
Unstable Majorities

In *Unstable Majorities* Fiorina makes a series of very important arguments about the American electoral process and the role of the public in it. Although completed not long after the election, Fiorina is able to offer early wisdom about the Trump election and the Trump era. The public, he demonstrates, has long been and continues to be basically moderate in its ideological and policy views. The public votes with high degrees of consistency in large part because the parties so consistently select the same kinds of candidates—liberal Democrats facing off against conservative Republicans. Given the same alternatives, the public tends to vote the same from election to election. Trump's victory, in his view, was essentially continuous with the series of elections in the twenty-first century. In net, only a small proportion of the electorate changed its choices from 2012 to 2016. It is the nature of simple majority rule that, in reasonably close contests, yields the vast changes we observe, such as between Trump and Obama.

—**John Aldrich**, *Pfizer-Pratt University Professor of Political Science, Duke University*

In this impassioned yet scholarly book Fiorina explores the instability that has resulted in recent American politics, as a generally moderate and conflicted electorate has been forced to choose among options served up to them by increasingly polarized political parties and activists. The paradox is that voters increasingly follow the party line but that political outcomes have become wildly oscillating and unpredictable. As Fiorina explains we can only understand voters in the context of the choices they face.

—**Andrew Gelman**, *Professor, Department of Statistics and Department of Political Science, Columbia University*

Few, if any, write as clearly and persuasively about politics as Mo Fiorina. Many will pick up this book thinking that polarization in the electorate is as obvious as the fact that the sun rises in the east, but they will immediately find themselves on their heels. Excellent scholarship causes us to question what we were sure was true, and no one causes us to do that as reliably as Fiorina.

—Marc J. Hetherington, *Vanderbilt University*

Once again Mo Fiorina shows us how institutions matter by reminding readers that voters are only as good as the choices in front of them. The implication in the wake of the 2016 presidential election is important: voters haven't failed democracy, party leaders have failed voters. To rehabilitate the reputation of voters in America, political elites must recruit and nominate candidates worthy of being chosen who, once elected, may actually reflect the positions of most voters—near the middle. *Unstable Majorities* is a classic Fiorina antidote to the hysteria of cable news and the panic among those who tend only to talk to others just like themselves.

—Lynn Vavreck, PhD, *UCLA Political Science & Communication Studies*

Here Fiorina zeroes in on the most significant and distinctive features of the contemporary US political landscape: tenuous party control of government, nationalized elections, and dissatisfied voters. The book is highly readable, rich with insight, packed with concise figures and data, and likely to interest broad audiences inside and outside academia.

—Frances Lee, *University of Maryland*

Are Americans and their political parties highly polarized? Fiorina set off a great debate over this question in *Culture Wars?* Now, after an intervening decade of turbulent politics, he revisits the question in *Unstable Majorities*. Whether or not you arrive at the same answers about polarization that he does, his thought-provoking analysis is must reading for anyone seriously interested in American politics.

—James E. Campbell, *author of Polarized: Making Sense of a Divided America.*

UNSTABLE
MAJORITIES

UNSTABLE MAJORITIES

Polarization, Party Sorting, and Political Stalemate

Morris P. Fiorina

HOOVER INSTITUTION PRESS

STANFORD UNIVERSITY   STANFORD, CALIFORNIA

www.hoover.org

Hoover Institution Press Publication No. 685

Hoover Institution at Leland Stanford Junior University,
Stanford, California 94305-6003

First printing 2017
23 22 21 20 19 18 17   7 6 5 4 3 2 1

Manufactured in the United States of America

The paper used in this publication meets the minimum Requirements of
the American National Standard for Information Sciences—Permanence of
Paper for Printed Library Materials, ANSI/NISO Z39.48-1992. ∞

Cataloging-in-Publication Data is available from the Library of Congress.
ISBN: 978-0-8179-2115-6 (pbk. : alk. paper)
ISBN: 978-0-8179-2116-3 (epub)
ISBN: 978-0-8179-2117-0 (mobi)
ISBN: 978-0-8179-2118-7 (PDF)

To George P. Shultz,
American statesman,
in appreciation of his support.

Contents

List of Figures and Tables

Figures

Tables

Preface

In the spring of 2003, I began to outline an article on then contemporary American public opinion. Unlike most of my writing over the preceding three decades, that effort reflected more than the usual "academic" concern, namely, that in its coverage of contemporary politics the national media were "hurting America," as Jon Stewart would put it sometime later.[1] The media had accepted a toxic narrative promoted by numerous pundits and politicos. According to the narrative, red-state and blue-state residents were combatants in a culture war. The political middle had vanished as our country split into a so-called 50–50 nation. The United States of America had become the Divided States of America, "Two Nations Under God."[2] Party and issue activists promoted the narrative for their own reasons (fund-raising and membership-maximizing among other things). Because the narrative nicely fit the media's concept of newsworthiness—division, conflict, battles, and war—it had become the dominant frame through which to interpret American elections.[3]

1. Jon Stewart, interview by Tucker Carlson and Paul Begala, *Crossfire*, CNN, October 15, 2004, http://mediamatters.org/research/2004/10/15/jon-stewart-on-crossfire-stop-stop-stop-stop-hu/132095.

2. For citations to these and other similar claims, see Morris Fiorina, with Samuel Abrams and Jeremy Pope, *Culture War? The Myth of a Polarized America*, 2nd ed., chap. 1 (New York: Pearson-Longman, 2005).

3. On the increasing use of the polarization frame in the mass media, see Matthew Levendusky and Neil Malhotra, "Does Media Coverage of Partisan Polarization Affect Political Attitudes?" *Political Communication* 33, no. 2 (2016): 283–301, figure 1.

The problem was that scholars who studied public opinion could produce little systematic evidence that supported the narrative. In common parlance, polarization implies that the extremes gain at the expense of the middle. So, if polarization is defined in ideological terms, we would expect to find self-identified moderates in decline while avowed liberals and conservatives were on the rise. But the data indicated that the proportion of moderates had changed little, if at all, during the course of the past four decades. In the early 2000s, "moderate" was the modal position in the United States, just as it had been in 1976 when moderate Republican Gerald Ford ran against born-again Democrat Jimmy Carter, long before anyone had heard of an American culture war. Similarly, if polarization is defined in partisan terms, we would expect to find the proportion of political independents diminishing as they joined the ranks of Democrats and Republicans. But on the contrary, in recent decades the proportion of self-identified independents had risen, not fallen. And in the states, analysts pointed out that the proportion of citizens registering to vote as independent or "decline to state" had sharply increased, not decreased.[4]

Finally, if polarization is defined by reference to the positions held by Americans on specific matters of public policy, the picture was again the same. Even on so-called hot-button issues like abortion, Americans continued to favor something "in between" the positions of the parties. There was no evidence that they had abandoned the middle and moved toward the policy poles. In particular, colorful but unrepresentative media case studies had greatly exaggerated the differences between the residents of red and blue states.[5] Public opinion data indicated that majorities in red and blue states were nearly always on the same side of issues, although the size of these majorities generally differed.

The planned article expanded into a short book, *Culture War? The Myth of a Polarized America,* published in the early summer

---

4. Eric McGhee and Daniel Krimm, "Party Registration and the Geography of Party Polarization," *Polity* 41, no. 3 (July 2009): 345–367.

5. E.g., Jill Lawrence, "One Nation, Divided," *USA Today,* February 18, 2002.

of 2004.[6] The findings and arguments in the book met with skepticism by some members of the Washington-based commentariat, but there has been little by way of serious political science critique of the *findings* in *Culture War*.[7] The reason is that the discussion in the book was based on a survey of publicly available data that had not been selected, recoded, or otherwise transformed to support a case. Any undergraduate political science major can replicate the findings reported in the book. *Interpretations* of findings can differ, of course. Is a difference between groups big or little? Is a temporal change significant or not? Such differences in interpretations and evaluations are perfectly legitimate, but the data in the tables and figures that generate them are facts, not opinions.

I believe that a major reason that much political punditry has gone off track in recent years is its tendency to focus on the attitudes and behavior of ordinary citizens while overlooking the political context in which these citizens are operating. In normal times, voters are responders, not initiators, in the political process. They react to what parties and candidates do. Importantly, they can only choose between the candidates the parties nominate. If voters increasingly vote the same way for president, senator, US representative, and state legislator, it may indicate that the voters have become more partisan. But an alternative interpretation is that parties today are much better *sorted* on policy and ideology than they were prior to the 1980s.[8] Today's sorted parties increasingly offer voters a choice between a liberal Democrat and a conservative Republican for every office, so there is not as much reason for voters to split their tickets as there was in earlier decades when the parties were more heterogeneous.

6. Fiorina, et al., *Culture War?* A second edition appeared after the elections that fall and a third edition after the 2008 elections.

7. To our knowledge, the principal exception is the critique by Alan I. Abramowitz and Kyle L. Saunders, "Is Polarization a Myth?" *Journal of Politics* 70, no. 2 (April 2008): 542–555, which illustrates several of the misconceptions I discuss in the chapters that follow. For a response, see Morris P. Fiorina, Samuel J. Abrams, and Jeremy C. Pope, "Polarization in the American Public: Misconceptions and Misreadings," *Journal of Politics* 70, no. 2 (April 2008): 556–560.

8. Matthew Levendusky, *The Partisan Sort: How Liberals Became Democrats and Conservatives Became Republicans* (Chicago: University of Chicago Press, 2009).

Similarly, if each party nominates a nearly identical candidate from one election to the next, there is little reason to expect voters to change their votes from one election to the next, other things being equal. Democrats Al Gore in 2000 and John Kerry in 2004 received virtually identical percentages of the popular vote. In contrast, the difference between the popular vote for Democrats George McGovern in 1972 and Jimmy Carter in 1976 was 12.6 percentage points. Does this significant difference between the 1970s and the 2000s mean that "swing voters" had disappeared and the country was much more set in its partisan ways in the 2000s than in the 1970s? Possibly, but it would be crazy to ignore the fact that Al Gore and John Kerry were much more similar to each other than were George McGovern and Jimmy Carter. That Carter won the presidency four years after McGovern lost in a landslide may not mean that the voters were less partisan in the 1970s (although they may have been), but only that they had very different alternatives to choose from than voters do today when most Democratic candidates look pretty much the same, as do most Republicans.

In the long decade since the publication of *Culture War,* political journalists have carried on a lively debate about the state of the American electorate and social scientists have produced a great deal of new research on questions raised in that debate. I have actively participated in that discussion, contributing another book, numerous short articles and op-eds, and dozens of presentations and lectures. As the 2016 election season approached, it seemed like an appropriate time to summarize and synthesize what we have learned in the past decade, to address several important misunderstandings that persist, and to examine the contemporary American electorate as it elected another president and Congress.

Chapters 1–9 were originally posted as essays on the Hoover Institution website between Labor Day and the November elections. They have been slightly revised and updated. Chapters 10–12 were written in the spring and early summer of 2017 after I had some time to digest the election results.

This book draws on the work of many people who have contributed to a very active and progressive research program. In particular, I thank my local colleagues Douglas Ahler, Shanto Iyengar,

Doug Rivers, Paul Sniderman, and Guarav Sood, whose questions forced me to sharpen the arguments, and David Brady for almost daily conversations about the matters covered in the pages that follow. Thanks also to John Aldrich, Paul Beck, Bruce Cain, and Sandy Maisel, who read and commented on earlier versions of the essays. Questions by Eileen Burgin, James Campbell, and participants at numerous seminars helped improve the discussion.

Morris P. Fiorina
Stanford, California
June 2017

CHAPTER I

An Era of Tenuous Majorities

The United States is one of a minority of world democracies that elect their chief executives independently of the legislature. The United States is even more unusual in having two equally powerful chambers of the legislature, separately elected for different terms of office. Moreover, as British analyst Anthony King notes, the two-year term of members of the US House of Representatives is the shortest among world democracies, where terms of four to five years are common.[1] Putting all this together, a US national election every two years can generate any one of eight patterns of institutional control of the presidency, House, and Senate (D=Democratic, R=Republican):

1. RRR
2. RDR
3. RRD
4. RDD
5. DDD
6. DRD
7. DDR
8. DRR

The 2004 elections generated pattern 1, unified Republican control under President George W. Bush, but the Democrats captured

This chapter extends an argument first outlined in Morris P. Fiorina, "America's Missing Moderates," *The American Interest* 8, no. 4 (March/April 2013): 58–67.

1. Anthony King, *Running Scared: Why America's Politicians Campaign Too Much and Govern Too Little* (New York: Free Press, 1997).

both houses of Congress two years later, moving the country to pattern 4. The 2008 elections generated pattern 5, unified Democratic control under President Barack Obama, but the Republicans took back the House in 2010, moving the country to pattern 6, and the Senate in 2014, moving the country to pattern 8. Donald Trump's election in 2016 completed the circle, moving the country back to pattern 1.

Although an election can produce any of these eight patterns of party control, elections are not independent events like coin tosses; rather, they reflect underlying cleavages that tend to persist over time. Thus, elections in any historical period tend to produce only a few patterns of control. Consider the period known to political historians as the Third Party System. After the devastating depression of the mid-1890s, the Republicans captured the presidency and both chambers of Congress in 1896: see pattern 1, RRR. They retained full control through the next six elections, fourteen consecutive years in all. A split between progressive and conservative factions of the Republican Party enabled the Democrats to capture the House of Representatives in the 1910 midterm elections and to elect Democrat Woodrow Wilson in 1912 and reelect him in 1916. But the Republicans regained unified control in 1920 and maintained it for the next four elections. As table 1.1 summarizes, the Republicans enjoyed full control of the federal government for twenty-four of the thirty-four years between the 1896 and 1930 elections; the seventeen elections held during that period produced only four patterns of institutional control.

Following the stock market crash of 1929 and the onset of the Great Depression, the Republicans lost the House in the elections of 1930 and then all three elective institutions in 1932.[2] Like the McKinley Republicans, the New Deal Democrats enjoyed full control for fourteen consecutive years, until they lost Congress in the election of 1946. But they recaptured Congress two years later when Harry Truman was elected in his own right and they held it until 1952. As table 1.2 summarizes, the Democrats controlled all three

2. The Republicans actually came out of the November 1930 general election with a one-seat majority in the House, but by the time the new Congress convened, special elections had given a narrow majority to the Democrats.

TABLE 1.1. **An Era of Republican Majorities**

	President	House	Senate
1896	R	R	R
1898	R	R	R
1900	R	R	R
1902	R	R	R
1904	R	R	R
1906	R	R	R
1908	R	R	R
1910	R	D	R
1912	D	D	D
1914	D	D	D
1916	D	D	D
1918	D	R	R
1920	R	R	R
1922	R	R	R
1924	R	R	R
1926	R	R	R
1928	R	R	R
1930	R	R/D	Tie

TABLE 1.2. **An Era of Democratic Majorities**

	President	House	Senate
1932	D	D	D
1934	D	D	D
1936	D	D	D
1938	D	D	D
1940	D	D	D
1942	D	D	D
1944	D	D	D
1946	D	R	R
1948	D	D	D
1950	D	D	D
1952	R	R	R

elective branches for eighteen of the twenty years between the 1932 and 1952 elections; nine out of ten elections produced the same pattern of institutional control.

The Republicans under Dwight Eisenhower captured all three branches in 1952 but lost Congress to the Democrats in 1954. So

began an era of divided government.[3] Although losing control of
Congress in the off-year elections was nothing new historically, the
1956 election that followed was. For the first time in American history, the popular vote winner in a two-way presidential race failed to
carry the House; only in 1880 had such a winner failed to carry the
Senate.[4] An interlude of unified Democratic control occurred from
1960 until 1968,[5] but the 1968 election marked a resumption of the
pattern first observed in the 1950s, when split control of the presidency
and Congress became the norm. As table 1.3 summarizes, between
1954 and 1992 thirteen of twenty elections resulted in split control
of the presidency and at least one chamber of Congress; after 1968,
only four years of unified control during the Carter presidency inter-
rupted what otherwise would have been a twenty-four-year pattern
of divided party control under a Republican president. Significantly,
however, while government control usually was split during this
forty-year period, institutional control remained relatively stable.
The Democrats controlled the House throughout the period and the
Senate for all but six years. Meanwhile, the Republicans won the
presidency seven times in ten tries, including three by landslides, with
only a narrow victory by Jimmy Carter in 1976 interrupting what
might well have been a string of six consecutive Republican victories.[6]

3. For a more detailed discussion of this period, see Morris Fiorina, *Divided
Government*, chap. 2 (New York: Macmillan, 1992).

4. In the three-way election of 1848, former Democratic president Martin Van
Buren ran on the Free Soil ticket, enabling Whig Zachary Taylor to narrowly win
the presidency while the Democrats won both chambers of Congress. The election of
1880 resulted in a tied Senate. Samuel Tilden in 1876 and Grover Cleveland in 1888
won the popular vote but lost in the Electoral College. In both years, Democrats
carried the House.

5. Some analysts argue that John Kennedy actually lost the popular vote in
1960—not because of fraud in Illinois as often charged, but because Dixiecrat candidate Harry Byrd's votes were allocated to Kennedy in some Southern states. Various
methods of allocating Byrd's votes between Nixon and Kennedy take away the latter's narrow popular vote majority. See Brian Gaines, "Popular Myths about Popular
Vote–Electoral College Splits," *PS: Political Science & Politics* 34, no. 1 (March
2001): 71–75; and Gordon Tullock, "Nixon, Like Gore, Also Won Popular Vote, but
Lost Election," *PS: Political Science & Politics* 37, no. 1 (January 2004): 1–2.

6. In retrospect, Carter's narrow victory looks like something of a fluke. He barely
defeated the Republican incumbent, Gerald Ford, who had been appointed to the vice
presidency upon the resignation in disgrace of Vice President Spiro Agnew and who

TABLE 1.3. **An Era of Different Institutional Majorities**

	President	House	Senate
1954	R	D	D
1956	R	D	D
1958	R	D	D
1960	D	D	D
1962	D	D	D
1964	D	D	D
1966	D	D	D
1968	R	D	D
1970	R	D	D
1972	R	D	D
1974	R	D	D
1976	D	D	D
1978	D	D	D
1980	R	D	R
1982	R	D	R
1984	R	D	R
1986	R	D	D
1988	R	D	D
1990	R	D	D
1992	D	D	D

Nineteen elections produced only three different patterns of institutional control.

As a consequence, even during this long period of divided government there still was a large degree of predictability. With Republicans generally in control of the executive branch, tax increases were unlikely; with Democrats in control of Congress, spending cuts were unlikely.[7] This was bad news for the budget, but the parameters within which deals would be struck were generally understood.

Bad news for the budget was good news for H. Ross Perot, who made budget deficits an issue in the 1992 election. Although it is doubtful that Perot cost George H. W. Bush the election, he probably

then ascended to the presidency upon the resignation in disgrace of President Richard Nixon. Ford then committed the electorally harmful action of pardoning Nixon.

7. Mathew McCubbins, "Party Governance and U.S. Budget Deficits: Divided Government and Fiscal Stalemate," in *Politics and Economics in the Eighties*, ed. Alberto Alesina and Geoffery Carliner (Chicago: University of Chicago Press, 1991), 83–111.

TABLE 1.4. **An Era of Unstable Majorities**

	President	House	Senate
1992	D	D	D
1994	D	R	R
1996	D	R	R
1998	D	R	R
2000	D/R*	R	Tie
2002	R	R	R
2004	R	R	R
2006	R	D	D
2008	D	D	D
2010	D	R	D
2012	D	R	D
2014	D	R	R
2016	D/R*	R	R

*Popular vote winner lost the electoral vote

didn't help.[8] The reestablishment of unified Democratic control under Bill Clinton began a two-decade-long (and counting) period of electoral outcomes that defy generalizations like those describing the three previous eras. Juxtaposed against the relatively stable institutional majorities that characterized the three previous eras, since 1992 the country has experienced an era of unstable institutional majorities. The Democrats have held the presidency for sixteen of the twenty-four years; but neither party has held the office longer than eight years, the popular vote margins have been relatively narrow, and twice the winner of the popular vote lost the electoral vote, an event that had not happened since 1888. Even the reelected presidents (Bush in 2004 and Obama in 2012) have won by relatively narrow margins. Republicans have had an advantage in the House since their 1994 takeover, but the Democrats won majorities twice. Control of the Senate has been almost evenly split. In contrast to the relative stability of institutional control in the three previous eras, the most recent twelve elections have generated six different patterns of control (see table 1.4).

Let us take a closer look at this recent electoral history. Table 1.5 lists the unusual developments that have occurred since 1992. The

8. Tim Hibbitts, "The Man Who Supposedly Cost George H. W. Bush the Presidency," *The Polling Report,* January 30, 2012, www.pollingreport.com/hibbitts1202.htm.

TABLE 1.5. An Era of Instability and Pattern-Breaking

1992: Ross Perot—19% / Clinton—43%
1994: Democrats lose House—first time in 40 years
1996: Democratic President / Republican Congress
1998: President's party gains seats in the House!
2000: Chaos
2002: President's party gains seats again!
2004: Consolidation of the Reagan Revolution?
2006: No—Republican thumpin'
2008: The New Deal returns?
2010: No—Democratic shellacking I
2012: Status quo (but historically unprecedented)
2014: Democratic shellacking II
2016: Trump

current era began with the 1992 election itself, of course, when Perot won almost 19 percent of the popular vote, the largest vote for a third place finisher since Theodore Roosevelt split the Republican Party in 1912. Similarly, Bill Clinton became president with 43 percent of the vote, the smallest popular vote percentage for a winner since Wilson's election in 1912. Then in 1994 the Republicans captured Congress for the first time in forty years, beginning a six-year period of divided government with a Democratic president and a Republican Congress—a reversal of the previous pattern of divided government that blew up a number of political science theories that attempted to explain why Americans supposedly liked Republican presidents and Democratic Congresses.[9] After a failed Republican attempt to impeach President Clinton, the Democrats gained House seats in 1998, violating perhaps the hoariest of all generalizations about American politics: that the party of the president loses seats in midterm elections.[10] The bitterly contested 2000 elections followed,

9. As pointed out above, the 1956 election was the first time in American history that a victorious president of *any* party failed to carry the House in a two-way race. The 1996 election was the first time in American history that a *Democratic* president failed to carry the House, although Perot received 8 percent of the popular vote, meaning it was not quite a two-way race.

10. This was the second time in thirty-five midterm elections since the Civil War that the midterm loss did not occur (1934 was the other case). A technical quibble: in 1902 the House was expanded and both parties gained seats, but the president's (Republican) party gained only nine seats whereas the opposition Democrats gained twenty-five, so the Republican percentage of the House declined.

with a tie in the Senate and the loser of the popular vote elevated to the presidency via the Supreme Court. In 2002, the party of the president again gained seats in a midterm election.

For a brief period, the 2004 elections appeared to put an end to this electorally turbulent decade. After the elections, Republicans of our acquaintance were dancing in the streets (figuratively, at least). Although George W. Bush did not win by a landslide, in capturing the Senate and the House as well as retaining the presidency the Republicans won full control of the national government for the first time since the election of Dwight Eisenhower in 1952, a half century earlier.[11] Even in the landslide reelections of Richard Nixon in 1972 and Ronald Reagan in 1984, Republicans had not been able to capture both chambers of Congress.[12] In the afterglow of the elections, many Republicans hoped (and some Democrats feared) that Karl Rove had achieved his professed goal of building a generation-long Republican majority, much as Mark Hanna had done for the McKinley Republicans in the 1890s.[13]

Such hopes and fears proved unfounded, however, as a natural disaster (Hurricane Katrina), a series of political missteps,[14] and the weight of an unpopular war in Iraq took their toll on the president's public standing. In the 2006 elections, which President Bush characterized as a "thumpin'" for his party, the Democrats took back the House and the Senate and netted more than three hundred state legislative seats. Republican fortunes continued to deteriorate in the remaining two years of President Bush's term. Following an economic collapse in 2008, the Democrats won the presidency to restore the unified control they had lost in 2000. In the short span of four years, party fortunes had completely reversed.

11. Yes, strictly speaking, the Republicans won full control in 2000, but the Democrats won the popular vote that year and the Senate was tied, with Vice President Dick Cheney in the position of tiebreaker. Unlike this messy 2000 outcome, the 2004 election rendered an unambiguous verdict.

12. Republicans won the Senate in the 1980, 1982, and 1984 elections.

13. Nicholas Lemann, "The Controller," *New Yorker,* May 12, 2003, www.new yorker.com/magazine/2003/05/12/the-controller.

14. Political junkies will remember (among other things) the ill-fated proposal of Social Security private accounts, the ill-fated nomination of Harriet Miers to the Supreme Court, and the ill-fated proposal to sell US ports to Dubai.

Now it was the Democrats' turn. Six months after the 2008 elections, Democratic politico James Carville published *40 More Years: How the Democrats Will Rule the Next Generation.*[15] By no means was Carville alone in his triumphalism. After the elections, pundits and even some political scientists speculated that the 2008 presidential outcome was "transformative" in the sense that it represented an electoral realignment similar to that of Franklin Roosevelt's New Deal in the 1930s.[16] Again, such hopes and fears proved unfounded, as the (politically) misplaced priorities of the new administration led to a massive repudiation in the 2010 midterm elections, which President Obama characterized as a "shellacking" for his party.[17] The Democrats lost the House of Representatives and more than seven hundred state legislative seats.[18] The loss of sixty-three seats in the House was the largest midterm seat loss since 1938, three-quarters of a century earlier—a far cry from the return to the 1930s that the Democrats had anticipated after the 2008 victories.

Republicans had high hopes of winning back the presidency and the Senate in 2012. But although President Obama managed the nearly unprecedented feat of winning reelection by a smaller popular vote margin than in his initial election, he beat back the challenge.[19] In other respects, the 2012 elections continued the status

15. James Carville, *40 More Years: How the Democrats Will Rule the Next Generation* (New York: Simon & Schuster, 2009). After the 2010 elections, Amazon offered a 60 percent discount on the book.

16. Thomas B. Edsall, "Permanent Democratic Majority: New Study Says Yes," *Huffington Post,* May 14, 2009, www.huffingtonpost.com/2009/04/13/pemanent -democratic-major_n_186257.html. The November 24, 2008, cover of *Time* magazine pictured a cigarette-smoking Obama as FDR riding in a 1930s car.

17. Namely, cap and trade and health care rather than jobs and the economy. The argument that the administration's priorities were (electorally) misplaced will be advanced in chapter 5, "The Temptation to Overreach." For an analysis of the electoral costs of these votes, see David Brady, Morris Fiorina, and Arjun Wilkins, "The 2010 Elections: Why Did Political Science Forecasts Go Awry?" *PS: Political Science & Politics* 44, no. 2 (April 2011): 247–250.

18. Not counting New Hampshire. That state's legislature is so large that including it skews the numbers.

19. Obama in 2012 was the first president since Andrew Jackson in 1832 who was reelected by a smaller margin than in his initial election. Two more technical quibbles: first, this factoid does not count Franklin Roosevelt's second and third reelections in 1940 and 1944, only his first in 1936; and second, Grover Cleveland

quo of a divided national government with a divided Congress, as the Democratic majority hung on in the Senate.[20] Still, looking ahead to 2014, Republican Senate prospects looked bright because the Democrats were defending two-thirds of the seats in the states where elections would be held, with seven of these elections in states carried by Republican Mitt Romney in 2012. In other respects, not a great deal of change was anticipated.

Election Day 2014 came as something of a shock, then, when an unexpected Republican wave rolled across the electoral landscape. Suffering their second consecutive midterm shellacking, the Democrats lost the Senate by a larger margin—nine seats—than most forecasters and prognosticators had predicted. Although the Republicans gained only thirteen seats in the House, their post-election majority was the largest after any election since 1928. The Democratic House delegation was reduced to the party's strongholds in the big cities, university towns, and majority-minority districts. Along the same lines, with the gain of another three hundred state legislative seats, the Republicans took control of sixty-eight of the ninety-eight partisan state legislatures—again, their strongest showing in the state legislatures since the 1920s.[21]

In sum, beginning in 1992, twelve elections have produced six different patterns of majority control of our three national elective institutions. In particular, the four consecutive elections of 2004–10 produced four different patterns of institutional control; extending that recent series through 2014 yields five distinct patterns in six elections. The United States did not experience any comparable period of majoritarian instability in the entire twentieth century.[22] We need to look back to the so-called Period of No Decision of the late nineteenth century that preceded the McKinley presidency to find a series of elections that showed this level of electoral instability:

---

won the popular vote in 1888 by a smaller margin (0.3 of a percentage point) than in his initial election in 1884, but he was not reelected; he lost in the Electoral Collège.

20. For the second election in a row, Republican primary voters chose several candidates whose out-of-the-mainstream remarks during the campaign very likely cost the party several eminently winnable Senate seats.

21. Only ninety-eight because Nebraska is unicameral and ostensibly nonpartisan.

22. Fiorina, "America's Missing Moderates."

TABLE 1.6. The Era of No Decision: 1874–1894

	President	House	Senate
1874	R	D	R
1876	D/R*	D	R
1878	R	D	D
1880	R	R	Tie
1882	R	D	R
1884	D	D	R
1886	D	D	R
1888	D/R*	R	R
1890	R	D	R
1892	D	D	D
1894	D	R	R

*Popular vote winner lost the electoral vote

the elections of 1886–94 produced five different patterns of institutional control as shown in table 1.6. This precedent shows several interesting similarities to the present period; I will return to this historical comparison in chapter 9.

Some analysts suggest that our recent electoral experience is simply the reverse of the era of divided government; in a mirror image of that period, Democrats now have the edge in presidential contests and Republicans in congressional contests, especially the House. There are similarities, to be sure, but the differences are more noteworthy. As noted above, the past twelve elections have produced six different patterns of institutional control, whereas the nineteen elections in the Divided Government Era produced only three patterns. Recent presidential elections have been closely contested; there have been no Democratic landslides comparable to those rung up by Republicans Eisenhower, Nixon, and Reagan in the Divided Government Era. Conversely, control of the Senate has been up for grabs in recent elections, unlike the pronounced Democratic advantage in the previous era. Some analysts talk about a Republican lock on the House, but only a few years ago—2007–8—the Democrats held a seventy-eight-seat majority.[23] As yet, there is nothing remotely

23. Alan I. Abramowitz and Steven Webster, "Explaining the Republican 'Lock' on the House," *Sabato's Crystal Ball*, April 23, 2015, www.centerforpolitics.org/crystal ball/articles/explaining-the-republican-lock-on-the-u-s-house-of-representatives/.

comparable to the four-decade-long string of Democratic House majorities in the second half of the last century.[24]

The electoral chaos of the past quarter century showed no sign of abating in 2016. Insurgent presidential candidacies rocked the parties, defeating the establishment in the case of the Republicans and disrupting Hillary Clinton's glide path to the nomination on the Democratic side. Donald Trump dispatched a dozen and a half competitors, almost every one of whom would have been preferred by the Republican establishment. Democrats had high hopes of retaking the Senate, and in the run-up to the election some analysts sketched out admittedly long-shot paths for the Democrats to win the House.[25] Although neither outcome came to pass, few analysts considered the Democratic hopes crazy. And looking ahead, while Democratic capture of the Senate in 2018 seems a very long shot, they only need twenty-four seats to capture the House, an outcome well within the range of midterm elections in this unstable era. Thus, recent election outcomes more closely resemble the electorally chaotic late nineteenth century (table 1.6) when presidential elections were virtual coin tosses: the Republicans had an edge in the Senate and the Democrats in the House, so the patterns of institutional control regularly changed.[26]

24. Many commentators believe that Republican control of redistricting following their 2010 electoral triumph has created an insuperable obstacle for the Democrats. Political scientists generally find redistricting to be a much less important factor than pundits think. The relatively greater geographic concentration of Democratic voters is the primary factor in the current Republican advantage in House elections. For a discussion, see John Sides and Eric McGhee, "Redistricting Didn't Win Republicans the House," *Washington Post*, February 17, 2013, www.washingtonpost.com/blogs/wonkblog/wp/2013/02/17/redistricting-didnt-win-republicans-the-house/.

25. See Kyle Kondik, "House 2016: Is it Possible for Republicans to Kick Away Their Majority?" *Sabato's Crystal Ball*, October 8, 2015, www.centerforpolitics.org/crystalball/articles/house-2016-is-it-possible-for-republicans-to-kick-away-their-majority/; and Lisa Hagen and Cristina Marcos, "Ten House Seats Dems Hope Trump Will Tilt," *The Hill*, April 3, 2016, http://thehill.com/homenews/campaign/274952-ten-house-seats-dems-hope-trump-will-tilt?utm_source=&utm_medium=email&utm_campaign=1087.

26. In the five presidential elections between 1876 and 1892, no candidate reached 51 percent of the popular vote and four winners received less than 50 percent. Two plurality losers won Electoral College majorities, something that did not happen again until 2000.

Interestingly, the instability of institutional control described in the preceding pages contrasts with the stability of voting patterns in recent national elections. Research indicates that individual voters are more consistent in their partisan voting choices now than several decades ago, but this apparent increase in micro-level stability in the electorate contrasts sharply with the increase in macro-level instability shown in the elections of the early twenty-first century.[27] Some analysts suggest that in a deeply divided country, a few centrist, cross-pressured, or clueless voters can swing control of government institutions from one party to the other, but (as shown in the next chapter) research does not support the assumption of a deeply divided country.[28] Others attribute the macro-instability to variations in turnout.[29] It is true that, in a period of evenly matched parties, shifts in partisan preference or turnout by a relatively small number of voters can change the outcomes of elections; after every close election there are print and online commentaries pointing out how a shift of a few votes in a few states could have changed the Electoral College majority or party control of the Senate.

But my belief is that the observed stability of voting patterns is more contingent than generally appreciated. Political pundits and even many political scientists tend to overlook the political context in which citizens vote. In general, voters are responders, not initiators, in the political process. They react to what parties and candidates

27. E.g., Larry Bartels, "Partisanship and Voting Behavior, 1952–1996," *American Journal of Political Science* 44, no. 1 (January 2000): 35–50. It is unclear whether the impact of partisanship itself has strengthened or whether factors associated with partisanship have become stronger and more consistent (see chapter 3), but there is little doubt that partisan consistency in voting has increased, at least for Democrats. With the sole exception of the 1964 elections, Republicans have always been very consistent. See Samuel Abrams and Morris Fiorina, "Party Sorting: The Foundations of Polarized Politics," in *American Gridlock: The Sources, Character, and Impact of Political Polarization,* ed. James Thurber and Antoine Yoshinaka (New York: Cambridge University Press, 2015), 113–29.

28. E.g., Michael Kazin, "The Trouble with Independents," *New Republic,* April 25, 2011, www.newrepublic.com/article/not-even-past/87379/republican-demo crats-independents-dewey-lippmann.

29. Samuel Best, "Why Democrats Lost the House to Republicans," CBS, November 3, 2010, www.cbsnews.com/news/why-democrats-lost-the-house-to-republicans/.

say and do. More important, they can only choose between the candidates the parties nominate.

Suppose that every Saturday night you and your partner go to dinner at a restaurant that serves only two entrées: beef and chicken.[30] Every week you order beef and your partner orders chicken. Many of today's political pundits would infer that you are strongly committed to beef and your partner is similarly committed to chicken. They predict that next week you will choose beef and your partner will choose chicken as you always do. But suppose next week the waiter tells you that the beef entrée is liver. On reflection, you decide to have chicken. Think of George McGovern as liver. Although you may have a general preference for beef (Democrats), that general preference may not extend to every specific instance of it like, say, liver (McGovern). Alternatively, imagine that the waiter tells you that in addition to the beef and chicken entrées, salmon is being served. Both of you happily order the salmon. Think of Ross Perot (or Donald Trump) as salmon. Between beef and chicken, you generally prefer beef and your partner chicken. But if salmon is on the menu, it's the preferred dish for both of you. The point of these fanciful analogies is to emphasize that our choices depend on the offered alternatives. Our choices between beef and chicken did not reflect only our culinary preferences but also the fact that they were the only two alternatives available to us. The same holds for choices between candidates.

If each party nominates a nearly identical candidate from one election to the next, there is little reason to expect voters to change their votes every four years (other things being equal). Democrats Al Gore in 2000 and John Kerry in 2004 received virtually identical percentages of the popular vote. In contrast, the difference between the popular vote for Democrats George McGovern in 1972 and Jimmy Carter in 1976 was 12.6 percentage points. Does this significant difference between the 1970s and the 2000s mean that swing voters had disappeared and the country was much more set in its partisan ways in the 2000s than in the 1970s? Possibly, but Al

---

30. Why would you patronize such a restaurant? It is the only restaurant in town. If you want to dine out, you must go to this restaurant.

Gore and John Kerry were much more similar Democrats than were George McGovern and (pre-presidency) Jimmy Carter.[31] Moreover, Gore and Kerry were running against the same Republican, George W. Bush, whereas McGovern and Carter faced different Republican opponents—Richard Nixon and Gerald Ford. That Carter won the presidency four years after McGovern lost in a landslide may not mean that voters were less partisan in the 1970s (although they may have been) but only that they had very different alternatives to choose from than voters do today, when most Democratic candidates look pretty much the same, as do most Republican candidates.

Similarly, if voters increasingly vote a straight ticket for president, senator, US representative, and state legislator, it may mean that voters have become more partisan. But it may also mean that today's homogeneous parties increasingly offer them a choice between a liberal Democrat and a conservative Republican for every office, so there is not as much reason for voters to split their tickets now as there was in earlier decades when the parties offered conservative and liberal Democrats and liberal and conservative Republicans.

My argument, developed in later chapters, is that party sorting is the key to understanding our current political turbulence. At the higher levels the parties have sorted; each party has become more homogeneous internally and more distinct from the other. Voter behavior does not change much because the alternatives voters face do not change much. Most voters, however, are not as well sorted as party elites and many voters do not identify with the parties at all; hence, they are increasingly dissatisfied with the choices the party system offers. The strong insurgent primary campaigns waged by Senator Bernie Sanders and Trump are reflections of these facts.

---

31. The current image of Jimmy Carter is that of a liberal Democrat, but in 1976 he was viewed as a respectable alternative to George Wallace. "Carter would not have been the establishment's first choice as a nominee, but as a less toxic conservative he had the best chance to defeat Wallace in major contests on their shared home turf in the South. Some of the more moderate and liberal candidates stayed away from the Florida primary to benefit Carter, who won there." PrimaryCaucus (a map-based history of the presidential nominating process), https://sites.google.com/site/primarycaucus/home/democrats1976.

With close electoral competition between two ideologically well-sorted parties, political overreach has become endemic, resulting in predictable electoral swings. By overreach I mean simply that a party governs (or attempts to) in a manner that reflects the preferences of its base but alienates the marginal members of its electoral majority, who then withdraw their support in the next election. Overreach is not new, but a number of developments have made it a normal feature of politics today. The consequence is unstable majorities. Looking ahead to the 2018 elections, Democrats should hope that this argument is correct.

Before developing the argument, it will be helpful to digest three chapters that describe the contemporary American electorate, correct some common misconceptions about that electorate, and describe some of the ways in which it has changed (or not) since the mid-twentieth century.

CHAPTER 2

Has the American Public Polarized?

> *It is time for our society to acknowledge a sad truth: America*
> *is currently fighting its second Civil War. In fact, with the*
> *obvious and enormous exception of attitudes toward slavery,*
> *Americans are more divided morally, ideologically and*
> *politically today than they were during the Civil War.*
>
> —Dennis Prager

What Is Polarization?

Claims like that quoted above became commonplace in the early years of the new century. Consequently, anyone who pays even casual attention to discussions of American politics in the media is likely to believe that American politics has polarized.[1] But although assertions about polarization often are made in unconditional form, such claims can be true or false depending on what aspect of American politics we consider. The US Congress, for example, clearly supports the contention that American politics has polarized. Keith Poole and Howard Rosenthal have developed a statistical methodology for estimating the ideological positions of legislators from their roll

---

Quotation from conservative talk show host Dennis Prager, "America's Second Civil War," *Real Clear Politics*, January 24, 2017, http://www.realclearpolitics.com/articles/2017/01/24/americas_second_civil_war_132880.html.

1. On the increasing use of the polarization frame by the media since 2002, see Matthew Levendusky and Neil Malhotra, "Does Media Coverage of Partisan Polarization Affect Political Attitudes?" *Political Communication* 33, no. 2 (2016): 283–301, figure 1.

call votes.[2] For much of American history, especially in more recent decades, members of Congress can be placed on a single ideological dimension, generally considered to incorporate economic issues, particularly redistribution. Figure 2.1 compares the Congress elected in 1960 with that elected in 2008. Evidently the Congress faced by Barack Obama in his first year as president was far more polarized than the one faced a half century earlier by John Kennedy in his first year—more members were on the left and right of the ideological spectrum in 2009–10 than in 1961–62 and fewer were in the middle. Moreover, the partisan distributions have become more distinct. In sharp contrast to Congresses elected a half century ago, in most recent Congresses the party distributions do not overlap: the most liberal Republican falls to the right of the most conservative Democrat. Poole and Rosenthal date the start of this polarizing trend to the early 1970s.

Many American state legislatures show the same polarizing trend.[3] Utah, Washington, and California, for example, are now more polarized than the US House. Other polarized statehouses include Colorado, New Mexico, Wisconsin, Michigan, Arizona, Maryland, Texas, and Minnesota. Most state senates are even more polarized than the US Senate. For reasons as yet unknown, a few state legislatures—like Louisiana, Rhode Island, Massachusetts, and West Virginia—seem to have bucked the polarizing trend.[4]

2. Keith T. Poole and Howard Rosenthal, *Ideology & Congress* (New Brunswick, NJ: Transaction Publishers, 2007), 82. Other scholars have developed alternative methodologies, but the Poole-Rosenthal method is the most well known and widely used. All methodologies that rely on roll call votes as data likely overestimate the extent of actual polarization because party leaders try to prevent issues that divide their party from coming to the floor. In addition, there is some difficulty in differentiating pure partisan "teamsmanship" from ideological disagreement. See Frances E. Lee, *Beyond Ideology: Politics, Principles, and Partisanship in the U.S. Senate* (Chicago: University of Chicago Press, 2009); and Laurel Harbridge, *Is Bipartisanship Dead? Policy Agreement and Agenda-Setting in the House of Representatives* (New York: Cambridge University Press, 2015).

3. Boris Shor and Nolan McCarty have provided the relevant analyses: "New Update of State Legislative Data Released," July 24, 2014, https://research.bshor.com/category/ideology/.

4. Interestingly, some of the least polarized legislatures have a reputation for petty corruption. Possibly, legislators who are skimming off the top are more likely to make bipartisan deals to keep the gravy train running smoothly.

FIGURE 2.1 Parties in the House of Representatives, Then and Now

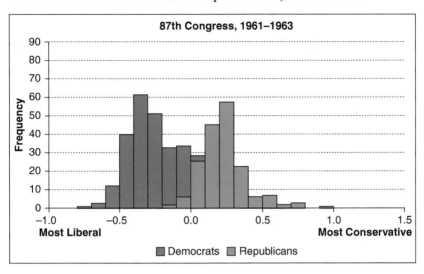

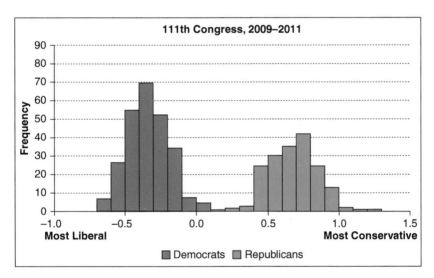

Data on other important political actors are less extensive, but figure 2.2 shows trends similar to those for members of Congress. Party
and issue activists, for example, have moved further apart in the past
several decades. Here party activists are those who self-identify as a
Republican or Democrat and report that they worked for a candidate

FIGURE 2.2 **Partisan Activists Are Polarizing**

Party activists are strong and weak identifiers who worked for a party or
candidate.

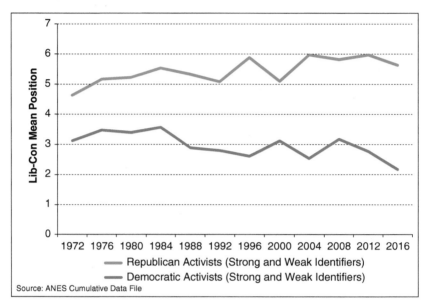

Source: ANES Cumulative Data File

or party.[5] Such individuals typically make up less than 5 percent of
the eligible electorate. In 1972, such activists were 1.53 units apart on
the standard seven-point ideological scale included in the American
National Election Studies (ANES). As figure 2.2 shows, that distance
more than doubled, to 3.45 units, by 2016 as each party's activists
moved a full scale unit toward their respective poles. Fewer activists
fall in the moderate middle today; more position themselves toward
the extremes. The same is true for campaign contributors, another
class of important political actors.[6] Generally they make up about
10 percent or so of the eligible electorate. As shown in figure 2.3,
donors too have become more polarized during the past several
decades. In the case of donors, Republicans clearly contribute more

5. As Carmines and Stimson note, working in the campaign "is a close concep-
tual fit to the ordinary connotation of 'activist.'" Edward G. Carmines and James
A. Stimson, *Issue Evolution: Race and the Transformation of American Politics*
(Princeton, NJ: Princeton University Press, 1989), 93.

6. There is less overlap between donors and those who work in campaigns than
one might expect—one-third to two-thirds depending on the election.

FIGURE 2.3 **Partisan Donors Are Polarizing**
Donors are strong and weak partisans who donated to a campaign.

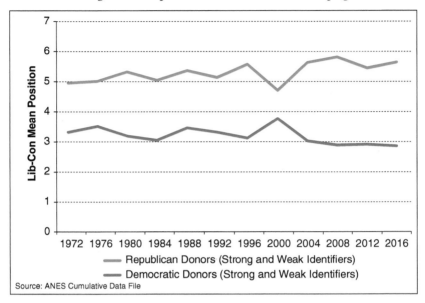

Source: ANES Cumulative Data File

to the increase in polarization, but for activists the polarization is more symmetric, with Democrats moving sharply left after 2008. The 2012 Cooperative Congressional Election Study surveyed 35,000 people, a large enough sample to include numerous donors at all levels. That survey found that relative to those who do not contribute, donors—whether big or small—tend to come from the ideological poles, a tendency that research indicates is increasing.[7]

The preceding figures capture our intuitive understanding of the concept of polarization: the middle loses to the extremes. There is a great deal of evidence that at the highest levels of political involvement—elected officials and candidates, donors, party and issue activists—the claim of increased polarization is accurate. In what follows, I will call this rarefied stratum of political actors the political

7. As demonstrated by an extensive study of polarization in Congress and state legislatures over the past two decades by Raymond J. La Raja and Brian F. Schaffner, *Campaign Finance and Political Polarization: When Purists Prevail* (Ann Arbor, MI: University of Michigan Press, 2015). See also Adam Bonica, "Mapping the Ideological Marketplace," *American Journal of Political Science* 58, no. 2 (April 2014): 367–86.

FIGURE 2.4 Americans Correctly See That the Parties Have Become More Distinct

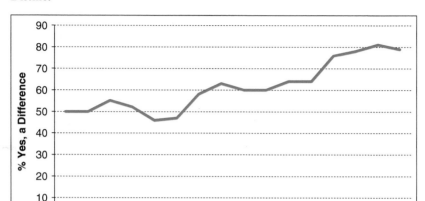

Source: ANES Cumulative Data File

class, as compared to the rest of the electorate, whom I will refer to as normal people.[8]

Figure 2.4 indicates that the American people recognize the polarizing trends shown in the preceding figures. The proportion believing that there are important differences between the two parties has risen 30 percentage points in the past half century. In 1968, almost half the electorate agreed with American Independent Party candidate George Wallace when he scoffed that there was not a "dime's worth of difference" between the Republicans and the Democrats, but a much smaller proportion agrees with such an assertion today. As the parties became more distinct, more and more Americans naturally came to believe that the outcome made a difference to them: more people care about the outcome of elections today than did before the election of Bill Clinton (figure 2.5). According to the ANES, from

8. The political class numbers 15 percent or so of the American citizenry, meaning that the members are abnormal in a statistical sense. James Davison Hunter, "The Culture Wars Reconsidered," in *Is There a Culture War? A Dialogue on Values and American Public Life*, ed. E. J. Dionne Jr. and Michael Cromartie (Washington, DC: Brookings Institution, 2006), 27.

FIGURE 2.5 **Americans Increasingly Care about the Outcome of the Presidential Election**

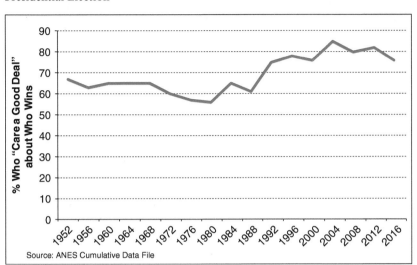

Source: ANES Cumulative Data File

Dwight Eisenhower in 1952 through George H. W. Bush in 1988, the proportion of people reporting that they "cared a good deal" about the outcome of the presidential election ranged between 56 and 67 percent. Since 1992 it has never fallen below 75 percent and has ranged between 75 and 85 percent.

Many politicos and pundits believe that trends in the beliefs and positions of normal people look like figures 2.1–2.3. James Pierson claims, "The number of people and the percentage of the electorate at the center has gradually diminished over time. Public opinion now appears to divide us up to the point that we have a couple of lumps— a liberal lump on one side and a conservative lump on the other."[9] Such claims are false. Given the trends pictured in figures 2.1–2.3, most readers will be surprised to learn that we do not see analogous trends when we look at distributions of normal people—typical Americans who are not deeply involved in politics. On the contrary,

9. Quoted in Andrew Soergel, "Divided We Stand," *U.S. News & World Report,* July 19, 2016, https://www.usnews.com/news/articles/2016-07-19/political -polarization-drives-presidential-race-to-the-bottom.

FIGURE 2.6 **Normal Americans Have Not Polarized Ideologically**

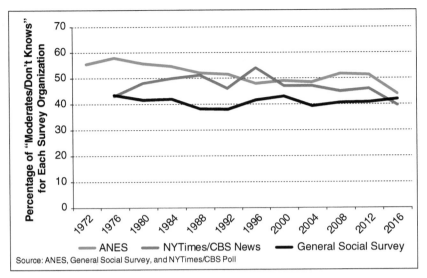

when Americans are asked to classify themselves ideologically, we do not find them moving away from the middle and lumping up at the liberal and conservative poles. Instead, as figure 2.6 shows, the way that Americans self-categorize their ideological positions has changed little in four decades.[10] The General Social Survey (GSS) series is flat, showing nothing beyond sampling variability. The CBS News/New York Times series fluctuates more, but the proportion of moderates in the two Obama elections is about the same as in the two Carter elections.[11] The ANES series shows a drop of about

10. "Liberal" has always been the least popular category in the American context. Although more popular, "conservative" typically trails "moderate," which normally occupies the modal position. On the historical popularity of the conservative label, see Lloyd A. Free and Hadley Cantril, *The Political Beliefs of Americans: A Study of Public Opinion* (New Brunswick, NJ: Rutgers University Press, 1967). Research by Ellis and Stimson shows that liberal is a more precisely defined category than conservative. That is, people who self-classify as liberals have liberal policy preferences, but many of those who self-classify as conservatives fail to hold consistently conservative policy preferences. See Christopher Ellis and James A. Stimson, *Ideology in America* (New York: Cambridge University Press, 2012).

11. The CBS News/New York Times series is based on the poll conducted closest to the election.

11 percentage points, but this decline probably is more apparent than real—the drop in moderates in the ANES series is due mostly to a drop in "don't know" and "haven't thought much about this" responses, which are typically classified as moderate.[12]

Knowing that Americans historically have not been particularly ideological, we might conceptualize polarization in partisan rather than ideological terms. If so, over the years independents should have been migrating to the Democratic and Republican camps. But partisanship data are even less kind to the polarization claim than ideological data. Figure 2.7 shows that it is partisans, not independents, who have lost ground: independents are now the largest single "partisan" category.[13] Moreover, Americans increasingly act as they talk. Administrative officials in states with party registration (currently twenty-one states and the District of Columbia) report a sharp rise in the proportion of Americans registering as "decline to state" (DtS) or some other term for independent, despite potential restrictions on their opportunity to vote in semi-closed or closed primaries.[14] Between 1976 and 2008, the average DtS registration increased from 12 to 18 percent across 1,200 counties in party

12. To explain, survey response rates have declined over the period covered by these time series. Converse cautions that contemporary survey samples capture a more informed and interested slice of the electorate than those taken at the dawn of the survey research era when response rates were over 80 percent, because "one major source of refusal to answer a political questionnaire (or to join a second-wave panel) is lack of interest in, or sense of competence about, the subject matter." Consistent with his observation, the GSS response rate dropped only 5 percentage points between the first and last observations in figure 6 whereas the ANES dropped sharply after 1994 and was 35 ·percentage points lower in 2012 than in 1972. See Philip Converse, "Democratic Theory and Electoral Reality," *Critical Review* 18, no. 1–3 (2006): 312–13. *Contra* Converse, James Campbell takes the declines in the time series at face value but even he notes, "Despite the substantial seven percentage point shift away from the center, the 2012 distribution does not look much different from the 1972 distribution and is not remotely close to being bimodal or even flat." James E. Campbell, *Polarized: Making Sense of a Divided America* (Princeton NJ: Princeton University Press, 2016), 69.

13. The interpretation of the large increase in independents is controversial in political science. I address this in chapter 6.

14. Eric McGhee and Daniel Krimm, "Party Registration and the Geography of Party Polarization," *Polity* 41, no. 3 (July 2009): 345–67.

FIGURE 2.7 **Normal Americans Have Not Divided into Two Partisan Camps**

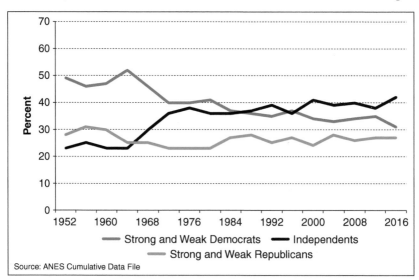

Source: ANES Cumulative Data File

registration states.[15] The trend is nationwide and shows no sign of abating.[16] Independents constitute a plurality of registrants in twelve states scattered across the country.[17]

Alternatively, if one thinks that—despite the negative picture presented by general orientations like ideology and partisanship— Americans have polarized around certain key issues, one again will search in vain for supporting evidence. Consider abortion, an issue that has roiled American politics since the 1970s and again came to the fore in the 2016 presidential primaries. Despite the polar positions advocated by the pro-choice and pro-life groups, the Gallup

15. Samuel J. Abrams and Morris P. Fiorina, "The Big Sort That Wasn't: A Skeptical Reexamination," *PS: Political Science & Politics* 45, no. 2 (April 2012), https://www.cambridge.org/core/journals/ps-political-science-and-politics/article/the-big-sort-that-wasnt-a-skeptical-reexamination/0FEA9EB647CC86566040BA95C6C9C83F.

16. Alex Gauthier, "Independents Exceed Party Registration in Key States," Independent Voter Project, June 18, 2013, http://ivn.us/2013/06/18/independents-exceed-party-registration-in-5-states/.

17. As of 2014, these were Alaska, Arizona, Arkansas, Colorado, Connecticut, Idaho, Iowa, Maine, Massachusetts, New Hampshire, New Jersey, and Rhode Island.

FIGURE 2.8 Most Americans Believe Abortion Should Be Legal Only in Certain Circumstances, with Little Change in Forty Years

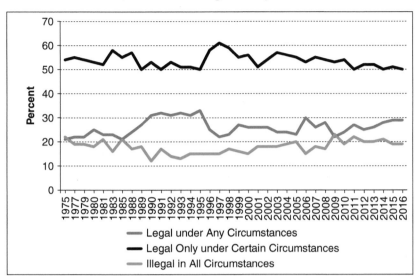

Poll data plotted in figure 2.8 indicate that most Americans continue to fall between the two poles. For four decades, the majority position in the United States has been that abortion should be legal only under some circumstances. Moreover, the proportions who truly believe that abortion should always or never be legal are actually significantly fewer than the proportions reported in the Gallup data.[18]

By no means is the abortion issue unrepresentative. In every presidential year since 1984, the ANES has measured respondents' positions on five policy issues: private insurance versus government-provided health insurance, lower government spending versus more government services, more or less government aid to minorities, lower or higher defense spending, and whether or not

18. Morris P. Fiorina with Samuel J. Abrams, *Disconnect: The Breakdown of Representation in American Politics* (Norman, OK: Oklahoma University Press, 2009), 35; Lynn Vavreck, "Candidates Fight Over Abortion, but Public Has Surprising Level of Harmony," *New York Times*, May 6, 2015, https://www.ny times.com/2015/05/06/upshot/candidates-disagree-on-abortion-but-public-is-in -surprising-harmony.html.

FIGURE 2.9 **Normal Americans Continue to Be Issue Centrists**
"Haven't thought much about it" responses are recorded as position 4.

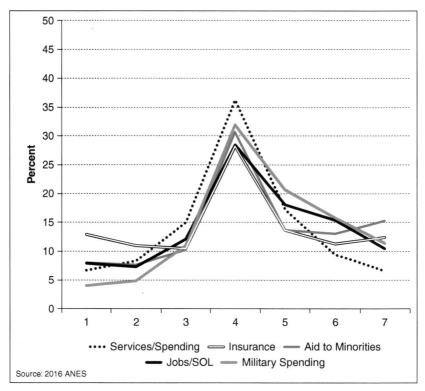

government should guarantee jobs and living standards. For each issue respondents are asked to place themselves on a seven-point scale running from extremely liberal to extremely conservative. As depicted in figure 2.9, the distributions in 2016 maintain the same generally centrist shape as they did in 1984. Although there are somewhat fewer people in the center on several issues in 2016, it is not because they shifted away from the middle toward both extremes. Rather, there is a notable rightward shift on aid to minorities and a smaller one on defense spending but leftward shifts on health insurance and more government spending versus fewer services.[19] Public opinion on specific issues changes in response to real-

19. Cynics might suspect that the rightward shift on aid to minorities was a reaction to Obama's presidency, but the shift actually began in the mid-'90s.

world developments, but it changes gradually and inconsistently and shows no polarizing trend comparable to those shown by members of the political class.

Finally, since 1987 the Pew Research Center has been conducting major surveys of forty-eight political beliefs and values held by Americans. Here is the summary statement from the most recent (2012) release:

> The way that the public thinks about poverty, opportunity, business, unions, religion, civic duty, foreign affairs and many other subjects is, to a large extent, the same today as in 1987. The values that unified Americans 25 years ago remain areas of consensus today, while the values that evenly divide the nation remain split. On most of the questions asked in both 1987 and 2012, the number agreeing is within five percentage points of the number who agreed 25 years ago. And on almost none has the basic balance of opinion tipped from agree to disagree or vice versa.[20]

All in all, the data compiled by academic and commercial survey organizations indicate that in broad outline the American public has changed little in the past four decades. In the aggregate, the public today looks much the same as the one that chose between Gerald Ford and Jimmy Carter in 1976, well before the polarization era. This inconvenient fact makes it hard to argue—as some pundits and a few political scientists continue to do so—that polarization in Congress and state legislatures and among party activists and donors has been driven by the polarization of the vast majority of Americans who do not belong to the political class.[21]

---

20. Pew Research Center, "Partisan Polarization Surges in Bush, Obama Years," June 4, 2012, www.people-press.org/2012/06/04/partisan-polarization-surges-in-bush -obama-years/.

21. Campbell is one of the few political scientists who reject the scholarly consensus, arguing that "polarization in the electorate preceded the greater polarization of party elites." Campbell, *Polarized*, 52.

False Polarization

In response to the question "Has the American electorate polarized?" the data presented above clearly answer no.[22] The American public, however, believes that the answer is yes. Although normal Americans who are largely uninvolved in politics correctly recognize (figure 2.4) that the political class has polarized (figures 2.1–2.3), they incorrectly believe—contrary to figures 2.6–2.9—that they have polarized as well. As the headline on a recent Pew Research Center report read, "On Eve of Inauguration, Americans Expect Nation's Deep Political Divisions to Persist."[23] A number of academic studies have documented such incorrect beliefs. Moreover, *these studies consistently report that it is the members of the political class who have the least accurate perceptions and beliefs.* Ironically, the great majority of Americans whose lives do not revolve around politics are more accurate in their political perceptions than their more politically involved compatriots who—wrongly—consider themselves well informed.

In a widely noted line of research, Westfall, Van Boven, Chambers, and Judd find that the more partisan or ideological the respondents, the more they exaggerate the differences between themselves and their political adversaries.[24] The research is based on the ANES conducted between 1970 and 2008. Considering issues like those graphed in figure 2.9, the researchers compare the actual positions reported by people in specific partisan categories to the perceptions of those positions held by people in other categories. They find systematic exaggeration of polarization: the positions actually held by

22. Other recent studies that show similarly negative findings are reviewed in Claude S. Fischer and Greggor Mattson, "Is America Fragmenting?" *Annual Review of Sociology* 35 (August 2009): 435–455.

23. Pew Research Center, January 19, 2017, www.people-press.org/2017/01/19/on-eve-of-inauguration-americans-expect-nations-deep-political-divisions-to-persist/.

24. Jacob Westfall, Leaf Van Boven, John R. Chambers, and Charles M. Judd, "Perceiving Political Polarization in the United States: Party Identity Strength and Attitude Extremity Exacerbate the Perceived Partisan Divide," *Perspectives on Psychological Science* 10, no. 2 (March 2015): 145–58.

Republicans, for example, are not as extreme as Democrats think they are, and vice versa. Consistent with various psychological theories, the tendency to push the other side further away is stronger than the tendency to exaggerate the extremity of one's own side. Not surprisingly, the exaggeration of the extremity of one's political opponents is positively related to one's own extremity: stronger partisans are less accurate than weaker partisans who are less accurate than independents. The perceptions held by party activists and donors are the least accurate of all.

Similarly, Graham, Nosek, and Haidt examine the "moral stereotypes" held by liberals and conservatives.[25] Do liberals lack respect for authority and tradition, as conservatives think, and do conservatives lack compassion and a sense of fairness, as liberals think? They report findings consistent with those of Westfall et al. on issue perceptions.[26] Both liberals and conservatives exaggerate the prevalence of moral stereotypes on both their side (the in-group) and the other side (the out-group). Contrary to popular stereotypes, self-identified liberals exaggerate moral differences more than do conservatives. Moderates are the most accurate.

Levendusky and Malhotra investigate false polarization using both surveys and laboratory experiments. The surveys show that Americans believe the country is more polarized than it is, by a factor of two on average.[27] Again, distorted perceptions are most common among party and issue extremists. People with extreme positions on issues are the most likely to exaggerate polarization, especially in regard to the positions of people on the other side of the issue, compared to those on their side. Additionally, the laboratory experiments Levendusky and Malhotra perform indicate that

25. Jesse Graham, Brian Nosek, and Jonathan Haidt, "The Moral Stereotypes of Liberals and Conservatives: Exaggeration of Differences across the Political Divide," *PLoS ONE* 7, no. 2 (December 2012), https://papers.ssrn.com/sol3/papers .cfm?abstract_id=2027266.

26. See Jonathan Haidt, *The Righteous Mind: Why Good People Are Divided by Politics and Religion* (New York: Pantheon, 2012).

27. Matthew Levendusky and Neil Malhotra, "(Mis)Perceptions of Partisan Polarization in the American Public," special issue, *Public Opinion Quarterly* 80 (2016): 378–91.

media coverage contributes to such false polarization, which in turn is associated with "affective polarization"—the tendency to dislike the other side over and above their policy differences.[28] (Chapter 3 will consider the subject of affective polarization.)

Finally, Ahler reports findings from two California surveys that are similar to the preceding findings based on national samples in surveys and laboratory experiments.[29] Both liberals and conservatives exaggerate the extremity of the positions held by members of their own group as well as those held by the opposing group. Again, moderates have the most accurate perceptions.

All in all, the evidence indicates that those most psychologically involved in politics have the least accurate perceptions of the views held by their fellow citizens. False polarization is widespread. The most recent contribution to this area of research suggests a mechanism to explain the prevalence of this false polarization. Ahler and Sood asked a representative national sample to estimate the social characteristics of people in the two parties.[30] To wit, what proportion of Republicans are senior citizens, Southern, evangelicals, or earn upward of $250,000? What proportion of Democrats are black, atheists or agnostics, union members, or LGBT? The results are mind-boggling. Misperception is massive. For example, Democrats think that 44 percent of Republicans make more than $250,000 per year, when the actual percentage is 2, and that 44 percent of Republicans are senior citizens, when the actual percentage is 21. For their part, Republicans think that 36 percent of Democrats are atheists or agnostics, when the actual percentage is about 9, and that 38 percent of Democrats are LGBT, when the true percentage is about 6. Once again, the more politically involved the respondent, the greater the misperception. The tendency of political media to highlight the most colorful and controversial personalities in the two parties ("exemplification") likely contributes to this state of extreme

---

28. Levendusky and Malhotra, "Media Coverage of Partisan Polarization."

29. Douglas J. Ahler, "Self-Fulfilling Misperceptions of Public Polarization," *Journal of Politics* 76, no. 3 (July 2014): 607–20.

30. Douglas J. Ahler and Gaurav Sood, "The Parties in Our Heads: Misperceptions about Party Composition and Their Consequences," May 22, 2016, http://www .dougahler.com/uploads/2/4/6/9/24697799/ahlersood_partycomposition.pdf.

misperception of the social composition of the parties.[31] The very vocal and visible activist groups who shape the parties' agendas are another likely contributor.[32]

In sum, Americans believe that the country is polarized even though studies consistently show that the perception of polarization far outstrips the reality. It is especially disconcerting to learn that the members of the political class who dominate politics in America not only are unrepresentative of the country at large, but also have the most distorted view of their country.

False Consensus

Not only do partisans and ideologues misperceive the extremity of the other side, resulting in a perceptual gap much larger than the objective gap (false polarization), they similarly misperceive how typical they are of their own side (false consensus). Some four decades ago Noelle-Neumann wrote of the *Spiral of Silence*.[33] People who believe they are in the minority in their group often refrain from expressing their disagreement for fear of being shunned or otherwise sanctioned by the group. Left unchecked, this dynamic leads the majority to believe that there are no dissidents, whereas members of the dissident minority believe that they are alone in their views.[34] As a result, both majority and minority members of a group

31. Dolf Zillmann and Hans-Bernd Brosius, *Exemplification in Communication: The Influence of Case Reports on the Perception of Issues* (London: Routledge, 2000); and Michael McCluskey and Young Mie Kim, "Moderatism or Polarization? Representation of Advocacy Groups' Ideology in Newspapers," *Journalism & Mass Communication Quarterly* 89 (September 6, 2012): 565–84.

32. After viewing these figures on misperception at one of my talks, a recently defeated Blue Dog Democratic congressman commented (paraphrasing from memory) that it was perfectly rational for people to infer that most Republicans were rich since Republicans spent so much time talking about tax rates, and it was perfectly rational for people to infer that a large proportion of Democrats must be gay because Democrats put so much emphasis on LGBT issues.

33. Elisabeth Noelle-Neumann, *The Spiral of Silence*, 2nd ed. (Chicago: University of Chicago Press, 1993).

34. On several occasions after giving a public lecture, I have been contacted by Republicans who express disbelief that one-fifth of strong Republicans believe that abortion should always be a matter of a woman's choice or that 40 percent of strong

come to believe—erroneously—that the group is politically homogeneous. This finding is consistent with the persuasive research of Diana Mutz.[35] Unlike political junkies, normal Americans get little pleasure out of political argument. On hearing an argument in the workplace with which they disagree, for example, they are likely to avoid the argument.

An online study by Yahoo! researchers illustrates the results of this process. In early 2008, approximately 2,500 Facebook users answered issue items adapted from the General Social Survey (GSS). They were also asked how their Facebook friends felt about these issues. Not surprisingly, friends agreed more than non-friends—by an average of 17 percentage points. But even close friends disagreed nearly 30 percent of the time, although they did not perceive this level of disagreement: "It appears that much of the diversity of opinions that exists in social networks is not apparent to their members."[36] Thus, surveys reporting that Americans have homogeneous friendship networks should not be taken at face value. People *think* their friends agree with them more than they actually do.

Maybe We're Not Polarized Yet

On digesting the negative evidence about polarization presented above, some believers in the polarization narrative suggest that the public just has not polarized *yet*. Surely, they say, the polarization of

Republicans believe that federal gun control laws should be stronger (both were facts in 2008 according to the ANES). "I don't know *any* Republicans who believe that," they write. In all likelihood, Republicans out of step with their fellow partisans on abortion or gun control do not advertise that fact.

35. "People entrenched in politically heterogeneous social networks retreat from political activity mainly out of a desire to avoid putting their social relationships at risk." Diana Mutz, *Hearing the Other Side: Deliberative versus Participatory Democracy* (New York: Cambridge University Press, 2006).

36. Shared Goel, Winter Mason, and Duncan J. Watts, "Real and Perceived Attitude Agreement in Social Networks," *Journal of Personality and Social Psychology* 99 (October 2010): 611–21. Consistent with these results, a more recent study of Facebook users reported that more than 20 percent of users' friends were from a different party. Eytan Bakshy, Solomon Messing, and Lada Adamic, "Exposure to Ideologically Diverse News and Opinion on Facebook," *Science* 348 (May 7, 2015): 1130–32.

the political class eventually will produce a reflection in the electorate. Contributing to that expectation is the vast increase in partisan and ideological programming on cable television and, more recently, the explosion of Internet sites that allow individuals to monitor only those news sources compatible with their political biases—if they so desire.[37] As social media, personalized search, and other technological "advances" proliferate, concerned observers have expressed the fear that Americans will isolate themselves in "ideological silos" or "echo chambers" that reinforce their views and insulate them from the views of the other side.[38] Given these technological trends, is there a serious danger that Americans gradually will balkanize into two nonoverlapping universes, each of which has its own facts and its own interpretations of reality?

Such questions fall under the rubric of what is known as the segregation hypothesis, which in this context has nothing to do with race. Rather, the hypothesis addresses biased information sources and their consequences for democratic societies. The concerns incorporated in the segregation hypothesis are real and the hypothesis intuitively plausible. Moreover, in laboratory experiments the effect is usually demonstrable. Studies like those of Iyengar and Hahn report that, in controlled conditions, subjects show a preference for information that is consistent with their prior political attitudes.[39] Levendusky's experiments show that partisan media make those who hold extreme views even more extreme.[40] Other laboratory studies report conflicting results, however, particularly when people are given the option of avoiding political news altogether.[41] Fortunately

37. According to some analysts, such "motivated reasoning" is not only common but biologically automatic. See Milton Lodge and Charles S. Taber, *The Rationalizing Voter* (New York: Cambridge University Press, 2013).

38. Cass Sunstein, *Republic.com* (Princeton NJ: Princeton University Press, 2001); Eli Pariser, *The Filter Bubble: What the Internet Is Hiding from You* (New York: Penguin, 2011).

39. Shanto Iyengar and Kyu S. Hahn, "Red Media, Blue Media: Evidence of Ideological Selectivity in Media Use," *Journal of Communication* 59 (2009): 19–39.

40. Matthew Levendusky, "Why Do Partisan Media Polarize Voters?" *American Journal of Political Science* 57, no. 3 (February 26, 2013): 611–23.

41. Kevin Arceneaux and Martin Johnson, *Changing Minds or Changing Channels? Partisan News in an Age of Choice* (Chicago: University of Chicago Press, 2013).

for American politics, studies undertaken in real-world conditions provide much more limited support for the segregation hypothesis than do some laboratory studies.[42]

Those who write about the dangers of ideological segregation are generally themselves well informed and highly interested in public affairs. They have a natural inclination to assume that most people are like them. But that assumption seriously overestimates the extent to which normal Americans follow politics. Historically, many social scientists have worried less about Americans getting their political information from biased sources than about them not getting any information at all. Research finds that, despite the increase in educational levels in recent decades, and despite the explosion of information sources, Americans are at best no worse informed than they were a generation ago, a conclusion that especially holds for younger people.[43] The simple fact is that most Americans do not follow politics closely, and surveys overestimate the proportion that does: Markus Prior documents that Americans claim to follow public affairs at much higher rates than objective measures show.[44] Table 2.1 provides some data on actual media usage by the contemporary American public.

42. Laboratory experiments in political science have exploded in popularity in recent years. The methodology has undeniable strengths, especially the capacity to pin down causal relationships. But problems of external validity are often severe. Effects produced in tightly controlled conditions with strong manipulations may not generalize to complex and confusing real-world contexts when numerous forces are at work simultaneously.

43. Michael X. Delli Carpini and Scott Keeter, *What Americans Know about Politics and Why It Matters* (New Haven, CT: Yale University Press, 1996); Markus Prior, *Post-Broadcast Democracy: How Media Choice Increases Inequality in Political Involvement and Polarizes Elections* (New York: Cambridge University Press, 2007); Martin P. Wattenberg, *Is Voting for Young People?* chap. 3 (New York: Pearson, 2012); Jennifer L. Lawless and Richard L. Fox, *Running from Office: Why Young Americans Are Turned Off to Politics*, chap. 4 (New York: Oxford University Press, 2015).

44. Markus Prior, "The Immensely Inflated News Audience: Assessing Bias in Self-Reported News," *Public Opinion Quarterly* 73, no. 1 (March 18, 2009): 130–43. John Sides notes that according to a 2008 Pew survey, one-third of the American public regularly watches cable news, but Nielsen reports that only 6 percent of the public actually watches cable news one hour in total each week. John Sides, "Can Partisan Media Contribute to Healthy Politics?" *The Monkey Cage*, March 10, 2013, http://themonkeycage.org/2013/03/can-partisan-media-contribute-to-healthy-politics/.

TABLE 2.1. The Public's (232 Million) Interest

	Millions of Viewers/Readers
NBC, CBS, ABC Nightly News	20.4
Meet the Press	3.9
USA Today	3.6
Wall Street Journal	2.4
New York Times	2.8
O'Reilly	3.7
Fox News	2.4
Rachel Maddow	2.4
PBS NewsHour	1.1
AC 360	1.0
Summer Olympics	28.8
Sunday Night Football	23.6
Big Bang Theory	18.3
Dancing with the Stars	10.3

Source: Nielsen Media Research.

There are upwards of 230 million eligible voters in the United States. On average, a bit less than 10 percent of the electorate watches any of the network evening news shows. The combined print and online circulation of the top national newspapers is between 1 and 2 percent of the electorate. Liberals gnash their teeth about Fox News and *The O'Reilly Factor* (until recently the top-rated political show on cable television), probably an overreaction given that the viewing audience of these shows is less than 2 percent of the electorate.[45] Some conservatives think that Rachel Maddow should be tried for treason (or at least have her Stanford degree revoked), surely an overreaction given that her viewing audience recently doubled to about 1 percent of the electorate. In contrast to these small numbers, sports and pop culture have audiences that are many times larger. Seven times as many people watch NBC's *Sunday Night Football* as watch NBC's Sunday morning *Meet the Press*, and six times as many people watch the *Big Bang Theory* as subscribe to the *New York Times*.

45. Liberals are finally beginning to realize this. See Frank Rich, "Stop Beating a Dead Fox," *New York* magazine, January 26, 2014, http://nymag.com/news/frank -rich/fox-news-2014-2/; Jack Shafer, "What Liberals Still Don't Understand about Fox News," *Politico*, May 25, 2015, www.politico.com/magazine/story/2015/05 /fox-news-liberals-118235.html#.VWT-Bc-6eUk.

Given these numbers, it is not surprising that studies of the segregation hypothesis based on real-world data rather than laboratory experiments offer a more reassuring picture. Beginning with the oldest of the new media, cable television, Webster notes, "Dystopian portrayals of the new media environment often envision the mass audience disaggregating into more or less self-contained communities of interest: The common public sphere is broken into many 'sphericules' or 'enclaves.'"[46] He analyzes Nielsen Media Research data on the audiences and viewing habits of sixty-two top television networks and finds that although the television audience is highly fragmented, evidence of polarization is modest. "Even the audience for Fox News, with its high TSV [time spent viewing], spends 92.5% of its [viewing] time watching something else on television. The rest of their time is widely distributed across the channels they have available."[47]

Martin and Yurukoglu report somewhat stronger evidence supporting the proposition that ideologically slanted news can affect citizens' opinions.[48] They estimate that someone who watched Fox News for four additional minutes per week increased her or his probability of voting Republican in 2000 by 0.9 of a percentage point; someone who watched MSNBC for four additional minutes increased his probability of voting Democratic by 0.7 of a percentage point. Although these are small numbers, particularly in view of the small audiences for those shows, the authors note that in extremely close elections they can make a difference. According to their estimates, for example, if Fox News had been removed from cable TV in 2000, it would have reduced the vote for George W. Bush in the average county by 1.6 percentage points, other things being equal. The electoral impact of such an effect would depend on the population of the county and whether the changes would have changed the winner in a state.

46. James G. Webster, "Beneath the Veneer of Fragmentation: Television Audience Polarization in a Multichannel World," *Journal of Communication* 55, no. 2 (2005): 379, http://onlinelibrary.wiley.com/doi/10.1111/j.1460-2466.2005.tb02677.x/epdf.

47. Ibid., 380.

48. Gregory J. Martin and Ali Yurukoglu, "Bias in Cable News: Persuasion and Polarization," NBER Working Paper 20798, December 2014, www.nber.org/papers/w20798.

Political blogs have proliferated in the past decade or so. Most blogs have small readerships—the vast majority of Americans never click on a political blog.[49] But one study finds that blog readers do focus their attention on blogs that are congenial with their prior political commitments.[50] Moreover, direct readership is not the only way that blogs could be influential. Farrell and Drezner conducted an online survey in the winter of 2003–4 and found that more than 80 percent of media employees report using blogs, more than 40 percent of them every week.[51] So blogs could indirectly affect a larger proportion of the population through stories and columns that later appear in the media. Liberal and conservative blogs link to others within their ideological camps (conservative blogs more so than liberal blogs), suggesting that blogs could have an echo chamber effect.[52]

Still, a study by Gentzkow and Shapiro again suggests that such effects are limited.[53] The authors investigate the ideological segregation of the audiences of 119 of the largest national news sites, a sample that includes important blogs as well as mainstream sites like the *New York Times, USA Today,* Yahoo!, and so forth. They report that although ideological segregation on the Internet is higher than in offline media, it remains low in absolute terms and is considerably lower than in people's face-to-face networks. Part of the reason for the failure of the segregation hypothesis is that people with extreme views "tend to consume more of everything, including centrist sites and occasionally sites with conflicting ideology. Their omnivorousness

49. The 2006 Comparative Congressional Election Study (CCES) reported that 14 percent of the respondents in a large Internet panel read political blogs. Eric Lawrence, John Sides, and Henry Farrell, "Self-Segregation or Deliberation? Blog Readership, Participation, and Polarization in American Politics," *Perspectives on Politics* 8, no. 1 (March 2010): 145. More generally, see Matthew Scott Hindman, *The Myth of Digital Democracy* (Princeton, NJ: Princeton University Press, 2009).

50. Lawrence et al., "Self-Segregation or Deliberation?"

51. Henry Farrell and Daniel W. Drezner, "The Power and Politics of Blogs," *Public Choice* 134 (2008): 15–30.

52. Lada Adamic and Natalie Glance, "The Political Blogosphere and the 2004 U.S. Election: Divided They Blog," proceedings of the 3rd international workshop on Link discovery, 2005, www.maths.tcd.ie/~mnl/store/AdamicGlance2004a.pdf.

53. Matthew Gentzkow and Jesse M. Shapiro, "Ideological Segregation Online and Offline," *Quarterly Journal of Economics* 126, no. 4 (November 2011): 1799–1839.

outweighs their ideological extremity, preventing their overall news diet from becoming too skewed."[54] Reassuringly, the researchers find that, if anything, segregation is lessening as the Internet news audience expands. In a later paper, Boxell, Gentzkow, and Shapiro report a puzzling finding that further undermines the argument that social media will create filter bubbles and lead to increased polarization. Looking at trends in nine different measures of polarization/sorting they find that polarization has increased significantly more among older cohorts than younger cohorts, despite the fact that use of social media is much more common among younger cohorts.[55]

One of the exciting features of some of the research discussed in this section is the exploitation of research designs that were unimaginable scarcely a decade ago. More data than ever are now available on the Internet, computing power has multiplied exponentially, and powerful new statistical techniques have been developed. Microsoft researchers provide another illustration in a study that touches on several of the points made in the previous discussion. The researchers monitored the search behavior of 1.2 million users of the Bing toolbar over a three-month period (March–May) in 2013.[56] The original database consisted of 2.3 billion page views of the top one hundred news sites, a median of 992 per user. This suggests an impressive appetite for news among these Bing search users, but on closer examination the vast majority of the pages visited concerned sports, weather, entertainment, and other subjects that are irrelevant to the segregation hypothesis. So the researchers developed a machine learning algorithm to identify page views of what is often referred to as "hard" news: government, economics, foreign affairs, and so on. Only 14 percent of the sample clicked on as many as ten such news articles during the three-month period—less than

54. Ibid., 1832.

55. Levi Boxell, Matthew Gentzkow, and Jesse Shapiro, "Is the Internet Causing Political Polarization? Evidence from Demographics," http://web.stanford.edu/~gentzkow/research/age-polar.pdf.

56. The Bing users had given consent. Seth Flaxman, Sharad Goel, and Justin M. Rao, "Ideological Segregation and the Effects of Social Media on News Consumption," 2013, https://bfi.uchicago.edu/research/working-paper/ideological-segregation-and-e%EF%AC%80ects-social-media-news-consumption.

one such visit a week, on average. Moreover, since the focus was the segregation hypothesis, people would have to visit "opinion" sites for their views to be affected. Only 4 percent of the sample that was tracked clicked on at least two such sites in the ninety-day period; that is, 96 percent of the sample read zero or only one opinion piece in three months. Only a few Americans are even very occasional readers of a Paul Krugman or George Will column. Although the trace element of those who visit opinion sites does show ideological segregation, the researchers conclude that the numbers are so small that the fears encapsulated in the segregation hypothesis are largely unwarranted.

Along similar lines, Barbera reports the results of an extensive study of Twitter users in the United States, Germany, and Spain.[57] Network diversity is correlated with political moderation—those with more diverse networks become more moderate over time and, importantly, Twitter networks tend to be fairly heterogeneous politically, in part because many of those in them are connected by only "weak ties."[58] Contrary to the fears expressed by those worried about ideological segregation, social media actually may lessen people's tendency to live in echo chambers: "Citizens are now exposed not only to their close friends' opinions, but also to political content shared by their co-workers, childhood friends, distant relatives, and other people with whom they form weak ties."[59]

To be sure, research on social media use and its effects is only in the early stages, but thus far careful empirical studies suggest that the worst fears about the consequences of the media revolution are not coming to pass.[60] In a recent review, Prior characterizes the

57. According to Barbera, Twitter is the leading social media source of political news, slightly exceeding Facebook. Pablo Barbera, "How Social Media Reduces Mass Political Polarization: Evidence from Germany, Spain, and the U.S.," paper presented at the annual meeting of the American Political Science Association, San Francisco, 2015.

58. Mark Granovetter, "The Strength of Weak Ties," *American Journal of Sociology* 78, no. 6 (May 1973): 1360–1380.

59. Barbera, 4.

60. This negative conclusion echoes that of studies of media influence on elections. As Diana Mutz comments, "Public perceptions of the power of media in elections, and the academic evidence of its influence, could not be further apart." Diana

rapidly expanding research in this area as follows: "Ideologically one-sided news exposure may be largely confined to a small, but highly involved and influential, segment of the population. There is no firm evidence that partisan media are making ordinary Americans more partisan."[61] To which one can add, no firm evidence exists that ideological media are making ordinary Americans more extreme.

All in all, contrary to clear trends in the political class, the American public is not "more divided morally, ideologically and politically today than they were during the Civil War," and there is no sign as yet that the public will become so. Mr. Prager (quoted at the beginning of this chapter) can rest more easily.[62]

Mutz, "The Great Divide: Campaign Media in the American Mind," *Daedalus* 141, no. 4 (2012): 83.

61. Markus Prior, "Media and Political Polarization," *Annual Review of Political Science* 16 (May 2013): 101–27.

62. Setting aside the question of how polarized Americans were during the Civil War, given that no survey evidence was available then.

CHAPTER 3

The Political Parties Have Sorted

When we speak of political polarization, it is more a matter of Democrats and Republicans becoming more homogeneous in their lives and basic beliefs than it is of the nation as a whole becoming fundamentally divided.

—Andrew Kohut

I'm here to insist that we are not as divided as we seem. And I know that because I know America.

—Barack Obama

The previous chapter noted that the American public believes that it has polarized despite evidence that in the aggregate the public looks much as it did in the 1970s and 1980s, long before polarization became a staple of political commentary.[1] Such perceptions are not surprising. Although many Americans are not interested in politics and make little effort to consume political news and commentary, it is hard to avoid getting some exposure to the widespread polarization meme. Even if only in passing, ordinary citizens are likely

Quotations are from Andrew Kohut, "The Political Middle Still Matters," Pew Research Center, August 1, 2014, www.pewresearch.org/fact-tank/2014/08/01/the-political-middle-still-matters/; and Barack Obama, "Remarks by the President at Memorial Service for Fallen Dallas Police Officers," July 12, 2016, www.whitehouse.gov/the-press-office/2016/07/12/remarks-president-memorial-service-fallen-dallas-police-officers.

1. Even some sophisticated observers share this misconception. An important reason is failure to consider the candidates. Partisan and ideological divisions will be much less apparent in an election featuring a moderate Midwestern Republican and a born-again Southern Democrat (1976) than in an election contested by a liberal Democrat and a conservative Republican (2000–2012).

to hear the extreme and uncivil remarks of members of the political class.[2] After all, that sort of rhetoric is what the media consider newsworthy. Moreover, the media regularly report the dysfunctional behavior of some of the people who participate in politics and serve in governmental positions—opposition for opposition's sake, refusal to compromise, threats to shut down the government or take the country over a "fiscal cliff."[3] Although negative political rhetoric and actions are not as common as media treatments make them seem, there is certainly plenty of reason for ordinary citizens to believe that the country has polarized.

The Difference between Sorting and Polarization

What people are actually seeing, however, is different, albeit real and important: the consequences of *partisan sorting* that has been going on for nearly five decades.[4] This sorting process flies in the face of long-standing political science generalizations about parties in countries like the United States that have single-member districts and majoritarian electoral rules, contrasted with parties in countries that have proportional electoral rules, like most European democracies. For decades, both theory and empirical research concluded that countries with majoritarian electoral rules tended to have two broad-based parties, often termed "catch-all" parties, whereas countries with proportional electoral rules tended to have more than two parties, all of which had clear ideological hues.[5] As Clinton

2. Matthew Levendusky and Neil Malhotra, "Does Media Coverage of Partisan Polarization Affect Political Attitudes?" *Political Communication* 33, no. 2 (2016): 283–301.

3. As Mutz writes, "One might say that mass media may not be particularly influential in telling people what to think, or perhaps even what to think about, but media are tremendously influential in telling people what others are thinking about and experiencing." Diana Mutz, *Impersonal Influence: How Perceptions of Mass Collectives Affect Political Attitudes* (New York: Cambridge University Press, 1998), 5.

4. Matthew Levendusky, *The Partisan Sort: How Liberals Became Democrats and Conservatives Became Republicans* (Chicago: University of Chicago Press, 2009).

5. The *locus classicus* is Maurice Duverger, *Political Parties: Their Organization and Activity in the Modern State* (New York: Wiley, 1954), 216–28, 245–55, passim.

Rossiter wrote about the United States in a standard 1960s political parties textbook, "There is and can be no real difference between the Democrats and the Republicans, because the unwritten laws of American politics demand that the parties overlap substantially in principle, policy, character, appeal, and purpose—or cease to be parties with any hope of winning a national election."[6] The validity of this conventional wisdom was shown by the electoral drubbings suffered by Republican Barry Goldwater, who gave the country "a choice, not an echo" in 1964, and Democrat George McGovern, who did the same with a similar result in 1972.

By the turn of the century, however, a new conventional wisdom had taken hold, one which asserted that the public had polarized and elections were now about maximizing the turnout of the "base," not about appealing to centrist voters—because the latter had virtually disappeared. As the previous chapter showed, that conclusion is unwarranted. We can argue about the size of the middle, which depends on how we define it (whether in terms of ideology, partisanship, or specific issues). But once we settle on a definition, the data reported in chapter 2 do not show any decline in its size. Rather, what is true today is that the middle has no home in either party. Political parties in the United States have come to resemble parties in proportional electoral systems. A process of sorting during the past several decades has resulted in a Democratic Party that is clearly liberal and a Republican Party that is clearly conservative.

In a 1998 article, Alan Abramowitz and Kyle Saunders showed that the American electorate was undergoing an "ideological realignment."[7] In an earlier, highly influential work, Carmines and Stimson demonstrated that Democrats and Republicans in Congress began to polarize after the election of a large class of liberal Democrats

---

For a contemporary treatment, see Gary Cox, *Making Votes Count: Strategic Coordination in the World's Electoral Systems* (New York: Cambridge University Press, 1997).

6. Clinton Rossiter, *Parties and Politics in America* (Ithaca, NY: Cornell University Press, 1960), 108.

7. Alan I. Abramowitz and Kyle L. Saunders, "Ideological Realignment in the U.S. Electorate," *Journal of Politics* 60, no. 3 (August 1998): 634–52.

in the 1958 elections, with racial issues being the apparent cause.[8] Abramowitz and Saunders concluded, however, that in the general electorate, "this process did not begin until the 1980s and that Civil Rights was only one of a host of issues involved in the realignment."[9] Whereas partisanship was only loosely correlated with ideology and issue positions for much of American history (as the mid-twentieth-century conventional wisdom held), the correlations increased dramatically between the late 1970s and the mid-1990s.

As electoral majorities have become more short-lived, the realignment concept has fallen out of favor, so it is more common today to use the term "party sorting" to describe the changes that Abramowitz and Saunders identified. Sorting and polarization are logically independent processes, although they may be empirically related. To illustrate, here is an example of pure polarization:

Time 1	*Democrats*	*Independents*	*Republicans*
	70 liberals	100 moderates	30 liberals
	30 conservatives		70 conservatives
Time 2	*Democrats*	*Independents*	*Republicans*
	105 liberals	—	45 liberals
	45 conservatives		105 conservative

Between time 1 and time 2 the electorate polarizes, both ideologically (as all moderates move to the liberal and conservative camps) and in partisan terms (as all independents become partisans). As fig-

8. Edward G. Carmines and James A. Stimson, *Issue Evolution: Race and the Transformation of American Politics* (Princeton, NJ: Princeton University Press, 1989).

9. Abramowitz and Saunders, "Ideological Realignment," 649. Using a different methodology, Hill and Tausanovitch confirm that sorting in the public first became apparent in the early 1980s. In another paper they report that the process began earlier with sorting of primary electorates in the South that spread beyond the South. Seth J. Hill and Chris Tausanovitch, "A Disconnect in Representation? Comparison of Trends in Congressional and Public Polarization," *Journal of Politics* 77, no. 4 (October 2015): 1058–75. Hill and Tausanovitch, "Southern Realignment, Party Sorting, and the Polarization of American Primary Electorates, 1958–2012," unpublished paper, June 3, 2016, http://sjhill.ucsd.edu/HillTausanovitch_Primaries.pdf.

ures 2.5 and 2.6 in the previous chapter show, this has *not* happened in the United States.

The preceding example shows polarization without sorting: although the middle has vanished (polarization), the parties are no better sorted at time 2 than at time 1—each party still has an ideological minority wing comprising 30 percent of the party. Consider an alternative time 2*:

Time 2*	Democrats	Independents	Republicans
	100 liberals	100 moderates	100 conservatives

This alternative time 2* shows pure sorting: there are the same numbers of liberals, moderates, and conservatives as at time 1 and the same numbers of Democrats, independents, and Republicans as at time 1, but now the parties are perfectly sorted—all liberals are in the Democratic camp, all conservatives in the Republican camp, and all moderates remain as independents.

Of course, the two processes are not mutually exclusive. Consider another alternative time 2**. If at time 2 above, conservative Democrats and liberal Republicans realize that they are hopelessly in the minority in their parties and migrate to the party in which their views predominate, we would have polarization *and* sorting:

Time 2**	Democrats	Independents	Republicans
	150 liberals	—	150 conservatives

To a less extreme degree this is the case in Congress, where we clearly observe sorting (resulting from the replacement of conservative Southern Democrats by Republicans and of liberal Northeastern Republicans by Democrats) and polarization (reflecting the decline of the moderates within each party).

Obviously sorting produces *partisan* polarization—when conservative Democrats leave the Democratic Party, the party becomes more liberal. When liberal Republicans leave the Republican Party, the party becomes more conservative. The problem with using the term "partisan polarization" is that in common usage the modifier "partisan" often gets omitted and then forgotten. Given that as much as 40 percent of the electorate claims not to be partisan, casual references to polarization exaggerate the divide in public opinion. (This brings up the whole question of what are independents, leaning and otherwise, which is considered in chapter 6.) The term "sorting" helps us keep in mind that we are focusing only on the two-thirds of the electorate that claims to have a partisan identity.

Different individual-level processes can produce both sorting and polarization.[10] One way is conversion, which in turn can occur in either of two ways. If partisan identity is extremely strong, people can change their ideological positions: liberal Republicans can become conservative Republicans and conservative Democrats can become liberal Democrats. Alternatively, if ideologies are strongly held, people can change their partisanship: liberal Republicans can become Democrats and conservative Democrats can become Republicans.[11] In addition, sorting may occur through population replacement without any individuals changing at all: during the course of several decades, liberal Republicans and conservative Democrats die off and younger voters who replace them join the party consistent with their views, if either. Especially when viewed over generation-long periods, each of these processes is probably at work to some extent.

According to Poole and Rosenthal, there is little evidence of conversion in the Congress: individual-level stability is the rule in con-

---

10. Levendusky, *The Partisan Sort,* chaps. 4–6.

11. The empirical evidence suggests that the first possibility is more common—people change their issue and ideological positions rather than their partisanship. See Levendusky, *The Partisan Sort,* chap. 6; Thomas M. Carsey and Geoffrey Layman, "Party Polarization and Party Structuring of Policy Attitudes: A Comparison of Three NES Panel Studies," *Political Behavior* 24, no. 3 (2002): 199–236; Geoffrey Layman and Thomas Carsey, "Party Polarization and 'Conflict Extension' in the American Electorate," *American Journal of Political Science* 46, no. 4 (October 2002): 786–802. Killian and Wilcox, however, report that on abortion people were more likely to switch parties than switch their positions on the issue. Mitchell Killian and Clyde Wilcox, "Do Abortion Attitudes Lead to Party Switching?" *Political Research Quarterly* 61, no. 4 (December 2008): 561–73. And most recently, a larger study by Goren and Chapp finds that positions on abortion and gay rights have a larger effect on party identification than vice-versa. Paul Goren and Christopher Chapp, "Moral Power: How Public Opinion on Culture War Issues Shapes Partisan Predispositions and Religious Orientations," *American Political Science Review* 111, no. 1 (February 24, 2017): 110–28.

gressional voting.[12] Thus, replacement is the dominant process in both party sorting and polarization in Congress. Republicans have replaced conservative Democrats and Democrats have replaced liberal Republicans (sorting), but in addition more extreme members have replaced less extreme ones, resulting in a loss of moderates in both parties (polarization). In contrast, as seen in figures 2.1–2.3 of chapter 2, in the public there is little or no increase in polarization; rather, sorting is the dominant process underlying the increased partisan conflict in recent decades, and both conversion and replacement appear to be at work.[13] As Andrew Kohut, former director of the Pew Research Center, commented, "When we speak of political polarization, it is more a matter of Democrats and Republicans becoming more homogeneous in their lives and basic beliefs than it is of the nation as a whole becoming fundamentally divided."[14]

Three Features of Party Sorting in the United States

Research to date supports three propositions that we can accept with some confidence. First, members of the political class initiate the process—they do not sort as a response to popular demand; rather, they sort first and the (attentive) public takes note and sorts later.[15] Second, sorting increases with the level of political involvement—the

12. Keith Poole and Howard Rosenthal, *Ideology and Congress,* chap. 4 (New Brunswick, NJ: Transaction Publishers, 2011).

13. After an intensive and extensive statistical analysis, Baldassarri and Gelman conclude that sorting is the primary explanation for changes in public opinion between 1972 and 2008. Krasa and Polborn concur that sorting is the dominant mechanism between 1976 and 2004, but find somewhat surprisingly that sorting and polarization are of about equal importance in 2008. Delia Baldassarri and Andrew Gelman, "Partisans without Constraint: Political Polarization and Trends in American Public Opinion," *American Journal of Sociology* 114, no. 2 (September 2008): 408–46; Stefan Krasa and Mattias Polborn, "Policy Divergence and Voter Polarization in a Structural Model of Elections," *Journal of Law and Economics* 57, no. 1 (2014): 31–76.

14. Andrew Kohut, "The Political Middle Still Matters," Pew Research Center, August 1, 2014, www.pewresearch.org/fact-tank/2014/08/01/the-political-middle-still-matters/.

15. Carmines and Stimson, *Issue Evolution;* Abramowitz and Saunders, "Ideological Realignment"; Levendusky, *The Partisan Sort.* Cf. James Campbell's "revealed polarization theory" in *Polarized: Making Sense of a Divided America* (Princeton NJ: Princeton University Press, 2016).

higher the level of political activism, the more distinct (better sorted) are Republicans and Democrats.[16] Third, related to the second proposition, among typical partisans in the public, sorting has increased but remains far below the levels exhibited by those in the political class. Consider the abortion issue on which the party platforms are polar opposites.

The General Social Survey (GSS) carried out by the National Opinion Research Center at the University of Chicago has been asking the same abortion question since 1972. The question reads:

Please tell me whether or not you think it should be possible for a pregnant woman to obtain a legal abortion if
  1. The woman's health is seriously endangered
  2. She became pregnant as a result of rape
  3. There is a strong chance of serious defect in the baby
  4. The family has low income and cannot afford any more children
  5. She is not married and does not want to marry the man
  6. She is married and does not want any more children[17]

This survey item avoids emotionally and politically charged oversimplifications like "pro-life" and "pro-choice" and asks directly

16. "No knowledgeable observer doubts that the American public is less divided than the political agitators and vocal elective office-seekers who claim to represent it." William A. Galston and Pietro S. Nivola, "Delineating the Problem," in *Red and Blue Nation*, vol. 1, ed. Pietro S. Nivola and David W. Brady (Washington, DC: Brookings Institution, 2006). See also John H. Aldrich and Melanie Freeze, "Political Participation, Polarization, and Public Opinion: Activism and the Merging of Partisan and Ideological Polarization," in *Facing the Challenge of Democracy: Explorations in the Analysis of Public Opinion and Political Participation*, ed. Paul M. Sniderman and Benjamin Highton (Princeton, NJ: Princeton University Press, 2011), 185–206. Most recently Hill and Huber conclude, "Thus we observe increasing extremism and homogeneity within each party as participation increases (from vote to general election voting to primary voting to contributing)." Seth J. Hill and Gregory A. Huber, "Representativeness and Motivations of the Contemporary Donorate: Results from Merged Survey and Administrative Records," *Political Behavior*, 2016, http://link.springer.com/article/10.1007/s11109-016-9343-y.

17. In 1977 the GSS added a seventh option, "The woman wants it for any reason." This option lacks the specificity of the previous six, and ANES data show that about a third of those who choose this option reject it when asked about gender selection. Thus, I omit this option from the analysis.

FIGURE 3.1. **Abortion Should Be Legal When**

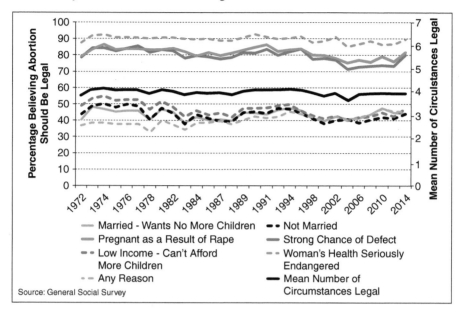

Source: General Social Survey

about the specifics of people's views. As shown in figure 3.1, in the aggregate Americans' views have changed little during the course of more than forty years. Large majorities favor legal abortion in the three cases of fetal birth defects, pregnancies resulting from rape, and dangers to the woman's health (the so-called traumatic circumstances).[18] On the other hand, the population is closely divided in the three cases of single motherhood, low income, and enough children already (the so-called elective circumstances). On average, the public believes in legal abortion in four of the six circumstances (the heavy middle line in the figure), with little change over the course of four decades.[19]

Figure 3.2 plots the average number of circumstances in which Democrats, independents, and Republicans favor legal abortion.

18. The terms "traumatic" and "elective" are not used in any evaluative sense. These terms are commonly used in the literature.

19. A small recent downturn is evident in the figure. Some analysts attribute it to the controversy over intact dilation and extraction, or "partial birth abortion." Descriptions of the procedure are graphic and gruesome and may have led some people to modify their views.

FIGURE 3.2. **Partisans Eventually Sorted on Abortion**

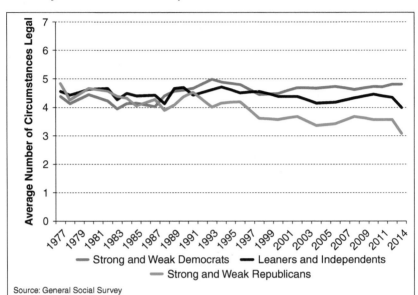

Source: General Social Survey

The Supreme Court decided *Roe v. Wade* in 1973. The delegates to the presidential nominating conventions had begun to diverge even earlier,[20] but it took nearly two decades for Democrats and Republicans in the public to get on the "correct" side of the issue. Republicans and Democrats, who began to separate after 1992, continue to do so. This illustrates the first proposition: that the political class sorts first, the public follows.

With the addition of some background information, figure 3.2 also illustrates the third proposition: that although better sorted than they used to be, ordinary partisans are still imperfectly sorted. In 2012 and 2016, the national platforms adopted by the two presidential nominating conventions could not have been more different on the subject of abortion. The Republican platform said, essentially, "never, no exceptions."[21] The Democratic platform said, essentially,

20. Kira Sanbonmatsu, *Democrats, Republicans, and the Politics of Women's Place* (Ann Arbor, MI: University of Michigan Press, 2002), 96–97.

21. Even "to save the life of the mother" is not explicitly included.

"at any time, for any reason."[22] Thus, it seems reasonable to conclude that a majority of Republican convention delegates would have
answered the General Social Survey question "none of these circumstances" and a majority of Democratic convention delegates "all of
these circumstances." But self-identified Democrats in the public are
only at 4.8 circumstances, not 6, and self-identified Republicans at
3.1 circumstances are nowhere near the zero circumstances position that a majority of Republican convention delegates presumably
holds. Put another way, after more than two decades of sorting, the
gap between partisans on this issue is less than two of the six circumstances whereas the gap between majorities of convention delegates
arguably is six circumstances.

To illustrate the second proposition with its finer gradation of
comparisons, consider an abortion item included on the quadrennial
American National Election Studies. This item reads, "Which one of
the opinions on this page best agrees with your view?"

 1. By law, abortion should never be permitted.
 2. The law should permit abortion only in case of rape, incest,
    or when the woman's life is in danger.
 3. The law should permit abortion for reasons other than
    rape, incest, or danger to the woman's life, but only after
    the need for the abortion has been clearly established.
 4. By law, a woman should always be able to obtain an abor-
    tion as a matter of personal choice.

Figure 3.3 contains the responses to the unconditional pro-choice
category for different levels of political involvement. In 1980, the
differences between weak partisans, strong partisans, and members
of the political class (donors and activists) were 10 percentage points
or less. By the early 1990s larger differences were apparent, and
these have continued to grow in the years since. But weakly committed Republicans and Democrats have sorted much less than strongly
committed ones—a 25 percentage point difference in 2016 in the

22. And, contrary to majority opinion, the procedure would be covered by government health programs.

FIGURE 3.3. **When Should Abortion Be Permitted?**
"Always as a Matter of Personal Choice"

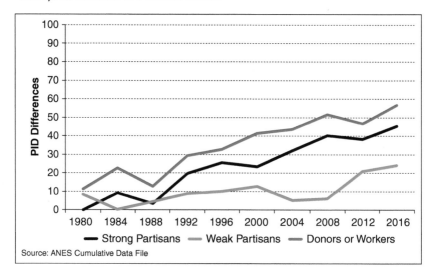

Source: ANES Cumulative Data File

Workers are strong and weak partisans who worked for a party or candidate. Donors are strong and weak partisans who donated to a party or candidate.

former category versus a 45 percentage point difference in the latter category; the donors and activist categories of each party have sorted even more than strong partisans—the former are now nearly 60 percentage points apart.

Like the GSS data in figure 3.2, the data underlying figure 3.3 also provide an illustration of the third proposition. Even at the level of strong partisans, the lack of sorting may surprise some. As table 3.1 shows, in 2016 one out of five strong Democrats believed that abortion should never be permitted or only permitted in the cases of rape, incest, or a threat to the woman's life, a position closer to the Republican position than that of their own party. Perhaps even more surprising, nearly one-third of strong Republicans believed that abortion should always be allowed as the personal choice of the woman or when there is "a clear need." Such positions obviously are very distant from that stated in the Republican platform.[23] Why

23. It may surprise some readers to learn that in 2004, at least, abortion was the issue on which most partisans were out of line with their parties. Hillygus and

TABLE 3.1. **When Should Abortion Be Permitted?**

When Should Abortion Be Permitted?	Strong Democrats	Strong Republicans
Never permitted	7%	26%
Only in case of rape, incest, or the woman's life is in danger	15%	43%
For a clear need	12%	14%
Always as a personal choice	64%	16%

Source: 2016 ANES

do such "unsorted" Republicans and Democrats stay in their respective parties given their views on the issue? Part of the answer is that contrary to widespread impressions from media coverage of politics, most Americans do not consider abortion (and other social issues) to be nearly as important as activist groups in the two parties do, a matter discussed in chapter 5.

Studies that measure constituent preferences on a single left-right dimension generally report "asymmetric polarization": both parties have moved toward the poles since the 1970s, but Republicans have moved further right than Democrats have moved left.[24] Opinion on specific issues, however, shows more variation. On same-sex marriage, for example, sorting appears to be due primarily to Democrats adopting a more liberal stance, although both parties have become more accepting (figure 3.4). On gun control, sorting seems to be entirely a matter of Republicans becoming more supportive of gun rights (figure 3.5); Democrats have scarcely moved at all. To complicate matters, sometimes survey items on the same subject support contradictory conclusions. On the GSS survey item graphed in

Shields reported that in 2004 nearly half of all partisans disagreed with their parties' positions on one or more issues. Abortion led the list. D. Sunshine Hillygus and Todd G. Shields, *The Persuadable Voter: Wedge Issues in Presidential Campaigns,* chap. 3 (Princeton, NJ: Princeton University Press, 2008).

24. A longer time perspective offers a somewhat more complex picture. Democrats began moving left in the 1950s as the South realigned. Republicans actually moved in a more centrist direction before making a sharp right turn in more recent decades. See Campbell, *Polarized,* chap. 7; Devin Caughey, James Dunham, and Christopher Warshaw, "Polarization and Partisan Divergence in the American Public, 1946–2012," unpublished paper, 2016.

FIGURE 3.4. Party Sorting on Same-Sex Marriage: Democrats Move More

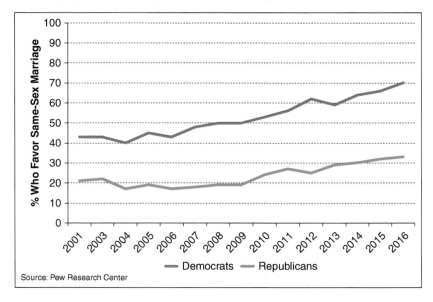

FIGURE 3.5. Party Sorting on Gun Ownership: Republicans Move More

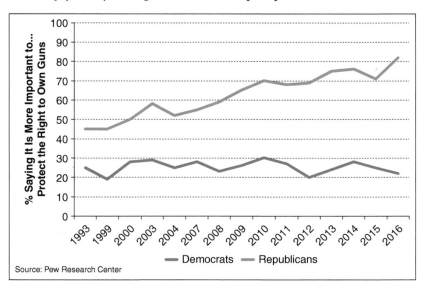

FIGURE 3.6. Partisan Sorting on Abortion: Democrats Move More

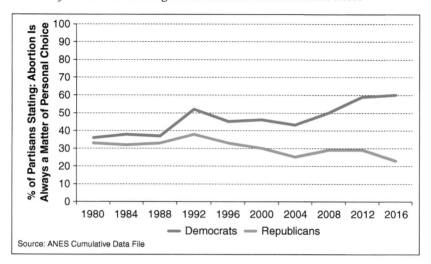

Source: ANES Cumulative Data File

figure 3.2, for example, the sorting seems to be primarily created by Republicans moving to a more restrictive stance. But as figure 3.6 shows, on the ANES item reported in figure 3.3, Democrats' support for abortion always being a matter of personal choice has nearly doubled, whereas Republicans have become only slightly less opposed to that position. The one thing we can say for sure is that partisans are further apart on most issues today than they were a generation ago.

A great deal of public opinion research shows that what has happened in the case of the issues examined above is the rule, not the exception. On issue after issue, Republicans increasingly find themselves on one side and Democrats find themselves on the other side, although the extent of disagreement often is not great. Sorting has significantly increased; but among typical Americans, even strong partisans, it remains far from perfect. A recent Pew Research Center report provided a wealth of information in support of this conclusion.[25] During the past two decades, partisans have increasingly sorted. Looking at

25. Pew Research Center, "Political Polarization in the American Public: How Increasing Ideological Uniformity and Partisan Antipathy Affect Politics, Compromise and Everyday Life," June 12, 2014, www.people-press.org/2014/06/12/political-polarization-in-the-american-public/.

opinions on ten issues, the researchers found that the proportion of extremely consistent Americans doubled from 10 percent to 21 percent and the proportion of mixed or inconsistent Americans declined from 49 percent in 1994 to 39 percent in 2014.[26] But as the authors cautioned, "These sentiments [those of uncompromising ideologues] are not shared by all—or even most—Americans. The majority do not have uniformly conservative or liberal views. Most do not see either party as a threat to the nation. And more believe their representatives in government should meet halfway to resolve contentious disputes rather than hold out for more of what they want."[27]

Party Sorting and Affective Polarization

Culture War? The Myth of a Polarized America took note of Samuel Popkin's suggestion that even if there were little evidence of increased polarization on the issues, perhaps voters on opposite sides had come to dislike each other more.[28] At that time there was only a modicum of evidence consistent with Popkin's suggestion, but research since then suggests that such "affective" partisan polarization has increased: Democrats and Republicans appear to dislike each other more than they did a generation ago.[29]

Cognitive and affective polarization are not mutually exclusive, of course. If human beings dislike others the more they disagree with them—a reasonable supposition, *ceteris paribus*—standard

26. The report was widely misinterpreted as showing that partisans had become more extreme, when the actual finding was that they had become more consistent. See Morris Fiorina, "Americans Have Not Become More Politically Polarized," *Washington Post*, June 23, 2014, www.washingtonpost.com/blogs/monkey-cage/wp/2014/06/23/americans-have-not-become-more-politically-polarized/.

27. Pew Research Center, "Political Polarization," 7.

28. Morris Fiorina, with Samuel J. Abrams and Jeremy C. Pope, *Culture War? The Myth of a Polarized America* (New York: Longman, 2011), 68–69.

29. Daron Shaw, "If Everyone Votes Their Party, Why Do Presidential Election Outcomes Vary So Much?" *The Forum* 10, no. 3 (October 2012), www.degruyter.com/view/j/for.2012.10.issue-3/1540–8884.1519/1540–8884.1519.xml; Alan I. Abramowitz, "The New American Electorate," in *American Gridlock: The Sources, Character, and Impact of Political Polarization*, ed. James A. Thurber and Antoine Yoshinaka (New York: Cambridge University Press, 2015).

spatial models would predict an increase in affective polarization.[30] Consider this pure sorting example:

Time 1	*Democrats*	*Independents*	*Republicans*
	50 liberals		25 liberals
	25 moderates	50 moderates	25 moderates
	25 conservatives		50 conservatives
Time 2	*Democrats*	*Independents*	*Republicans*
	75 liberals		75 conservatives
	25 moderates	50 moderates	25 moderates

If we assign liberals the value of −1 on a left-right scale, moderates 0, and conservatives +1, then as figure 3.7 shows, as the parties sort, the average Democratic position moves leftward from −.25 to −.75, the average Republican position moves rightward from .25 to .75, and the distance between them triples.[31] One need not conjure up esoteric social-psychological theories to suggest that the greater the policy or ideological differences between the average Democrat and the average Republican, the greater the dislike.

FIGURE 3.7. **Sorting Causes Partisan Polarization**

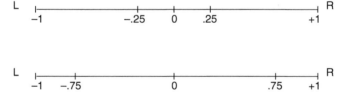

Moreover, the preceding observation carries over from conceptualization to measurement. One commonly used measure of affect is the "feeling thermometer."[32] Nearly forty years after their introduction, I

30. Alan I. Abramowitz and Steven Webster, "The Angry American Voter," *Sabato's Crystal Ball* 13, no. 30 (August 6, 2015): figure 2, www.centerforpolitics .org/crystalball/articles/the-angry-american-voter/.

31. The numbers are arbitrary, but the point is general.

32. The item reads as follows: "I'd like to get your feelings toward some of our political leaders and other people who are in the news these days. I'll read the name of a person and I'd like you to rate that person using something we call the feeling

think it is fair to say that no one really knows what these items measure. A voter may feel cold toward a candidate because she thinks he is a terrible human being. Alternatively, she may feel warmly toward him because she approves of his foreign policy. Nothing in the item allows us to separate the affective from the cognitive. The same is true for various other measures. A voter may say that Trump makes him feel "angry" because of Trump's persona or because of Trump's policy proposals.

This intermingling of the cognitive and affective is evident in a fascinating finding widely discussed in the media: partisans are now less likely to want to date or marry someone from the other party than they were in 1960.[33] As Iyengar, Sood, and Lelkes summarize,

> Democrats and Republicans not only increasingly dislike the opposing party, but also impute negative traits to the rank-and-file of the out-party. We further demonstrate that affective polarization has permeated judgments about interpersonal relations, exceeds polarization based on other prominent social cleavages, and that levels of partisan affect are significantly higher in America, compared to the United Kingdom.[34]

Not all data are consistent with such findings—a study comparing how Americans ranked the importance of eighteen traits in a marriage partner in 1939 compared to 2008 found that "similar political background" increased from eighteenth (dead last) only

---

thermometer. Ratings between 50 degrees and 100 degrees mean that you feel favorable and warm toward the person. Ratings between 0 degrees and 50 degrees mean that you don't feel favorable toward the person and that you don't care too much for that person. You would rate the person at the 50 degree mark if you don't feel particularly warm or cold toward the person. If we come to a person whose name you don't recognize, you don't need to rate that person. Just tell me and we'll move on to the next one."

33. Shanto Iyengar, Gaurav Sood, and Yphtach Lelkes, "Affect, Not Ideology: A Social Identity Perspective on Polarization," *Public Opinion Quarterly* 76, no. 3 (2012): 405–31.

34. Ibid., 407.

to seventeenth.[35] Still, if the findings of Iyengar and his collabora-tors are accepted at face value, party sorting provides a plausible explanation.

In 1964, what if a daughter came home from college and told her Democratic parents that she was engaged to a Republican? How might they have responded? They probably would have thought, "What kind of Republican?" A Western conservative like Barry Goldwater? A Northeastern liberal like Nelson Rockefeller? A Midwestern moder-ate like George Romney? Similarly, had a son come home from college and told his Republican parents that he was engaged to a Democrat, they likely would have wondered, "What kind of Democrat?" A union stalwart? An urban liberal? A Southern conservative? A Western prag-matist? In the unsorted parties of that time, no matter what kind of person you were, there were probably people with similar social char-acteristics and political views in the other party.

In the better-sorted parties of today (reinforced by the crude ste-reotypes common in the media and in political debate), it is unsur-prising that some parents might react very differently. If a son comes home and announces his engagement to a Democrat, his Republican parents might think, "You want to bring an America-hating atheist into our family?" Similarly, Democratic parents might react to their daughter's engagement to a Republican by asking, "We're supposed to welcome an evolution-denying homophobe into our family?" In the better-sorted parties of today, it would be surprising if affective partisan polarization has not increased.

Consistent with thought experiments like the one above, empirical research shows that party sorting contributes to the rise in affective polarization.[36] Still, at this time I would not argue that the increase in party and issue alignment is the entire explanation. Adopting

35. Ana Swanson, "What men and women wanted in a spouse in 1939—and how different it is today," *Washington Post*, April 19, 2016, www.washingtonpost.com /news/wonk/wp/2016/04/19/what-men-and-women-wanted-in-a-spouse-in-1939 -and-how-different-it-is-today/.

36. Lori D. Bougher, "The Correlates of Discord: Identity, Issue Alignment and Political Hostility in Polarized America," *Political Behavior*, November 2016, https:// link.springer.com/article/10.1007%2Fs11109-016-9377-1.

a social identity perspective, Mason argues that party sorting has increased the agreement between partisan and ideological identities, resulting in the strengthening of both:[37] "The effect is an electorate whose members are more biased and angry than their issue positions alone can explain."[38] This line of work is reminiscent of the studies reviewed in chapter 2 that show distorted perceptions of the actual positions held by members of the opposite party and those at the opposite end of the ideological spectrum. But these findings are stronger in that the inaccurate perceptions appear to increase emotional antagonism. If our present political difficulties have deep psychological roots that have little basis in objective reality, any attempt to overcome the difficulties through institutional reforms will face additional obstacles. As Mason comments, "It may therefore be disturbing to imagine a nation of people driven powerfully by team spirit, but less powerfully by a logical connection of issues to action."[39]

The critical question for the future is whether affective polarization will carry over into actual political behavior. Iyengar and Westwood report experimental evidence that partisan hostility and willingness to discriminate on partisan grounds today may be as pronounced in some respects as racial hostility (or at least that people are less inhibited about expressing the former compared to the latter).[40] A series of experiments reported by Lelkes and Westwood offers a more positive note. They find that affective polarization is associated with acceptance of hostile rhetoric, avoidance of members of the other party, and favoritism toward members of one's own party, but not with overt discrimination against members of

37. Lilliana Mason, "'I Disrespectfully Agree': The Differential Effects of Partisan Sorting on Social and Issue Polarization," *American Journal of Political Science* 59, no. 1 (January 1, 2015): 128–45.

38. Ibid., 140.

39. Ibid., 142.

40. Shanto Iyengar and Sean J. Westwood, "Fear and Loathing across Party Lines: New Evidence on Group Polarization," *American Journal of Political Science* 59, no. 3 (2015): 690–707. See also an interesting study of online dating that reports findings consistent with those of Iyengar and Westwood: Gregory Huber and Neil Malhotra, "Social Spillovers of Political Polarization," unpublished paper, 2015.

the other party. On the other hand, Miller and Conover report that controlling for issue and ideological distance, affective polarization increases the likelihood of voting and participating in the campaign, which would increase partisan polarization in elections.[41]

Party Sorting and Geographic Polarization

Whereas research on affective polarization delves into mental processes inside the voters' heads, a different line of research examines the physical location of voters' heads. Some years ago a book entitled *The Big Sort* received considerable popular and some scholarly attention.[42] The thesis of the book is that since the 1970s the United States has experienced a process of geographic political segregation:

> We have built a country where everyone can choose the neighborhood (and church and news shows) most compatible with his or her lifestyle and beliefs. And we are living with the consequences of this segregation by way of life: pockets of like-minded citizens that have become so ideologically inbred that we don't know, can't understand, and can barely conceive of "those people" who live just a few miles away.[43]

This argument is another version of the segregation hypothesis discussed in chapter 2 except that the hypothesized mechanism of voter homogenization is social pressure from one's neighborhood surroundings rather than the media. The arguments and analyses in *The Big Sort* are flimsy, ranging from anecdotal to impressionistic. Briefly, patterns in the presidential vote that are the basis of the argument often differ from patterns in votes for other offices and espe-

41. Yphtach Lelkes and Sean J. Westwood, "The Limits of Partisan Prejudice," unpublished paper, 2015; Patrick R. Miller and Pamela Johnston Conover, "Red and Blue States of Mind: Partisan Hostility and Voting in the United States," *Political Research Quarterly* 68 (2015): 225–39.

42. Bill Bishop, *The Big Sort: Why the Clustering of Like-Minded America Is Tearing Us Apart* (New York: Houghton Mifflin, 2008).

43. Ibid., 40.

cially in party registration, and most Americans don't know their neighbors, let alone feel pressure to conform politically.[44] Studies find that although many people profess a desire to live in politically compatible neighborhoods, their ability to realize those desires is limited by the fact that when making location decisions, liberals and conservatives alike privilege nonpolitical factors like good schools, low crime rates, stable property values, and commuting time, with political considerations ranking much lower.[45] After calculating the 2008 presidential vote for more than 120,000 precincts, Hersh concluded, "In this nationwide collection of precinct data it is clear that most precincts are quite mixed in terms of partisan supporters. Most voters live in neighborhoods that are not lopsidedly partisan."[46]

Still, since the 1960s there have been significant changes in the geographic locus of party competition in the country. Until the 1960s, Republican presidential candidates were not competitive in most of the South; today Democratic presidential candidates are not competitive in much of the South. That much is more or less a wash, however. More notably, in the mid-twentieth century most northern states were competitive. In particular, both parties had realistic chances of carrying big heterogeneous states such as New York, Pennsylvania, Illinois, and California. Today most of these states vote dependably for Democratic presidential candidates; in recent elections only a dozen or so states have constituted the Electoral College battleground that decides the presidential winner.

44. Samuel J. Abrams and Morris P. Fiorina, "The Big Sort That Wasn't: A Skeptical Reexamination," *PS: Political Science & Politics* 45, no. 2 (April 2012), https://www.cambridge.org/core/journals/ps-political-science-and-politics/article/the-big-sort-that-wasnt-a-skeptical-reexamination/0FEA9EB647CC86566040BA95C6C9C83F.

45. Iris Hui, "Who is Your Preferred Neighbor? Partisan Residential Preferences and Neighborhood Satisfaction," *American Politics Research* 41, no. 6: 997–1021; James G. Gimpel and Iris S. Hui, "Seeking Politically Compatible Neighbors? The Role of Neighborhood Partisan Composition in Residential Sorting," *Political Geography* 48 (2015): 130–42; Clayton Nall and Jonathan Mummolo, "Why Partisans Don't Sort: The Constraints on Political Segregation," *Journal of Politics,* 2016 (forthcoming).

46. Eitan D. Hersh, *Hacking the Electorate* (New York: Cambridge University Press, 2015), 93.

Party sorting very likely makes a significant contribution to this version of geographic polarization. Sixty-five years ago a committee of the American Political Science Association issued a report under the title, "Toward a More Responsible Two-Party System."[47] Among other things, the report called for more ideologically homogeneous parties that have the tools to discipline "heretical" members and force them to toe the party line. As various scholars have pointed out, much of what the committee desired has come to pass.[48] But, as critic Julius Turner predicted sixty-five years ago, one of the consequences of what we now call party sorting is a decline in party competition in many areas of the United States:

> The reforms which the Committee proposes would increase the tendency toward one-party districts. If local parties and candidates cannot be insurgent, if they cannot express the basic desires of their constituencies, then those local parties can have no hope of success. Regardless of the organization provided, you cannot give Hubert Humphrey [a liberal Democratic senator from Minnesota] a banjo and expect him to carry Kansas. Only a Democrat who rejects at least a part of the Fair Deal can carry Kansas and only a Republican who moderates the Republican platform can carry Massachusetts.[49]

Putting this argument in more contemporary terminology, a Democrat who is anti-fossil fuels and pro-gun control has little chance

47. American Political Science Association, "A Report of the Committee on Political Parties: Toward a More Responsible Two-Party System," *American Political Science Review* 44, no. 2 (September 1950).

48. E.g., Morris P. Fiorina with Samuel J. Abrams, *Disconnect: The Breakdown of Representation in American Politics*, chap. 7 (Norman: Oklahoma University Press, 2009).

49. Julius Turner, "Responsible Parties: A Dissent from the Floor," *American Political Science Review* 45, no. 1 (March 1951): 143–152. Our sense is that most political scientists, like Turner, believe that catch-all parties are in general electorally advantaged, but there are some dissenters. See, not surprisingly, Bernard Grofman, Samuel Merrill, Thomas L. Brunell, and William Koetzle, "The Potential Electoral Disadvantages of a Catch-All Party," *Party Politics* 5, no. 2 (1999): 199–210.

in the Appalachians, the South, and many areas of the Midwest and intermountain West. Similarly, a Republican who is strongly pro-life and opposes gay marriage has little chance in many areas of diverse urban states. Only if the parties nominate people whom Turner called "insurgents" in such areas do they have a chance to win, a fact well understood by Democratic Congressional Campaign Committee (CCC) chair Rahm Emmanuel when he engineered the most recent Democratic House majority in the 2006 elections. To the dismay of progressive Democrats, the CCC backed candidates who fit the district over more liberal rivals who were less likely to win.[50] If the parties were less well sorted than they now are, their candidates would be competitive in more districts and states than they now are, and geographical polarization would be less apparent.

50. Naftali Bendavid, *The Thumpin': How Rahm Emanuel and the Democrats Learned to Be Ruthless and Ended the Republican Revolution* (New York: Wiley, 2007).

CHAPTER 4

Party Sorting and Democratic Politics

*I believe that we have to end the divisive partisan politics that is
ripping this country apart. And I think we can. It's mean-spirited, it's
petty, and it's gone on for much too long. I don't believe, like some do,
that it's naive to talk to Republicans. I don't think we should look at
Republicans as our enemies. They are our opposition. They're not our
enemies. And for the sake of the country, we have to work together.*
—Joe Biden

The previous chapter described the ongoing process of party sorting that transformed the heterogeneous American parties of most
of the twentieth century into organizations that resemble the more
ideological parties that historically contested elections in parliamentary democracies. That chapter focused on the American public:
how much sorting had occurred, how much had normal Americans
sorted compared to members of the political class, and which partisans and which issues showed more sorting. This chapter takes a
more impressionistic stance and considers in broad brush the likely
consequences of party sorting for the larger political and governmental process.[1]

Quotation is from then vice president Joe Biden's announcement that he would not
be a presidential candidate in 2016, www.washingtonpost.com/news/post-politics
/wp/2015/10/21/full-text-bidens-announcement-that-he-wont-run-for-president/.
    1. The first part of this chapter extends the discussion that appears in Daniel
M. Shea and Morris P. Fiorina, "Party Homogeneity and Contentious Politics," in
Can We Talk?: The Rise of Rude, Nasty, Stubborn Politics, 1st ed., ed. Shea and
Fiorina (New York: Pearson, 2013), 142–53. Reprinted by permission of Pearson
Education, Inc. For an up-to-date discussion of the consequences of party sorting for

How Party Sorting Contributes to the State of
Contemporary American Politics

Chapter 1 noted that long periods of unified party control characterized American politics in the first half of the twentieth century. First
the Republicans dominated, then the Democrats. Governing a large
heterogeneous democracy like the United States is never an easy task
but, other things being equal, it probably never is easier than in periods like those. A single party controls the executive branch and the
Congress, enhancing the prospects of adopting the party program
without major compromises with the opposition party. Given that
they share the party label, most members of the congressional majority have an electoral incentive to make their president look good, not
bad.[2] The president appoints and his legislative party confirms the
judges and agency heads, who consequently are unlikely to hinder—
let alone sabotage—implementation of the party program. The congressional majority is less likely to investigate a president of its own
party.[3] It is very unlikely that the opposition will enjoy an electoral
triumph so sweeping that it can repeal the laws already passed. And
if part of the president's agenda does not pass in one Congress, it can
be carried over and finished up in the next one by a cast of charac-
ters that is largely the same. There is a high degree of predictability
surrounding policy making in stable one-party-dominated eras like
the two that prevailed in the first half of the twentieth century. So
long as the majority party governs competently and wins popular
approval, it continues in office.

---

the operation of our national institutions, see Steven E. Schier and Todd E. Eberly,
Polarized: The Rise of Ideology in American Politics (Lanham, MD: Rowman and
Littlefield, 2016).

2. Gary C. Cox and Mathew D. McCubbins, *Legislative Leviathan: Party
Government in the House* (Berkeley, CA: University of California Press, 1993).

3. Although Mayhew originally reported that investigations were about equally
likely in periods of unified and divided government during the period 1946–90,
the more recent experience with divided government found investigative activity
more likely than under unified government. David Mayhew, *Divided We Govern:
Party Control, Lawmaking, and Investigations, 1946–2002,* 2nd ed., chap. X (New
Haven, CT: Yale University Press, 2005.)

Divided government characterized the second half of the twentieth century.[4] Nevertheless, quite a bit still got done, although scholars continue to disagree about whether what got done was less than the American public wanted or the country needed.[5] During the Eisenhower administration, Congress funded construction of the interstate highway system and the Saint Lawrence Seaway, passed the first civil rights bill since Reconstruction, and adopted major labor legislation. Republican Richard Nixon has been called the "last liberal president."[6] His time in office saw the adoption of the alternative minimum tax and the establishment of the Environmental Protection Agency. Republican Ronald Reagan and the Democratic congressional leaders struck a grand bargain to save Social Security (at least temporarily) in 1983 and adopted a major tax reform in 1986. During the Divided Government era, cross-party coalitions formed to pass major legislation. But the parties then were not well sorted as they are now

Thomas Mann charges, "To treat polarization as 'mere sorting' is to trivialize, if not miss entirely, the biggest development in recent decades."[7] Mann's comment reflects a misunderstanding of my position.[8] Nothing I have written attaches the adjective "mere" to the process of party sorting. On the contrary, I agree with Mann that it is one of the most important developments in American politics in recent decades and that it makes a major contribution to the

4. For a more detailed discussion of this period, see Morris Fiorina, *Divided Government,* chap. 2 (New York: Macmillan, 1992).

5. Cf. Mayhew, *Divided We Govern;* and Sarah Binder, *Stalemate: Causes and Consequences of Legislative Gridlock* (Washington, DC: Brookings Institution, 2003).

6. John Fund, "Nixon at 100: Was He 'America's Last Liberal'?" *National Review,* January 11, 2013, www.nationalreview.com/article/337447/nixon-100-was-he-americas-last-liberal-john-fund.

7. Thomas Mann, "Admit It, Political Scientists: Politics Really Is More Broken Than Ever," *The Atlantic,* May 26, 2014, www.theatlantic.com/politics/archive/2014/05/dysfunction/371544/.

8. Mann links his criticism to a column discussing an essay of mine: Molly Ball, "5 False Assumptions Political Pundits Make All the Time," *The Atlantic,* February 27, 2013, www.theatlantic.com/politics/archive/2013/02/5-false-assumptions-political-pundits-make-all-the-time/273544/.

political conditions that he denounces. The consequences of sorting have become all too apparent in the political incivility that characterizes contemporary political discussion. Even more important, party sorting arguably makes a major contribution to the gridlock and stalemate that so many commentators—academic and otherwise— condemn.[9] Finally, while recognizing that party sorting has some positive consequences—it clarifies the choices facing the electorate and makes it easier for voters to assign political responsibility—I argue that, in addition to incivility and gridlock, sorting has negative representational consequences that cumulatively outweigh the benefits.[10] Admittedly, this is a normative judgment that some may contest.

Incivility and Gridlock Both academics and journalists decry the state of American politics today. To political scientists Thomas Mann and Norman Ornstein, "it's even worse than it looks."[11] To journalist Jon Terbush, the Congress that sat from 2014 to 2016 was "the worst ever."[12] Although such assertions are hyperbolic, anecdotal evidence does support them. During the ferocious congressional battle over the debt ceiling extension in 2011, for example, tea party Republicans in the House of Representatives took the country to the brink of default. Outraged politicos and pundits charged that those who marched under the banner of the tea party were "extortionists" and worse. They were a "small group of terrorists," "the Republican Taliban wing," "the GOP's Hezbollah faction," the "tea terrorist party," "a nihilistic caucus." According to their critics, the tea party had "waged jihad on the American people." Tea partiers donned political "suicide vests," "strapped explosives to the Capitol," and

---

9. Thomas E. Mann and Norman J. Ornstein, *It's Even Worse Than It Looks: How the American Constitutional System Collided with the New Politics of Extremism* (New York: Basic, 2012).

10. There are also claims that party sorting stimulates political participation but, as noted below in this chapter, such claims are empirically wrong.

11. Mann and Ornstein, *It's Even Worse Than It Looks.*

12. Jon Terbush, "Confirmed: This Is the Worst Congress Ever," *The Week*, December 26, 2013, http://theweek.com/articles/453744/confirmed-worst-congress-ever.

engaged in other "terrorist tactics" which ultimately forced the entire nation to eat a "sugar-coated Satan sandwich."[13]

In this particular episode, tea party Republicans were the recipients of incivility, but their members had often been the suppliers of incivility during the preceding years. An Iowa tea party billboard compared Obama to Hitler and Lenin.[14] Tea party posters depicted President Obama as the Joker in the popular Batman movies. A tea party heckler called Massachusetts Democratic Senate candidate Elizabeth Warren a "socialist whore" with a "foreign-born boss."[15]

For those old enough to have observed politics in the mid-twentieth century, there is little question that American politics now is more contentious and far less civil than it was then. Congressional scholars of that era wrote about the norms that mandated personal courtesy and institutional patriotism:

> A senator whose emotional commitment to Senate ways appears to be less than total is suspect. One who brings the Senate as an institution or senators as a class into public disrepute invites his own destruction as an effective legislator. One who seems to be using the Senate for the purposes of self-advertisement and advancement obviously does not belong.[16]

13. For wrap-ups of the uncivil nature of much of the discourse, see David Harsanyi, "America Can Thank the 'Terrorists,'" *Real Clear Politics,* August 3, 2011, www.realclearpolitics.com/articles/2011/08/03/when_we_balance_the_budget _the_terrorists_have_won_110810-comments.html; and James Taranto, "'Civility': The Denouement," *Wall Street Journal,* August 2, 2011, http://online.wsj.com /article/SB10001424053111903520204576484303256286950.html.

14. Meenal Vamburkar, "Tea Party Billboard Shows Obama alongside Hitler and Lenin," *Mediaite,* July 13, 2010, www.mediaite.com/online/tea-party-billboard -shows-obama-alongside-hitler-and-lenin/.

15. Aliyah Shahid, "Elizabeth Warren, Massachusetts Senate Candidate, Called a 'Socialist Whore' by Tea Party Heckler," *New York Daily News,* November 4, 2011, www.nydailynews.com/news/politics/elizabeth-warren-massachusetts-senate -candidate-called-a-socialist-whore-tea-party-heckler-video-article-1.972213?local LinksEnabled=false.

16. Donald R. Matthews, *U.S. Senators and Their World,* chap. 5 (Chapel Hill, NC: University of North Carolina Press, 1960). For a discussion of analogous norms prevailing in at least some committees in the House of Representatives, see Richard F. Fenno, "The House Appropriations Committee as a Political System: The Problem of Integration," *American Political Science Review* 56, no. 2 (June 1962): 310–24.

In that era, someone like Ted Cruz (R-TX), who called his own party leader a liar (among a series of other personal offenses), might well have been censured by a unanimous bipartisan vote.[17]

It is ironic that congressional politics in the 1960s was more civil than today, at a time when popular passions probably were at least equal and probably greater. Younger commentators sometimes talk about unprecedented political polarization, even comparing the current situation to the Civil War.[18] But in the 1960s, Vietnam War protests raged, strikes and demonstrations paralyzed campuses, major American cities burned during the summers, and assassins murdered political leaders. As chapter 2 discusses, however, today's electorate in the large is no more divided on the issues—and perhaps even less so—than the electorate of a half century ago. In the halls of government, however, civility prevails now to a much lesser degree than it did then.

As for gridlock, its relationship with party sorting is straightforward. Refer again to figure 2.1 of chapter 2. In the bottom panel of the figure, the average Democrat is further from the average Republican than in the top figure—the scope of partisan disagreement is wider. Moreover, the party distributions are more concentrated in contemporary Congresses, to the extent that in the bottom panel there is no overlap between the two parties: the most conservative Democrat is less conservative than the least conservative Republican. If a party offers proposals that reflect the central tendency of its members, it is more likely to propose policies that are strongly opposed by the other party than it would have in the Congress depicted in the top panel, and there are many fewer moderates who can threaten to defect to the other party, thus discouraging bipartisan compromise.

17. Further back, in 1954 the Senate censured Senator Joseph McCarthy (R-WI) by a vote of 67–22. The censure resolution said McCarthy had "acted contrary to senatorial ethics and tended to bring the Senate into dishonor and disrepute, to obstruct the constitutional processes of the Senate, and to impair its dignity; and such conduct is hereby condemned." The Senate was narrowly controlled by the Republicans at the time. All Democrats and half the Republicans voted for censure. One can hardly imagine a Senate resolution containing such terminology today.

18. George Stephanopoulos, "A Country Divided: Examining the State of Our Union," *ABC News*, June 30, 2006, http://abcnews.go.com/2020/print?id =2140483.

In addition, looking ahead to chapter 5, the contest for institutional control in each election creates an incentive for the minority to deny the majority any programmatic accomplishments and for the majority to resort to violations of traditional norms and procedures to implement its programs.

In his classic study of the late nineteenth-century Congress, David Brady describes the venomous politics of the era. Their opponents likened Populist leaders like William Jennings Bryan to Robespierre, Danton, and other leaders of the French Revolution who sent their political opponents to the guillotine. According to some commentators, the 1896 Democratic platform was "made in Hell" and Bryan, the Democratic candidate, was a "mouthing, slobbering demagogue whose patriotism is all in his jaw bone."[19] Brady argues that a major contributor to the historic levels of roll call polarization in the McKinley Congresses—levels not matched until very recently—was the distinct nature of the parties' electoral coalitions. An overwhelming majority of House Republicans represented industrial districts, and a solid majority of House Democrats represented agricultural districts.[20] In other words, the parties were well sorted: each party contained a heavy majority of members who represented a core interest that was opposed by the core interest of the other party.

The same situation characterizes the current era. Party coalitions have again become more homogeneous. Take regional strengths and weaknesses, for example. From the Civil War to the 1990s, Democratic representatives dominated the South; from the New Deal onward, they were elected from all regions of the country. The Republican congressional delegation in the twentieth century also came from all regions—except from the South (with a few minor exceptions). Today, the character of the Democratic congressional caucus is very different. What remains of the southern contingent consists primarily of liberal African American representatives from southern cities, and the party now enjoys its greatest strength in the liberal northeastern and western coastal regions. In a complete

19. These quotations are all taken from David Brady, *Congressional Voting in a Partisan Era: A Study of the McKinley Houses and a Comparison to the Modern House of Representatives* (Lawrence, KS: University of Kansas Press, 1973), 1–3.

20. Ibid., 102.

historical reversal, today's Republican Party now dominates the South and has almost disappeared from its historic stronghold in New England. Most of its members represent districts in the heartland—what coastal elites call the fly-over states.

Urban-suburban differences reinforce these regional differences in electoral support. Today's Democratic Party is an urban party, whereas the Republican Party is predominantly suburban and rural. Moreover, as Bruce Oppenheimer points out, many of the remaining southern Democratic districts are in the large cities of the Sunbelt, so that they are more similar to northern districts than southern Democratic districts were at mid-century.[21] The consequences of such differences in party support show up clearly in issues involving energy, the environment, and guns.

As parties become more homogeneous, political issues become more partisan and divisive. If both parties include representatives from urban and rural districts, both feel pressure to moderate their issue stances. The pressure comes from members associated with points of view that diverge from the party majority. Such members will defect on party proposals that are highly unpopular in their districts, and party leaders who wish to become or remain *majority* party leaders will hesitate to endanger such members by advocating proposals that harm those members' electoral chances. But when Democrats are largely an urban party and Republicans a suburban and rural party, why should anyone expect Republican representatives to worry about the problems of the cities? Urban districts only elect Democrats. And why should Democrats worry about the economic consequences of environmental laws for farmers and ranchers? Rural and farm districts consistently vote for Republicans. Party homogeneity encourages both parties to reject trade-offs and advocate one-sided programs that reflect the parties' preponderant interests.

The natural consequence of party sorting is that each party gradually comes to have less contact with, knowledge of, and sympathy

21. Bruce Oppenheimer, "Barack Obama, Bill Clinton, and the Democratic Congressional Majority," *Extensions* (University of Oklahoma), Spring 2009.

for the constituencies of the other (recall the discussion of partisan misperception in chapter 2). If one party is rooted in the predominantly white middle class, one should not expect its representatives to support policies that redistribute income or other resources from its voters to minorities who vote heavily for the opposing party. Conversely, if one party's adherents are heavily employed in the public sector or dependent on government benefits, one should not expect its representatives to favor policies that cut taxes and public spending.

Students today are surprised to learn that, until the feminist movement, Republicans had traditionally been somewhat more supportive of an equal rights amendment. And until the mid-1970s, the environmental issue was up for grabs, leading Republican president Richard Nixon to support the Clean Air Act. As pointed out in chapter 3, until the early 1990s Republicans and Democrats felt about the same on the issue of abortion. And until the 1992 election, the presidential vote division between regular churchgoers and seculars was small.[22] The natural result of such party heterogeneity was much less of a partisan divide on related issues. But once the advocates for a particular issue became exclusively associated with one party or the other, balance and moderation were the casualties. For several decades, Republican pro-life groups have advocated a constitutional amendment to prohibit abortion altogether while Democratic pro-choice groups defend the legality of third-trimester abortions for elective reasons. That almost 90 percent of the electorate falls between these polar positions gets overlooked in the partisan battle. Most recently, uncertain voters are offered a stark choice in regard to climate change: one party tells them that global warming is an imminent planetary threat, and the other party asserts that it is a gigantic hoax.

In recent decades, many commentators have identified another factor that contributes to contentious politics—the introduction of issues variously called moral, social, or cultural into the political

22. Morris P. Fiorina, with Samuel J. Abrams and Jeremy C. Pope, *Culture War: The Myth of a Polarized America*, chap. 7 (New York: Pearson, 2005).

agenda. This is the culture war argument that I have dealt with extensively in other writings.[23] Issues that can easily be framed in terms of moral and/or religious beliefs—racial equality, women's rights, traditional family values—are harder to compromise than economic issues, the argument goes, especially when framed in terms of fundamental rights protected by the US Constitution. One side asserts that affirmative action is a violation of racial equality while the other asserts to the contrary that it is an important means toward racial equality. One side contends that free access to abortion is a fundamental component of equal rights for women, while the other contends that abortion violates the right to life of the fetus. One side claims that same-sex marriage is a violation of traditional morality and religious principles while the other claims that it is a necessary component of personal dignity and equality.

Certainly these arguments have some validity, although the contending sides often underestimate the willingness of Americans to compromise on moral issues—they have little problem in the case of abortion, for example, as shown in chapters 2 and 3.[24] The important caveat, however, is that—contrary to the assumptions of many commentators—such issues are not new to the modern era. The New Deal period was historically unusual in that economic and, later, foreign policy issues crowded out moral issues. The latter have been staples of American political conflict through most of our history. From at least the time that large numbers of Catholic immigrants began arriving on American shores to the Great Depression, Protestant Americans worried about the moral "failures" of Catholic immigrants who drank and danced and in other ways violated the Sabbath. Regulating the use of foreign languages also is an old issue. Bilingual education—French and German long before Spanish—was controversial in the nineteenth century. But the parties of earlier periods were patronage based and generally kept such issues off the public agenda because of their (now and then demonstrated)

23. Ibid. See also Morris Fiorina, with Samuel Abrams, *Disconnect: The Breakdown of Representation in American Politics* (Norman: University of Oklahoma Press, 2009).

24. For a more detailed discussion, see Fiorina with Abrams, *Disconnect,* chap. 2.

potential to fracture party coalitions and jeopardize control of what was viewed as the real value of institutional control—jobs, contracts, and various forms of "honest graft."[25]

As I have discussed elsewhere, however, civil service, public sector unionization, conflict-of-interest laws, and investigative media have restricted the use of material incentives to generate political activity and support.[26] Partially in consequence, the parties have enlisted issue activists to serve as foot soldiers, thus rendering it impossible to keep their issues off the agenda. Substantive disagreement between the parties is greater now than half a century ago not only because of greater party differences but also because of a greater number of issues to disagree about.

In sum, in the mid-twentieth-century period when politics seemed less contentious than today, the American parties were considerably more heterogeneous. The result was party platforms that were less divergent and more balanced among various interests, allowing greater room for compromise. In the ensuing decades, the parties sorted along various regional, demographic, and issue lines.[27] The result is parties that are more homogeneous internally and more distinct from each other. Extreme partisans regard the members of the opposing party as "the other."

Politics for Higher Stakes For the reasons just outlined, party sorting has raised the stakes of politics.[28] In an era of heterogeneous parties and low party cohesion, party control of Congress makes relatively less difference in what kinds of policies emerge than in an era with the opposite characteristics. Party control always matters, to be sure. It matters for who gets various perquisites of office: committee and subcommittee chairmanships, control of staff, budgets, and other

25. For a discussion, see Joel H. Silbey and Samuel T. McSeveney, *Voters, Parties and Elections: Quantitative Essays in the History of American Popular Voting Behavior,* part 3 (Lexington, MA: Xerox College Publishing, 1972).

26. E.g., Morris Fiorina, "Parties, Participation, and Representation in America: Old Theories Face New Realities," in *Political Science: The State of the Discipline,* ed. Ira Katznelson and Helen Milner (New York: Norton, 2002), 511–41.

27. Alan I. Abramowitz, *The Polarized Public? Why American Government Is So Dysfunctional* (New York: Pearson, 2013).

28. Fiorina with Abrams, *Disconnect,* chap. 7.

institutional benefits. But party control matters relatively less for substantive policy outcomes when the parties are heterogeneous and fragmented.

Without a Democratic majority in Congress, the Democratic health care plan fails to pass in 2010. Without a Republican majority in the House, the debt ceiling extension passes easily in 2011. Without a Senate of his own party, President Obama's Supreme Court nomination is stymied rather than confirmed. The stakes of politics generally rise with substantive disagreement and, by whatever psychological mechanism(s), so does emotional involvement.[29] If I am forced to accept a compromise far from my preferred position, I will feel disappointed and frustrated. The more important the issue is to me, the greater the emotional reaction.

Party sorting heightens the frequency and intensity of such feelings. If activists and public officials associate only with people who agree with them politically—colleagues, other activists, campaign donors and workers—they will slowly lose understanding of, sympathy for, and eventually even tolerance of those who do not. They gradually will come to believe that their positions are so self-evidently correct that they will cease to critically evaluate their own positions and to recognize any validity in opposing positions. The arguments made by political opponents will be dismissed or ignored entirely, not rebutted with logic or facts. Contrary to Senator Moynihan's dictum, partisans ultimately feel entitled to their own facts.[30] And it becomes all too automatic to question the motives of opponents. Your political opponents advocate particular policies not because they honestly believe such policies address important public problems but because they are racists or are bought and paid for by Wall Street or the Koch brothers. Or they hate America and consciously plan to undermine it and establish a socialist state. And as for the hoi polloi who are taken in by the propaganda of the other side, they deserve no respect, only contempt. They are "bitter and cling to their

29. Alan Abramowitz and Steven Webster, "The Ideological Foundations of Affective Polarization," paper presented at the annual meeting of the Southern Political Science Association, Puerto Rico, 2016.

30. Daniel Patrick Moynihan is credited with the comment that "we are all entitled to our own opinions but not to our own facts."

gods and guns" and they are "deplorables." Or they are economic illiterates and "tax-eaters."

In sum, far from a "mere" sorting, the evolution of American political parties from loose coalitions of disparate interests to groups of like-minded people is a major factor contributing to the contentious and unproductive politics of today. Substantive differences between the parties are on average greater today, and as the political agenda has expanded ("the personal is the political") they have found more things to disagree about. And as noted in the previous chapter, substantive conflict generates emotional affect and personal animosity. Many political scientists of the 1950s looked at their parties and found them wanting. They wanted the parties to look more like they do today. But many of today's political scientists look at our parties and wonder whether it would be better for the country if they looked more like they did in the mid-twentieth century.[31]

Is Party Sorting All Bad?

As stated in the introduction to this chapter, I believe that party sorting is one of the principal underpinnings of our current political stalemate. I suspect that the great majority of observers would agree that the sorting described in the preceding chapter has had serious negative consequences. When ideology and issues crosscut party cleavages, party cohesion in Congress and other legislative bodies is difficult to maintain and cross-party coalition possibilities expand. This was the case in mid-twentieth-century America. Today, ideology and issues reinforce the partisan cleavage rather than cut across it. This restricts the possibilities for constructing cross-party compromises.

While I believe that the party sorting that has occurred during the past two decades has heightened the conflictual nature of American politics, making compromise more difficult and stalemate more likely, other scholars have noted some potentially positive aspects of sorting. Alan Abramowitz argues that today's sorted parties have produced a more engaged public and heightened political

31. Fiorina, "Old Theories Face New Realities."

participation: "Some Americans may be turned off by the sharp ideological divisions between the parties, but more Americans appear to be excited and energized by the choice between a consistently liberal Democratic Party and a consistently conservative Republican Party."[32] As Levendusky and I pointed out when Abramowitz first made this argument, the data fail to support it.[33] True, interest in the campaign rose slightly in 2004 and 2008 before receding in 2012, and more people reported attempting to persuade others how to vote in 2004 and 2008 before receding in 2012. But contrary to Abramowitz's claim that "every available indicator of public interest and involvement indicates that the level of engagement in the 2008 election was even greater than it was in 2004,"[34] American National Election Studies (ANES) measures show levels of activity and involvement that are well within the range established in past decades.

For example, despite the ease of donating to campaigns over the Internet and frequent claims by candidates about record-setting numbers of small donors, figure 4.1 shows that the proportion of Americans who report donating to a campaign has stayed roughly constant at about 10 percent. Similarly, despite myriad claims about Obamamania in 2008, figure 4.2 shows that the proportion of Americans who report attending a political meeting or rally has shown almost no movement over a sixty-year period. And the proportion of Americans who actually work for a party or candidate is no higher now than in the mid-twentieth century—less than 5 percent, as graphed in figure 4.3.

The serene stability of these figures is all the more surprising given that the political parties have conducted much more intensive "ground games" in the elections since the turn of the century, as reflected in figure 4.4. Even though today's sorted parties are more

32. Alan I. Abramowitz, *The Disappearing Center: Engaged Citizens, Polarization, and American Democracy* (New Haven, CT: Yale University Press, 2010), 33.

33. Alan I. Abramowitz, "Disconnected, or Joined at the Hip?" in *Red and Blue Nation? Characteristics and Causes of America's Polarized Politics*, vol. 1, ed. Pietro S. Nivola and David W. Brady (Washington, DC: Brookings Institution Press, 2006), 72–75; and Morris P. Fiorina and Matthew S. Levendusky, "Response to Abramowitz's Comments," in *Red and Blue Nation*, vol. 1, 95–108.

34. Abramowitz, *Disappearing Center*, 112.

The Proportion of Americans Who Are Campaign Donors Has Not Increased

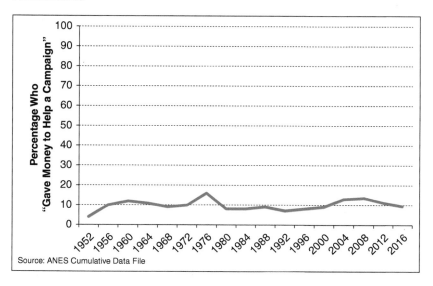

Source: ANES Cumulative Data File

The Proportion of Americans Who Attend a Political Meeting or Rally Has Not Increased

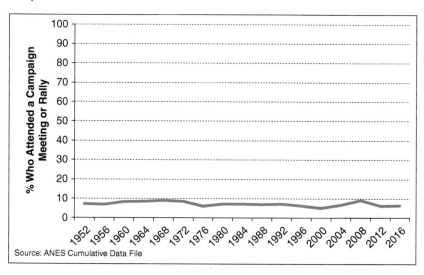

Source: ANES Cumulative Data File

FIGURE 4.3. The Proportion of Americans Who Work for a Party or Candidate Has Not Increased

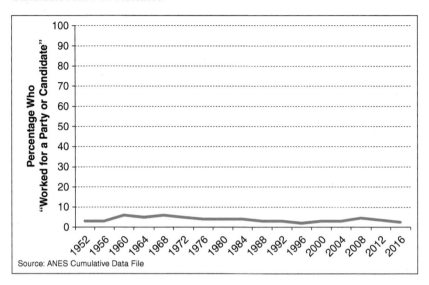

Source: ANES Cumulative Data File

FIGURE 4.4. Americans Increasingly Report Party or Campaign Contacts

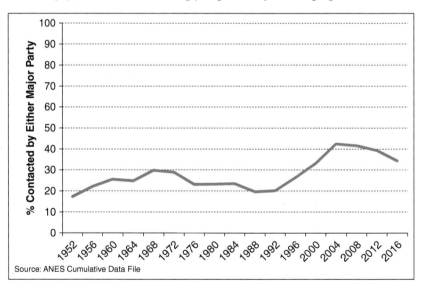

Source: ANES Cumulative Data File

likely to cajole voters to participate, aside from displaying more yard signs and campaign stickers, voters have only just maintained their previous levels of activity. Moreover, other data are even less consistent with the heightened engagement thesis. After noting the 2012 plunge in presidential primary turnout and the decline in turnout in the 2012 general election, Rhodes Cook asks, "Are Voters Drifting Away?" and notes that "in recent years it seems as though voters have become more attuned to what they do not like in American politics than what they do. Stark differences between the parties remain, but voters appear to be tiring of the shrill partisanship, 'my way or the highway' rhetoric, and the frequent examples of government dysfunction that follow."[35] Continuing that trend, turnout in the 2014 midterm elections was the lowest since 1942. In 2016, Republican primary turnout surged, a development that most observers attributed to the Trump candidacy. This may be the exception that proves the rule: as Republican elites complain, Trump does not represent the sorted Republican establishment very well—they feared and hated him in part because he is a party de-sorter.

Ironically, a number of analysts, notably Russell Dalton, are in partial agreement with Abramowitz that today's sorted parties have contributed to a change in political involvement, but the change is the opposite of the one Abramowitz imagined.[36] Dalton argues that traditional conceptions of citizenship are "duty-based" at their core. The good citizen is someone who performs the duties of citizenship—in particular, she pays attention to public affairs and votes. But Obamamania in 2008 notwithstanding, young people today—millennials—are less likely to follow public affairs and to participate in election activities. Disputing those who conclude that the young are unengaged, however, Dalton argues that they are "differently" engaged. They adhere to a conception of citizenship that focuses on the community more than the polity. They are skeptical of government. They favor participation in community life rather than in campaigns and elections. They sign online petitions, boycott

35. Rhodes Cook, "Are Voters Drifting Away?" *Sabato's Crystal Ball*, April 2, 2015, www.centerforpolitics.org/crystalball/articles/are-voters-drifting-away/.

36. Russell Dalton, *The Good Citizen: How a Younger Generation Is Reshaping American Politics* (Washington, DC: CQ Press, 2008).

corporations, and volunteer to help those less fortunate or those affected by natural disasters.[37] They are more tolerant and more compassionate.

Dalton suggests that part of the explanation of "young people's alienation from electoral politics" lies in the party sorting that Abramowitz celebrates: "Youth are drawn to political figures who appear to be forthright and not acting with ideological or partisan blinders . . ."[38] I do not need to take a side in this debate. Suffice it to say that not only has party sorting not produced any increase in political participation but, if Dalton is correct, as millennials become a steadily larger proportion of the electorate, citizen participation in campaigns and elections may actually decline.

A second argument in favor of party sorting does have the benefit of being empirically correct. As Levendusky notes, sorting simplifies the task facing the voter by making the alternatives very clear.[39] No longer are voters as confused about which party stands for what as they often must have been in the past. According to the ANES, in 1976, when moderate Republican Gerald Ford ran against moderate Democrat Jimmy Carter, only 54 percent of the public thought the Republican Party was the more conservative of the two parties, and 29 percent said they didn't know or there was no difference between them. By 2012, 73 percent of the public said the Republicans were more conservative and only 18 percent said they did not know or there was no difference.[40] The recognition of party differences on many individual issues has increased as well.

Not only does party sorting simplify the task facing the voter by making the alternatives very clear, but I would add that sorting may enhance electoral accountability as well since parties are less able

37. Research finds that this is true in Britain, Canada, and Australia, as well as in the United States. Aaron J. Martin, *Young People and Politics: Political Engagement in the Anglo-American Democracies,* chap. 5 (New York: Routledge, 2012).

38. Russell Dalton, "The Good News Is the Bad News Is Wrong: Another View of the Millennial Generation," *Extensions,* 2015: 10–13.

39. Matthew Levendusky, *The Partisan Sort: How Liberals Became Democrats and Conservatives Became Republicans* (Chicago: University of Chicago Press, 2009), 138–41.

40. A minority of 10 percent stubbornly continues to believe that the Democrats are the more conservative party.

to hide their positions in a "fog of ambiguity."[41] On the contrary, on many issues today there are very clear party differences that are generally recognized by voters. Moreover, as chapter 7 discusses, the electoral fates of individual candidates now rise and fall with the fortunes of their parties. Compared to the mid-twentieth century, candidates are less able to carve out a personal vote and insulate themselves from collective party responsibility.

But while recognizing that party sorting has a positive aspect, I believe that in a large, heterogeneous democracy like the United States, where people have different interests and values, the level of sorting that exists in the party system today on balance is a negative. Mann and Ornstein among others have pointed out that—given the American constitutional system with its separation of powers, checks and balances, and federalism— a party would have to win and retain an overwhelming majority to implement its platform given all the veto points that can be utilized by the opposition.[42] Failure to win and hold such overwhelming majorities produces the stalemate and gridlock that characterize contemporary politics.

To this, I would add that there is a significant cost on the representational side as well: As Ross Douthat wrote before the 2016 campaign formally began,

> But it [the two-party system] does mean certain ideologies and world views get marginalized in national political debate. The libertarian who wants to cut defense spending, the anti-abortion voter who favors a bigger welfare state, the immigration skeptic who wants to keep Social Security exactly as it is . . . all these voters and many others choose the lesser of two evils every November, because neither party's leadership has any interest in representing their entire world view.[43]

41. Downs argues that in two-party majoritarian systems like that in the United States, the parties have incentives to broaden their appeal by taking ambiguous positions. Anthony Downs, *An Economic Theory of Democracy* (New York: Harper and Row, 1957), 135–37.

42. Mann and Ornstein, *It's Even Worse Than It Looks*.

43. Ross Douthat, "Donald Trump, Traitor to His Class," *New York Times*, August 29, 2015, www.nytimes.com/2015/08/30/opinion/sunday/ross-douthat-donald -trump-traitor-to-his-class.html.

Quite right. It is not too much of a simplification to posit that there are three clusters of issues in the contemporary United States: foreign and defense issues, economic and social welfare issues, and cultural and moral issues.[44] For purposes of illustration, imagine that there are only two stances on each cluster: an assertive (A) or cautious (C) stance on defense and foreign policy issues, a preference for government control (G) or a free market (M) stance on economic issues, and a progressive (P) or traditional (T) stance on cultural issues. Then there are eight ($2 \times 2 \times 2$) possible platforms a party could espouse:[45]

	Platform							
	1	2	3	4	5	6	7	8
Foreign/Defense	C	C	C	C	A	A	A	A
Economic	G	G	M	M	G	G	M	M
Cultural	P	T	P	T	P	T	P	T

Contemporary Democratic candidates generally offer voters the first platform and contemporary Republican candidates the eighth platform. If you are a voter whose views fit any of the six platforms in between, you usually will have to choose between candidates who are wrong on at least one position you hold. With less well-sorted parties, however, New Deal Democrats could vote for a local congressional candidate who adopted platform 6, libertarian Republicans could vote for a local candidate who offered platform 3, and so on. No more.

44. A number of studies find that the views of ordinary Americans about domestic issues generally fall on two dimensions—economic and cultural—in contrast to the single ideological dimension that emerges in congressional voting. Foreign policy issues on which the public has less well-formed views normally are not even included in such analyses. Byron E. Shafer and William J. M. Claggett, *The Two Majorities: The Issue Context of Modern American Politics* (Baltimore: Johns Hopkins University Press, 1995); Edward G. Carmines, Michael J. Ensley, and Michael W. Wagner, "Who Fits the Left-Right Divide? Partisan Polarization in the American Electorate," *American Behavioral Scientist* 56, no. 12 (December 2012): 1631–53.

45. If we add a middle-of-the-road position on each cluster, there are 27 possible platforms. No need to go there; eight is enough to make the point.

The success of Donald Trump in the 2016 Republican nomination contests may be partially a reaction to this "two sizes fit all and you'd better like it" choice offered by the current sorted parties. To the surprise of many politicians, journalists, and academics, Donald Trump won the Republican presidential nomination. Reflecting on that development, Douthat writes:

> Trump proved that movement conservative ideas and litmus tests don't really have any purchase on millions of Republican voters. Again and again, Cruz and the other G.O.P. candidates stressed that Trump wasn't really a conservative; they listed his heresies, cataloged his deviations, dug up his barely buried liberal past. No doubt this case resonated with many Republicans. But not with nearly enough of them to make Cruz the nominee. . . .
>
> Trump proved that many of the party's moderates and establishmentarians hate the thought of a True Conservative nominee even more than they fear handing the nomination to a proto-fascist grotesque with zero political experience and poor impulse control. That goes for the prominent politicians who refused to endorse Cruz, the prominent donors who sat on their hands once the field narrowed, and all the moderate-Republican voters in blue states who turned out to be #NeverCruz first and #NeverTrump less so or even not at all.[46]

Trump offered something different to voters who don't fit happily in issue profiles 1 and 8 above. On foreign affairs, he was cautious about American involvement but assertive where critical American interests are at stake. On cultural issues, he was inconsistent, but seemed to lean traditional on abortion but progressive on gay rights. On economic issues, he attacked Wall Street but favored deregulation. But he promised to protect Social Security and Medicare, the major components of the welfare state. And he further muddied the choice by complicating the economic dimension—adding trade agreements to the more traditional issues of government regulation

46. Ross Douthat, "The Defeat of True Conservatism," *New York Times,* May 3, 2016, www.nytimes.com/2016/05/04/opinion/campaign-stops/the-defeat-of-true-conservatism.html?ref=opinion&_r=0.

TABLE 4.1. **Only Strong Partisans Feel Well Represented by the Contemporary Parties (Do Any of the Parties Represent Your Views Reasonably Well?)**

	2004	*2008*	*2015*
Strong Republicans	93%	85%	92%
Weak Republicans	83%	60%	63%
Independent Republicans	66%	49%	50%
Independents	47%	36%	11%
Independent Democrats	58%	53%	40%
Weak Democrats	72%	69%	46%
Strong Democrats	80%	81%	87%

Source: 2004 and 2008 data from Comparative Study of Electoral Systems; 2015 data from Polimetrix

and income redistribution. Whatever his many negatives, Trump has a potentially positive role as a de-sorting force in contemporary American politics.[47]

The simple fact is that the present condition of sorted parties primarily pleases a minority of Americans, mostly active partisans who are similarly well sorted. Table 4.1 contains the responses to a survey question included on the 2004 and 2008 Comparative Study of Electoral Systems (CSES) surveys and updated by Polimetrix in 2015. Strong partisans (about one-third of the eligible electorate) are quite happy with the contemporary parties (and no doubt some of those who are not may think their party is too moderate). Not-so-strong partisans (about one-quarter of the electorate) are significantly less enthusiastic about their parties. Only half of the leaning independents (about 30 percent of the electorate) feel reasonably well represented by either party, and a majority of pure independents (10 percent of the electorate) feel they were left out of the party system altogether, particularly in 2015. The sorted parties today represent the political class well, the larger country not so well.

In a recent survey of Americans' attitudes toward the political parties, Howard J. Gold concludes: "There is no question that public disdain for both the Democratic and Republican parties has grown considerably since the mid-1990s, and that the public understands

47. He is not the first to try, of course, but previous attempts by candidates like Rudy Giuliani and Jon Huntsman met with little success.

well the polarization that has gripped political elites. Increasing numbers of Americans have come to see the parties as ideologically far apart, with large percentages stating that the Republicans are too conservative and that the Democrats are too liberal."

Rather than being enthusiastic supporters of one or the other of the two parties, we suspect that many Americans wish they could divide their votes, say 65 percent for the Republican candidate, 35 percent for the Democrat, or vice-versa, rather than give an all-or-nothing endorsement to either side.[48] Two sizes don't fit all.

48. Howard J. Gold, "Americans' Attitudes toward the Political Parties and the Party System," *Public Opinion Quarterly* 79, no. 3 (2015): 815.

CHAPTER 5

The Temptation to Overreach

Things fall apart; the centre cannot hold; . . . The best lack all conviction, while the worst are full of passionate intensity.
—William Butler Yeats

It's hard not to think sometimes that the center won't hold and that things might get worse.
—President Barack Obama

No single factor explains the broad patterns that characterize early twenty-first-century politics, and electoral outcomes in particular states, districts, and localities have numerous specific causes. But my contention is that a significant component of the national pattern of majoritarian instability stems from today's close party divide combined with today's ideologically well-sorted parties. Briefly, neither party can win control without significant support from nonaligned citizens and even some defectors from the other party. But to attract those marginal supporters who are necessary for victory, the parties generally must soften some of their core positions and downplay some of the issues of most concern to their base supporters. After the election, however, base pressures reassert themselves, and the party in office operates in a manner that alienates marginal members of its electoral coalition. In short, the interaction between the close party divide and today's well-sorted parties leads to "overreach,"

Quotations are from William Butler Yeats, *The Second Coming;* and Barack Obama, "Remarks by the President at Memorial Service for Fallen Dallas Police Officers," July 12, 2016, www.whitehouse.gov/the-press-office/2016/07/12/remarks -president-memorial-service-fallen-dallas-police-officers.

with predictable electoral repercussions.[1] The center *does* hold, frustrating the governing attempts of both parties.

The Close Party Divide

Figure 2.8 (chapter 2) charts the partisanship of the American electorate. To review, since the Reagan era the national pattern has been relatively stable. Today, self-identified Republicans make up a bit less than 30 percent of the eligible electorate, Democrats about 35 percent, and independents about 40 percent.[2] When turnout is factored in, the proportions become closer, especially in midterm elections. The smallest partisan grouping, Republicans, turns out at the highest rate, whereas the largest grouping, independents, turns out at the lowest rate, with the Democrats in between. Thus, very roughly, the party divide in the electorate over the past three decades has been close to one-third/one-third/one-third with some year-to-year fluctuation (Republicans up in 2004, Democrats up in 2008).[3] The implication is clear. In contrast to, say, the 1950s, when Democrats could have won the presidency—hypothetically—with only the votes of self-identified Democrats, neither party today can win with only its own adherents.[4] Indeed, as shown in the next chapter, it is

1. Although used in slightly different ways, the term is common in the literature. See, for example, George C. Edwards, *Overreach: Leadership in the Obama Presidency* (Princeton, NJ: Princeton University Press, 2015). The general idea also runs through the works of James Stimson, e.g., *Tides of Consent: How Public Opinion Shapes American Politics* (New York: Cambridge University Press, 2004).

2. Once again, I note that the status of independents is somewhat controversial. The next chapter addresses this subject.

3. The Pew Research Center provides an alternative picture of the electorate based on ideology rather than partisanship. According to the Pew Political Typology, the Partisan Anchors comprise 36 percent of the eligible electorate (43 percent of registered voters), divided 22 percent conservative, 10 percent liberal. A majority of the electorate—57 percent of registered voters—falls into Pew's Less Partisan, Less Predictable categories. While this ideological distribution may be slightly more tilted to the right than the partisan distribution, conservatives, the largest group, still are nowhere near a majority. Andrew Kohut, "The Political Middle Still Matters," Pew Research Center, August 1, 2014, www.pewresearch.org/fact-tank/2014/08/01/the-political-middle-still-matters/.

4. Since Republican Dwight Eisenhower won in 1952 and 1956, the Democrats obviously did not hold all of their partisans when the latter entered the voting booths.

almost a necessary condition for a winning party to get a majority of the vote among independents. When this condition of close party balance combines with the sorted parties of today, it produces an increasingly common tendency for parties to overreach, leading in turn to the observed pattern of flip-flopping majorities.

Overreach

By overreach I mean simply that after it wins control of an elected institution, particularly when it wins control of all three elected institutions, a party attempts to govern in a manner that alienates the marginal members of its electoral majority.[5] Most commonly, a party that wins an election with the support of independents and some of the more loosely attached adherents of the opposition party overreaches by attempting to impose more extreme policies and/or a more partisan agenda than marginal voters anticipated. In consequence, the party suffers losses among these marginal supporters in the next election. Although he does not use the term, a recent study by Wlezien provides a statistical description of overreach in the post–World War II United States. Earlier research by Wlezien established that public opinion in America has a thermostatic quality.[6] That is, when the Democrats win control of the government, public opinion moves in a conservative direction, and when Republicans win, public opinion moves in a liberal direction, the obvious implication being that Democratic administrations are more liberal than the median voter wants, and Republican administrations more conservative. Wlezien's latest research shows that the loss in electoral support for an incumbent party is proportional to the net liberalism of laws passed by Congress during the party's hold on the presidency,

5. Martin Gilens concludes *ceteris paribus* that policy responsiveness is weakest when majority party control is strongest, consistent with our notion of overreach. He suggests, however, that uncertainty about future control will lead parties to be more responsive to popular preferences, whereas I argue the opposite below. Martin Gilens, *Affluence & Influence: Economic Inequality and Political Power in America,* chap. 7 (Princeton, NJ: Princeton University Press, 2012).

6. Christopher Wlezien, "The Public as Thermostat: Dynamics of Preferences for Spending," *American Journal of Political Science* 39, no. 4 (November 1995): 981–1000.

relative to measures of median public opinion.[7] The marginal voters are located near the center in a policy or ideological space, of course, between the two parties which stake out positions to the left and right. Put simply, the more a party's record and platform depart from the median, the greater the electoral loss.

Overreach is a more common danger in a two-party, single-member, simple-plurality (SMSP) electoral system like that in the United States than in multiparty proportional representation (PR) systems like those that exist in a majority of world democracies.[8] As I noted in chapter 3, as the American parties sorted, they have come to resemble the ideologically coherent parties that have long characterized European politics. In commenting on this development, most analysts have focused on the increased likelihood for stalemate such ideological parties pose in a governmental system rife with veto points like ours.[9] That is, in parliamentary systems which tend to be institutionally simpler than the US government, the government rules, but in our decentralized system the verb "rule" rarely is appropriate.[10] An independently elected executive and bicameral legislature make divided party control possible. The Senate filibuster, independent courts, federalism, and other features of American institutional structure pose further obstacles for governing majorities. These observations are widely accepted, but I believe that there

7. Christopher Wlezien, "Policy (Mis)Representation and the Cost of Ruling: The Case of US Presidential Elections," 2015, www.washingtonpost.com/blogs/monkey-cage/files/2015/04/Wlezien-Policy-Misrepresentation-and-the-Cost-of-Ruling-for-distribution.pdf.

8. Systems like that in the United States are referred to by the acronym SMSP—single-member, simple-plurality. Whichever person wins a simple plurality of the vote in each electoral district (state, congressional district, state legislative district, etc.) wins the office. A majority of world democracies use some version of proportional representation. There are many variations of the latter.

9. Thomas Mann and Norman Ornstein, *It's Even Worse Than It Looks; How the American Constitutional System Collided with the New Politics of Extremism* (New York: Basic Books, 2012).

10. In retrospect, the responsible two-party system of the United Kingdom for most of the twentieth century now seems to be something of an anomaly among world democracies, despite being taken as an ideal type by some political scientists of an earlier generation.

TABLE 5.1. **Most Advanced Democracies Have Coalition Governments**

	# of Parties in Governing Coalition	# of Parties with Seats but Not in Governing Coalition
Australia	3	7
Austria	2	6
Belgium	4	13
Czech Republic	3	7
Denmark	2 (6)	5
Finland	3	9
France	5	15
Germany	3	5
Ireland	2	8
Italy	4	13
Japan	2	9
Luxembourg	3	6
Netherlands	4	13
Poland	2	5
Spain	1	5
Sweden	2	8
United Kingdom	2	8

"Note: Denmark has two parties in the governing coalition (Social Democrats and Social Liberal Party) with six ancillary parties supporting it but they are in neither the actual governing or opposition coalitions"

Source: UN, CIA World Factbook, and representative parliament sites. Current as of March 2017.

is another important consequence of the development of European-style parties in the United States that is less often recognized.

In PR systems, one party rarely governs alone. Such systems generally have multiple parties, no one of which wins a majority of seats in Parliament, so parties usually must enter coalitions to form a government, as shown in table 5.1.[11] Such coalitions constitute something of a natural brake on overreach. While each party in the coalition would like to implement its ideologically most preferred policies, there will be less support for those policies among other parties in the coalition; moreover, the latter may fear the electoral consequences of any coalition member overreaching. When the governing coalition

11. Michael Laver and Kenneth A. Shepsle, *Making and Breaking Governments: Cabinets and Legislatures in Parliamentary Democracies* (New York: Cambridge University Press, 1996).

does agree to act, it does so with the support of a majority of the Parliament that represents a majority of the electorate (because of proportional representation).[12]

Two-party SMSP systems, in contrast, "manufacture" majorities. Whoever wins the most votes wins the contest. In the limit, just over 25 percent of the electorate could elect a majority of the legislature or parliament.[13] Thus, a majority party hypothetically could implement policies that were favored by much less than a majority of the electorate. That is essentially the definition of overreach.

I emphasize that the term overreach is used here in a value-neutral sense. By definition an overreach is electorally costly, but not necessarily bad from the standpoint of some moral or ethical standard. For example, after the landslide Democratic victory in 1964, the 89th Congress produced a series of landmark legislative enactments. But for their efforts, the Democrats lost forty-seven seats in the House of Representatives and four in the Senate in the 1966 elections.[14] Then (with the Vietnam War and urban disorder added to the mix), they lost more seats in both chambers as well as the presidency in 1968. This was political overreach in the sense that I am using the term, but I doubt that many Americans today would say that passage of the Voting Rights Act and Medicare was a bad thing.[15] History can judge the moral merits of political overreaches; we are focusing here on the electoral costs when overreaches occur.

As the example of the Johnson administration suggests, overreaches are nothing new, but they were once something that generally

---

12. To cite an extreme case, at the time of this writing Germany is governed by a coalition of the two biggest parties, the Christian Democratic bloc and the Social Democrats. One can hardly imagine how the US Congress might operate if it were organized by a coalition of Republicans and Democrats.

13. Just over 50 percent of the voters in just over 50 percent of the districts. Extreme distortions happen in practice, not just in theory. In the 2015 British general election, the Tories under David Cameron won an absolute majority of seats in Parliament despite winning only 36 percent of the popular vote.

14. Ellis and Stimson, *Ideology in America*, 75.

15. Of course, other Great Society initiatives were and remain matters of continuing partisan controversy. Consistent with this discussion of overreach, Gilens concludes that policy responsiveness to the public was quite low in the Johnson years. *Affluence & Influence*, 221–29.

happened in the aftermath of an electoral landslide. Now they have become standard operating procedure for today's parties. What follows are some recent examples.

In 1992, Bill Clinton led the Democrats out of the electoral wilderness where they had wandered since 1968. During the campaign Clinton emphasized the importance of hard work and individual responsibility and promised an administration that would reform welfare and be tough on crime—issues that had put the Democrats on the defensive for two decades. Although the Democrats won full control of the national government, Clinton received only 43 percent of the popular vote in a three-way election. Despite his centrist campaign appeals and winning only a minority of the vote, however, the new Clinton administration adopted a traditional Democratic agenda, including an attempt to overhaul the health care system, an effort that failed completely. The result of this overreach was Democratic calamity in the 1994 elections. The Republicans under Newt Gingrich gained fifty-four seats in the House of Representatives to win control of that body for the first time in forty years—and with a net gain of ten seats in the Senate won control of that body as well. In the year after the election, many in the commentariat viewed President Clinton as a mere placeholder.[16] The consensus held that Republican Senate leader Robert Dole was the "grown-up" in Washington and only the formality of the next election remained before President Dole took office.

But Newt Gingrich did not draw the obvious lesson from the Clinton administration's overreach. He resurrected Clinton's political fortunes and sank Dole's by using his House majority in an overreach of his own. A battle over cutting the federal budget led the federal government to shut down twice in the winter of 1995–96, with negative consequences for the Republican Party in the court of public opinion. Despite the monumental Republican victory in the 1994 elections, that result had by no means indicated that a majority of voters wanted cuts in popular programs like Medicare.

16. In one widely noted postelection press conference, President Clinton argued that he was still "relevant." *Time* magazine, "Clinton 'The President Is Relevant,'" April 18, 1995, http://content.time.com/time/nation/article/0,8599,3632,00.html.

The consequence of the Republican overreach was an easy Clinton reelection in 1996.

In 2004, the Republicans won full control of the national government for the first time in a half century. Given his narrow popular vote margin, many observers were surprised by the assertive tone adopted by President George W. Bush. In his postelection news conference, he stated, "I earned capital in the campaign, political capital, and now I intend to spend it."[17] The president announced that the United States would follow a freedom agenda in the international arena—the use of American power to actively promote democracy around the world. And in the domestic arena the president proposed the introduction of Social Security private accounts. Historically, presidents who win by large margins are likely to claim mandates, those who win by smaller margins not so much.[18] Today, as the Bush example illustrates, the simple fact of winning may be taken as a mandate.

More attuned to the next election than the lame-duck president, the Republican congressional majorities let the president's proposal to adopt Social Security personal accounts die a quiet death, and the Republican "thumpin'" in 2006 put an end to any lingering talk of a Bush mandate. In his memoirs, President Bush acknowledged the likelihood that he had overreached: "On social security, I may have misread the electoral mandate."[19] The American people rarely give mandates; generally they hire you on probation and renew your contract if you perform satisfactorily.[20]

As James Carville and numerous others noted, the 2008 election results were superficially consistent with the idea of a Democratic mandate, especially when considered together with the 2006

17. Marc Sandalow, "Bush claims mandate, sets 2nd-term goals/'I earned capital in this campaign, political capital, and now I intend to spend it,'" *San Francisco Chronicle*, November 5, 2004, www.sfgate.com/politics/article/Bush-claims-mandate -sets-2nd-term-goals-I-2637116.php.

18. On mandates, see Patricia H. Conley, *Presidential Mandates: How Elections Shape the National Agenda* (Chicago: University of Chicago Press, 2001); and Lawrence J. Grossback, David A. M. Peterson, and James A. Stimson, *Mandate Politics* (New York: Cambridge University Press, 2012).

19. George W. Bush, *Decision Points* (New York: Random House, 2010), 300.

20. And the mandate after landslide elections often is no more than "for God's sake, do something different."

"thumpin'" of the Republicans. But most political scientists took a more cautious position, pointing to the ongoing war in Iraq, President Bush's approval ratings (which were flirting with historical lows in 2008), and the September stock market crash more than any desire on the part of the American public to embark on a new liberal era as principal factors underlying the Democratic victories.

The warning signs of Democratic overreach were apparent early on. The night that he claimed the nomination Barack Obama stated,

> Generations from now, we will be able to look back and tell our children . . . that this was the moment when we began to provide care for the sick and good jobs for the jobless; this was the moment when the rise of the oceans began to slow and our planet began to heal.[21]

Had I been advising Obama I would have suggested replacing the semicolon in the preceding passage with a period and striking everything about the oceans and the planet that followed. The remarks suggest an administration itching to overreach, which in fact it did.[22]

At a time when many Americans felt that their economic condition was desperate, the new administration focused on issues of more concern to the Democratic base than the larger public. In an effort to address global warming, the House passed "cap and trade" energy legislation that was unpopular in coal- and oil-producing states. (The Senate, where carbon interests were stronger, refused to even consider the bill, meaning that some House Democrats had

21. *Huffington Post*, "Obama's Nomination Victory Speech in St. Paul," June 3, 2008, www.huffingtonpost.com/2008/06/03/obamas-nomination-victory_n_105028 .html.

22. Given that most professors spend their days in liberal university environments, I realize that many Democrats think of Obama as a moderate pragmatist rather than a liberal overreacher. But the opinions that matter are the voters'. According to the Gallup organization, when Obama was elected about 45 percent of the members of the electorate thought they had elected a moderate and similar numbers a liberal (nearly 10 percent thought they had elected a conservative). Nine months later 55 percent thought they had elected a liberal and only 35 percent a moderate—and voters' remorse began to set in.

been forced to cast an unnecessary, politically damaging vote.) But the Affordable Care Act obviously was the central element of the Democratic overreach. The legislation never enjoyed majority support in the population (although specific parts of it did), and the Democrats secured passage only via a series of side deals and parliamentary maneuvers that reflected poorly on the legitimacy of the process. An intensive statistical analysis indicated that the Democrats might have saved their House majority—just barely—in 2010 had marginal members of the party not been forced to cast a vote for the Affordable Care Act.[23]

After the 2014 elections, Democratic senator Chuck Schumer of New York created a stir in Democratic circles by stating publicly that his party had embraced the wrong priorities after the 2008 elections.[24] Health care had not been a major concern of the American public, although it was more important to the Democratic base.[25] Instead of putting all their efforts on the financial crisis and the resulting recession, "Democrats blew the opportunity the American people gave them. We took their mandate and put all of our focus on the wrong problem: health care reform."[26] Schumer's remarks were criticized by many Democrats, but I believe his analysis was correct.

The health care example makes an important point about overreach that is often overlooked. On reflection, there are two components of overreach, although they often occur together. The first, more widely noticed one is the tendency to take more extreme positions on issues than a majority of the public at large favors. Abortion is our running example. As noted earlier, the 2012 Democratic

23. David Brady, Morris Fiorina, and Arjun Wilkins, "The 2010 Elections: Why Did Political Science Forecasts Go Awry?" *PS: Political Science & Politics* 44, no. 2 (April 2011).

24. Schumer also noted that the botched rollout of Healthcare.gov, the Veterans Affairs scandals, and the child migrant border crisis had contributed to a general sense that the administration was incompetent.

25. Ryan D. Enos and Eitan D. Hersh, "Party Activists as Campaign Advertisers: The Ground Campaign as a Principal-Agent Problem," *American Political Science Review* 109, no. 2 (May 2015): 263–64.

26. Russell Berman, "Chuck Schumer's Cure for Democrats," *The Atlantic*, November 25, 2014, www.theatlantic.com/politics/archive/2014/11/chuck-schumers -cure-for-democrats/383175/.

platform plank amounted to "anytime, for any reason," while the Republican plank amounted to "never, no exceptions." While majorities of convention delegates supported these positions, 85 percent or more of the American public falls between these extremes. Much of the discussion of polarization in the United States focuses on this first component of overreach.

But Schumer's comments identify a second, perhaps equally important component. It is not just how parties position themselves on issues, but also which issues they place on the agenda. This second aspect of overreach entails the adoption of priorities that are important to the party base but of secondary importance to the public. The data indicate that the priorities of President Obama were out of step with those of the public for his entire administration, not just the first as Schumer charged. At his 2013 inauguration, Obama focused on issues vital to specific constituencies within his coalition.[27] The president emphasized issues like climate change, gay rights, immigration, gun control, and equal pay for women. Such issues are very important to the Democratic base. Two weeks before the president's inauguration, however, the Pew Research Center asked a representative sample of the American public what they believed should be the most important issues the Congress and the president should work on during the coming year. As table 5.2 shows, it is striking how little overlap there was between the priorities of the broader public and those enunciated by President Obama.

The priorities of the public were heavily focused on what are generally called bread-and-butter issues—the things that are important in the day-to-day lives of most Americans. Will I keep my job? Are my kids getting a decent education? Will Social Security and Medicare be there for me? Are we safe here in our country? As for Obama's priorities, immigration came in at seventeenth on the public's list, guns (only a month after the school massacre at Sandy Hook) at eighteenth, and global warming dead last at twenty-first.

I emphasize that I am not arguing that the public's priorities are always the ones that a governing party should follow. That is a

27. Tom Curry, "In Second Inaugural, Obama Appeals to His Progressive Base," NBC News, January 21, 2013, http://nbcpolitics.nbcnews.com/_news/2013/01/21/16627455-in-second-inaugural-obama-appeals-to-his-progressive-base?lite.

TABLE 5.2. The Public's Policy Priorities: January 2013

	% Saying each is a "Top Priority" for the President and Congress this year
Strengthening the economy	86
Improving the job situation	79
Reducing the budget deficit	72
Defending against terrorism	71
Making Social Security financially sound	70
Improving education	70
Making Medicare financially sound	65
Reducing health costs	63
Helping the poor and needy	57
Reducing crime	55
Reforming the tax system	52
Protecting the environment	52
Dealing with the energy problem	45
Reducing the influence of lobbyists	44
Strengthening the military	41
Dealing with the moral breakdown	40
Dealing with illegal immigration	39
Strengthening gun laws	37
Dealing with global trade	31
Improving infrastructure	30
Dealing with global warming	28

Source: Pew Research Center, "Deficit Reduction Rises on Public's Agenda for Obama's Second Term," January 24, 2013, www.people-press.org/2013/01/24/deficit-reduction-rises-on-publics-agenda-for-obamas-second-term/.

normative position that political philosophers have argued about for centuries. Surely there is a place for—indeed, a need for—leadership in a democracy. Farsighted leaders should work to counteract the bias toward short-term thinking and the preference for tangible versus abstract outcomes that seem to be part of human nature. Rather than a normative argument, I am simply observing that leaders who stray too far from the priorities of the public in democratic societies run the risk of becoming former leaders.

As the experience of the Bush administration showed, contemporary Republicans are just as prone to prioritizing issues differently from the way the broader public does. With one war already under way, there was no evidence in the polls that Americans were keen on

TABLE 5.3. The 2004 Presidential Election:
This Issue Is Extremely or Very Important

Issue	
Economy	91
Jobs	91
Education	88
Terrorism	87
Health Care	85
Iraq	82
Social Security	79
Taxes	77
Medicare	76
Budget Deficit	74
Foreign Affairs	71
Energy	71
Environment	70
Gay/Lesbian Policy	28

Source: Joseph Carroll, "Economy, Terrorism Top
Issues in 2004 Election Vote," Gallup, September 25,
2003, http://www.gallup.com/poll/9337/economy
-terrorism-top-issues-2004-election-vote.aspx.

investing more blood and treasure in pursuit of a freedom agenda,
but it was a policy favored by the neoconservative faction of the
party. And certainly, there was no widespread public demand for
Social Security personal accounts. Further back, a central part of the
2004 Republican campaign was an emphasis on anti-gay-marriage
initiatives, an issue designed to maximize turnout within the evan-
gelical community, although all reputable polls showed that it was
of minor import to the public at large (table 5.3).[28]

The 2016 election season provided numerous examples of a
misalignment of party and popular priorities, especially on the
Democratic side where Hillary Clinton was pulled to the left by
the Sanders challenge. Watching Clinton at a December 2015 town
meeting in New Hampshire, journalist Joe Klein noted:

28. And postelection analyses found little evidence that it had any significant
effect on the vote. Morris P. Fiorina with Samuel J. Abrams and Jeremy C. Pope,
Culture War? The Myth of a Polarized America, 2nd ed., chap. 8 (New York: Pearson,
2006).

And then she went straight to questions. Dozens were asked. And you might wonder how many concerned the topic of the moment, the need to rethink national security in an era when the terrorists have switched tactics and are attacking low security targets—theaters and restaurants in Paris, Christmas parties in San Bernardino.

The answer, as Bill Clinton used to say, was zee-ro. None. Not a single question about national security. Several times Clinton tried to steer her answers toward the topic, but the crowd resisted and it occurred to me that Clinton was actually taking a *risk* with the Democratic base.

What were the questions about? Genetically modified food. Climate change. Gun control. Whether Exxon Mobil suppressed information about carbon pollution. Voting rights. Mental health. Student loans. Immigration (pro-family preservation, not border control). Preserving Social Security and Medicare. Taking care of veterans.[29]

As Klein noted, some of these are important issues, but table 5.4 shows that most ranked far down the list of public priorities measured at about the same time that he was covering the Clinton campaign.

Why Do Today's Parties Overreach?

Given the availability of the kind of data presented above, as well as a wealth of internal polling data (not to mention the electoral experiences of some two decades), why did Barack Obama, Nancy Pelosi (Speaker of the House), and Harry Reid (Senate majority leader) not behave differently in 2009–10? Why did they overreach in both senses of the term? Today's sorted parties are an important part of the answer. Generally speaking, Democrats build their governing coalitions starting from the left, while Republicans build their coalitions starting from the right. Since neither party has a majority of the

29. Joe Klein, "Hillary Clinton and the Democrats' National Security Problem," *Time* magazine, December 11, 2015, http://time.com/4145735/hillary-clinton-demo crats-national-security/.

TABLE 5.4. The Public's Policy Priorities: January 2016

	% Saying each is a "Top Priority" for the President and Congress this year
Strengthening the economy	75
Terrorism	75
Education	66
Jobs	64
Social Security	62
Health Care Costs	61
Medicare	58
Reducing crime	58
Budget deficit	56
Poor and Needy	54
Immigration	51
Strengthening the military	49
Environment	47
Tax Reform	45
Criminal justice reform	44
Climate change	38
Gun policy	37
Dealing with global trade	31

Source: PEW Research Center. "Budget Deficit slips as Public Priority," January 22, 2016, http://www.people-press .org/2016/01/22/budget-deficit-slips-as-public-priority/.

electorate, each must capture enough votes among nonpartisans and otherwise nonaligned citizens—usually a majority of them—to win. Thus, one sees the well-known tendency for nominees to edge toward the political center following primary contests that take place largely on the left and right. (In today's wired world, where everything said finds its way to the Internet, that time-honored strategy has become increasingly difficult to implement.)

After the elections the vast majority of Americans return to their focus on their nonpolitical lives, leaving the political arena to the political class. But the victors face pressure from their base to enact the core policies and priorities of the party. In today's sorted parties, this means that Democratic officials face pressures coming almost entirely from the left, while Republican officials face pressures coming almost entirely from the right.[30] Given that activists typically have more extreme views than the public at large (chapter 2), the result is more extreme policy positions than favored by the broader public, as in the example of abortion. And given that political activists are often motivated by issues that are not the issues most important to the broader public, the result is a mismatch of priorities, as in the health care example. The result is overreach, followed by backlash at the next election.

Contrast the situation today with that of the unsorted parties of the mid-twentieth century. A Democratic president then could play off disparate elements in the party, telling Southern conservatives that the Northern liberals wouldn't stand for this, and telling the liberals that the Southerners wouldn't stand for that. Similarly, a Republican president could steer a course between the Northeastern liberals and the Midwestern conservatives in the party. But after several decades of party sorting, the party bases are now so homogeneous that all the pressures within each party come from the same side, pulling elected officials away from the electorally safer center ground.

Here is where the close party balance comes in again. The close balance between today's sorted parties reinforces the pressures coming from the left or the right in each party.[31] If a party is secure in its status as a majority party, it can afford to proceed deliberately, to gradually build support for a legislative initiative until adopting it no longer is an overreach. But if you cannot count on long-term majority control, better strike while the iron is hot—you may not have another opportunity for a long time. Given the close party balance,

30. For many elected officials in today's well-sorted parties, such pressures simply reinforce what they would personally like to do anyway.

31. Frances Lee provides excellent analyses of the consequences of the close party divide for congressional operations today. In addition to the general consequences I note, she emphasizes that the goal of winning the next election leads the congressional parties to posture rather than legislate and to eschew bipartisan compromises. See her "Legislative Parties in an Era of Alternating Majorities," in *Governing in a Polarized Age: Elections, Parties, and Political Representation in America*, ed. Alan Gerber and Eric Schickler (New York: Cambridge University Press, 2016); also see Frances E. Lee, *Insecure Majorities: Congress and the Perpetual Campaign* (Chicago: University of Chicago Press, 2016).

the party could lose the next election even if it does not overreach. A scandal, a foreign policy crisis, an economic downturn not of the administration's making—any unfavorable development might result in loss of control. Given this uncertainty about the electoral future, you might as well go for broke even if you suffer the consequences in the next election. I would love to know whether Pelosi would have driven health care through Congress had she known that the price would be a Republican House majority for six years and possibly longer. It would not be surprising if her answer were yes.[32]

These developments are further reinforced by two additional considerations. First, for most of American history the primary goal of parties was to win office and retain it. Policy implementation was sometimes important, but generally secondary to winning elections. Contemporary parties are different. Partly as a consequence of participatory reforms that changed the kind of people who constitute the parties, many of those active in today's parties consider material goals—winning office and all the perquisites that go with it—to be of relatively less importance than achieving desired policy ends.[33] Scholars of political parties have recently characterized contemporary parties as coalitions of "policy demanders."[34] Given the

32. According to the *New York Times*, Pelosi told President Obama, "We'll never have a better majority in your presidency in numbers than we've got right now," suggesting that she was well aware of the possible ephemeral nature of her majority. Sheryl Gay Stolberg, Jeff Zeleny, and Carl Hulse, "The Long Road Back," *New York Times*, March 21, 2010, http://query.nytimes.com/gst/fullpage.html?res=9C05EFDC 1039F932A15750C0A9669D8B63&pagewanted=all. Thanks to Eileen Burgin for pointing out this passage.

33. This is an argument developed in two earlier essays: Morris Fiorina, "Extreme Voices: A Dark Side of Civic Engagement," in *Civic Engagement in American Democracy*, ed. Theda Skocpol and Morris Fiorina (Washington, DC: Brookings Institution Press, 1999), 395–425; and Morris Fiorina, "Parties, Participation, and Representation in America: Old Theories Face New Realities," in *Political Science: State of the Discipline*, ed. Ira Katznelson and Helen V. Milner (New York: W. W. Norton, 2003), 511–41. For a recent argument that a little participatory reform is a good thing, but too much can be harmful, see Bruce E. Cain, *Democracy More or Less: America's Political Reform Quandary* (New York: Cambridge University Press, 2015).

34. Kathleen Bawn, Martin Cohen, David Karol, Seth Masket, Hans Noel, and John Zaller, "A Theory of Political Parties: Groups, Policy Demands and Nominations in American Politics," *Perspectives on Politics* 10, no. 3 (September

relatively greater importance of policy goals, the members of today's party bases are willing to run larger electoral risks—to overreach—than was the case when the party bases were less well sorted.[35] And they meet little intra-party opposition because the parties are even more well sorted at the higher levels of involvement.

A final consideration that increases the likelihood that today's sorted parties overreach is more impressionistic on my part—anecdotal, really. But in talking to activists and reading their blogs and other statements, it seems clear that many of them sincerely believe that if their party only nominated a true conservative (liberal), a large majority of the country would turn out and elect him or her. To such claims, most political scientists have a brief answer: Goldwater (McGovern).[36] But as discussed in chapter 2, although normal Americans inhabit heterogeneous information environments (to the extent that they are aware of the media at all), the highly involved members of the political class do inhabit homogeneous communications networks—*everyone* they talk to thinks as they do.[37] Moreover, their partisan and ideological blinders make them consider the other side so far out of the mainstream that people

2012): 571–97; Hans Noel, *Political Ideologies and Political Parties in America* (New York: Cambridge University Press, 2013).

35. In fact, they may be perfectly content to lose. This is not a phenomenon unique to the United States. In 2015, British Labour Party activists elected as their leader a far-left MP universally viewed as a certain loser in the next general election. One poll reported that only 10 percent of his supporters believed that electability was an important consideration in deciding to support him. See Alex Massie, "The Labour Party's Two Word Suicide Note," *The Daily Beast,* September 12, 2015, www.thedailybeast.com/articles/2015/09/12/labour-s-two-word-suicide-note.html.

36. Although according to Douglas Hibbs' parsimonious forecasting model, Goldwater did no worse and McGovern only a bit worse than economic conditions and international conflict would have indicated, www.douglas-hibbs.com/Election 2012/2012Election-MainPage.htm.

37. A study of delegates to the 2008 presidential nominating conventions—extremely high-level political activists—reports extreme partisan segregation of the delegates' organizational networks. See Michael T. Heaney, Seth E. Masket, Joanne M. Miller, and Dara Z. Strolovitch, "Polarized Networks: The Organizational Affiliations of National Party Convention Delegates," *American Behavioral Scientist* 56 (October 19, 2012): 1654–76.

could not possibly support them if only they were given a true liberal (conservative) to vote for.

For all of the above reasons, today's sorted parties competing for the votes of a closely divided electorate find the temptations and pressures to overreach nearly irresistible. Consequently, they do not hold their majorities for very long.

Postscript

Given the argument of this chapter, *under ordinary circumstances* I would expect the Republicans to overreach and suffer significant defeats in the 2018 midterm elections. For six years, a Republican House majority has chafed under a Democratic president. Senate Republicans endured not only six years of life under a Democratic president but in addition six years under a Democratic Senate majority. Now the 2016 elections have unleashed the pent-up ambitions of congressional Republicans. With full control of the national government, one would expect Republicans to repeal Obamacare, cut taxes, reform entitlements, deregulate the economy, reverse environmental policies, and adopt other prominent elements of the Republican agenda. A Democratic president's veto no longer stands in the way. But as this chapter argues, such a Republican legislative onslaught would likely alienate the marginal supporters of 2016 and result in significant congressional losses in 2018. Heavy Democratic exposure in Senate races (they will be defending twenty-five of thirty-four seats) probably will insulate the Republican Senate majority, but a twenty-four-seat loss in the House would mark a return to divided government.

Ironically, Trump could save congressional Republicans from themselves. Because his policy commitments do not neatly accord with those of today's sorted Republican Party, the likelihood of an overreach may be less than it would be under a more typical conservative Republican president. Already Trump's commitment to some of the most popular elements of Obamacare has made it difficult for congressional Republicans to construct a substitute health care bill that will neither bust the budget nor deny coverage to millions.

Trump disagrees with some elements of his party on foreign policy, trade policy, immigration, and other specific issues. His draconian budget proposals will put some Republicans in the awkward position of opposing cuts to programs and agencies important to their districts and he does not appear to be as socially conservative as many Republicans. With congressional Democrats unlikely to provide any help, it is possible that the Trump administration will accomplish less than Republicans initially hope and Democrats fear. Thus the irony—less Republican accomplishment on the policy front from 2016–18 would lead to lower Democratic gains on the electoral front in 2018.

CHAPTER 6

Independents: The Marginal Members of an Electoral Coalition

We will never have a time again, in my opinion, in this country when you are going to have a polarization of only Democrats versus Republicans . . . you are going to have the Independents controlling basically the balance of power.
—Richard M. Nixon

There are more independents than ever before. That means nothing.
—Aaron Blake

In recent elections, partisans have voted for the presidential candidates of their parties at rates exceeding 90 percent.[1] These figures lead many commentators to jump to the conclusion that the country is evenly divided into two deeply opposed partisan camps. But, as shown in chapter 3, party sorting in the general public remains far from perfect. Consider an analogy from the religious realm. Probably 90 percent of self-identified Catholics who attend church services attend Catholic services rather than those of other denominations, just as 90 percent of partisans who turn out cast their votes for the

Quotations are from former president Richard M. Nixon in an interview with Howard K. Smith of ABC News, March 22, 1971, *Public Papers of the Presidents of the United States: Richard M. Nixon* (Washington, DC: Office of the Federal Register), 460; and Aaron Blake, "There are more independents than ever before. That means nothing," *The Fix* (blog), *Washington Post*, April 7, 2015, www.washingtonpost.com/blogs/the-fix/wp/2015/04/07/there-are-more-independents-than-ever-before-that-means-nothing/.

1. These rates are slight overestimates of partisan loyalty because a few people will change their partisanship to reflect their vote choice, artificially inflating the figures.

party with which they identify. But at the same time we know from various public opinion surveys that a large majority of self-identified Catholics disagrees with the church's position on contraception, and a substantial minority disagrees with the church's position on abortion.[2] So, if one were to infer the birth control views of church-attending Catholics based on the pronouncements of Catholic bishops, the inference would be wildly inaccurate. Analogously, as discussed in chapter 3, the positions of substantial minorities of partisans on abortion are at odds with the positions taken by their party leaders. The vote is a binary choice, a blunt and often inaccurate way to express one's preferences on the issues. A given voter might repeatedly make the same decision in the voting booth even while disagreeing substantially with the party for whom she votes—so long as she disagrees even more substantially with the other party.[3] Many voters faced just such a situation in 2016 when they had to choose between the two most negatively viewed candidates in modern times (see chapter 10). Recent research on "negative partisanship" is consistent with the notion that many voters choose between the lesser of two evils.[4] Since the Reagan era, partisans have not registered increased favorability toward the party with which they identify, but they register greater antipathy toward the other party.[5] Such findings suggest that we should view the proportion of Americans who identify with the parties less as guaranteed levels of electoral support and more as upper limits on the proportion of the vote the parties can definitely

2. E.g., "Public Divided over Birth Control Insurance Mandate," Pew Research Center, February 14, 2012, www.people-press.org/2012/02/14/public-divided-over -birth-control-insurance-mandate/. In this 2012 survey, only 8 percent of Catholics thought contraception was morally wrong. Thirteen percent thought abortion was morally acceptable and 25 percent thought it was not a moral issue.

3. See Jeremy C. Pope, "Voting vs. Thinking: Unified Partisan Voting Does Not Imply Unified Partisan Beliefs," *The Forum: A Journal of Applied Research in Contemporary Politics* 10, no. 3 (October 2012).

4. Alan Abramowitz, "The New American Electorate: Partisan, Sorted, and Polarized," in *American Gridlock: The Sources, Character, and Impact of Political Polarization*, ed. James A. Thurber and Antoine Yoshinaka (New York: Cambridge University Press, 2015), 19–44.

5. Lori D. Bougher, "The Origins of Out-Party Dislike: Identity and Ideological Consistency in Polarized America," paper presented at the 2016 annual meeting of the Midwest Political Science Association, Chicago.

FIGURE 6.1. Self-Classified Independents Are at a Record High

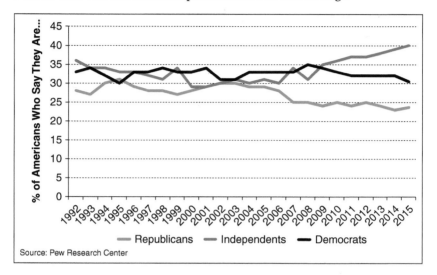

Source: Pew Research Center

count on. Given turnout differentials, that amounts to roughly one-third of the electorate that either party can absolutely count on (figure 2.7 of chapter 2 and the accompanying discussion).

In a two-party majoritarian system this means that the marginal voters in an electoral majority come from the ranks of the independents, with perhaps the addition of some weakly attached members of the opposing party. The proportion of the eligible electorate responding "independent" to survey questions has hovered around 40 percent in recent years, the highest levels recorded since the advent of modern survey research (figure 6.1). Independents clearly hold the balance of electoral power in the contemporary United States.

Some analysts dismiss numbers like these, contending that most independents are "closet," "hidden," or "covert" partisans.[6] According to Ruy Teixeira, "Numerous studies have shown that treating leaners as independents is 'the greatest myth in American politics' . . . Call them IINOs, or Independents in Name Only. IINOs who say

6. The seminal article is John Petrocik, "An Analysis of Intransitivities in the Index of Party Identification," *Political Methodology* 1, no. 3 (Summer 1974): 31–47. Also see Bruce Keith, David Magleby, Candice Nelson, Elizabeth Orr, Mark Westlye, and Raymond Wolfinger, *The Myth of the Independent Voter* (Berkeley, CA: University of California Press, 1992), 4, 23.

they lean toward the Republicans think and vote just like regular Republicans. IINOs who say they lean toward the Democrats think and vote just like regular Democrats."[7]

Teixeira's claim rests on the fact that when self-identified independents are asked whether they are closer to one party or the other, many will say yes. Following John Petrocik and Alan Abramowitz, he contends that these "leaners" actually are partisans who like the independent label.[8] If this claim is true, the actual proportion of independents—so-called "pure independents"—is no more than 10 percent of the eligible electorate, a far cry from the 40 percent registered in the polls. From the standpoint of my larger argument about overreach, it does not really matter whether the party balance is about 33/33/33 or 45/10/45; the marginal members of an electoral majority still must come from the ranks of the independents. But since I believe that much of the conventional wisdom about independents is wrong, or at least significantly overstated, the first part of this chapter makes a slight digression and examines them more closely.

How Do We Count Independents?

The American National Election Studies (ANES)—which provide much of the data discussed in this book—measure party identification with this survey question: "Generally speaking, do you usually think of yourself as a Republican, a Democrat, an independent, or what?" If the answer is Republican or Democrat, the respondent then is asked, "Would you call yourself a strong [Republican, Democrat] or a not-very-strong [Republican, Democrat]?" The resulting four categories are referred to in the political science literature as strong Democrats, strong Republicans, weak Democrats, and weak Republicans.

---

7. Ruy Teixeira, "The Great Illusion," *New Republic,* March 6, 2012, www.tnr.com/book/review/swing-vote-untapped-power-independents-linda-killian.

8. Petrocik, "An Analysis of Intransitivities"; Alan Abramowitz, "Setting the Record Straight: Correcting Myths about Independent Voters," *Sabato's Crystal Ball,* July 7, 2011, www.centerforpolitics.org/crystalball/articles/aia20110070702/.

Respondents who answer the first question as independent or something else, however, are then asked, "Do you think of yourself as *closer* to the Republican Party or the Democratic Party?" Those respondents who answer that they are closer to one party or the other are classified as Independent Democrats or Independent Republicans. These are the leaning independents or "leaners" whom analysts often combine with weak partisans. In justifying this common practice Abramowitz asserts, "Research by political scientists on the American electorate has consistently found that the large majority of self-identified independents are 'closet partisans' who think and vote much like other partisans."[9] And doubling down on his seminal 1974 contribution, Petrocik writes, "Leaners are partisans. . . . As an empirical matter, Americans who admit to feeling closer to one of the parties in the follow-up probe—the leaners—are virtually identical to those who are classified as 'weak' partisans . . . across a wide variety of perceptions, preferences, and behaviors."[10]

In my view, the preceding claims go well beyond anything the data justify. Rather than a large body of research that "consistently finds" that leaners are partisans, researchers cite the same handful of studies, all of which fail to deal with a serious methodological objection.[11] The basic problem with the claims made in such studies is their failure to deal with reverse causation or, in contemporary social science argot, endogeneity.[12]

Causal Confusion

More than three decades ago, W. Phillips Shively suggested that rather than covert partisanship causing their vote, independents may

9. Abramowitz, "Setting the Record Straight."

10. John Petrocik, "Measuring Party Support: Leaners Are Not Independents," *Electoral Studies* 28 (2009): 562.

11. Two studies receive the lion's share of the citations. As noted above, the seminal article is Petrocik, "An Analysis of Intransitivities." The other standard citation is Keith et al., *The Myth of the Independent Voter,* which devotes far more emphasis to the distinction between pure and leaning independents than to the similarity between leaning independents and partisans.

12. Given a system with two variables, x and y, if x causes y, x is exogenous and y is endogenous. If they cause each other, both are endogenous.

say how they lean based on how they plan to vote—the reverse of the standard causal assumption.[13] Consider a simple illustration. In a given election four independent leaners vote as follows:

Voter	Party Identification	Presidential Vote Report
1	Independent Democrat	Democratic
2	Independent Democrat	Democratic
3	Independent Republican	Republican
4	Independent Republican	Republican

So independent-leaning Democrats vote Democratic, and independent-leaning Republicans vote Republican, consistent with the covert partisanship view. But suppose in the next election the same four voters report the following patterns:

Voter	Party Identification	Presidential Vote Report
1	Independent Democrat	Democratic
2	Independent Republican	Republican
3	Independent Republican	Republican
4	Independent Democrat	Democratic

We still have a perfect relationship: voters vote the way they lean, but voters two and four changed their votes *and* changed their response to the "closer to" question to match the change in their votes. Rather than covert partisans, they are actually swing voters.

How can we determine whether real-world voting patterns reflect the first or second examples? One way would be to follow independent leaners over several elections to see if they consistently lean and vote in the same direction. Such an analysis has been done, and the reader interested in the details should digest Samuel J. Abrams and Morris P. Fiorina, "Are Leaning Independents Deluded or Dishonest Weak Partisans?" http://cise.luiss.it/cise/wp-content/uploads/2011

---

13. W. Phillips Shively, "The Nature of Party Identification: A Review of Recent Developments," in *The Electorate Reconsidered*, ed. John C. Pierce and John L. Sullivan (Beverly Hills, CA: Sage, 1980), 219–36.

/10/Are-Leaners-Partisans.pdf. For the more casual reader, a brief summary follows.

Leaning Independents Change Their Self-Identification More Than Weak Partisans Do

Presidential vote choice is the primary evidence cited by those who equate leaning independents and weak partisans.[14] Petrocik writes, "The almost indistinguishable voting choices of leaners and weak identifiers of the same party is datum number one for the proposition that leaners are partisans, even if their first inclination is to respond to the party identification question by calling themselves independents."[15] As figure 6.2 shows, independent leaners indeed are similar to weak partisans in their presidential voting choices. In fact, they often are *more* loyal than weak partisans, as in the 1964 Goldwater and 1972 McGovern electoral debacles. But these facts should immediately raise warning signs. According to the American National Election Studies, in 1964 weak Republicans abandoned Barry Goldwater in droves, but independent-leaning Republicans registered support almost 20 percentage points higher. Similarly, in 1972 George McGovern did not win even a majority of weak Democrats, but 60 percent of independent-leaning Democrats supported him. What might explain these puzzling contrasts? Well, perhaps independent Republicans voted more heavily for Goldwater not because they were closet Republicans; rather, they were independents who felt closer to the Republicans *in that election* because they had decided to vote for Goldwater. Analogously, the high level of independent Democratic support for McGovern may have been because they were independents who liked McGovern and consequently said they leaned Democratic.

In fifty-six of sixty comparisons of one-, two-, and four-year panel waves in the ANES database, leaners are less stable than weak partisans, often by significant margins—20 percentage points

---

14. They are less similar in their congressional voting behavior, particularly in midterm elections.

15. Petrocik, "Measuring Party Support," 566–67.

FIGURE 6.2. **Leaning Independents Vote Like Partisans**

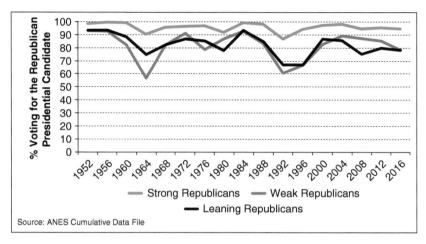

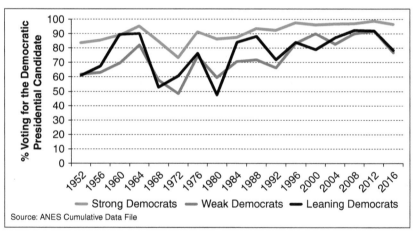

or more.[16] In the four major presidential election panel studies conducted by ANES (1956–60, 1972–76, 1992–96, and 2000–2004), nearly 70 percent of strong partisans give the same response when queried about their partisan identities during two presidential election campaigns four years apart. A bit less than 50 percent of weak

16. Samuel J. Abrams and Morris P. Fiorina, "Are Leaning Independents Deluded or Dishonest Weak Partisans?" In panel studies, the same individuals are surveyed two or more times, permitting analysts to track individual change rather than just net change.

partisans give the same response, and one-third of pure independents give the same response. But only 31 percent of independent Democrats and 38 percent of independent Republicans give the same response. Their partisan stability is closer to pure independents than to weak partisans.[17]

Such findings suggest that the causal arrow runs not only from partisanship to vote, but also from vote back to partisanship, particularly among citizens who choose the independent label. Some (unknown) proportion of leaners vote the way they lean because they tell us how they lean based on how they intend to vote. This endogeneity in the survey responses artificially exaggerates the apparent strength of party loyalty as an influence on the vote. And it misleads pundits and some political scientists to conclude that partisanship has become nearly universal.

Additional Evidence

Analysts simply have not looked hard enough for data that contradict the practice of treating leaning independents as hidden partisans. The Comparative Study of Electoral Systems module on the ANES included the following item in 2004 and 2008: "Do any of the parties represent your views reasonably well?" YouGov/Polimetrix asked a similar question in 2015. The responses in table 6.1 clearly indicate that leaning independents are less satisfied with the party toward which they lean than are weak partisans.

When third-party candidates appear on the scene, leaning independents also differentiate themselves from weak partisans. George Wallace in 1968, John Anderson in 1980, Ross Perot in 1992 and 1996, and Ralph Nader and Pat Buchanan in 2000 all received higher support among independent leaners than among weak partisans. When given the opportunity, independent leaners are more likely than weak partisans to opt for candidates outside the two-party duopoly (table 6.2).

All in all, there is little basis for blanket claims that leaning independents are merely closet partisans. I hasten to emphasize that I am not endorsing the opposite blanket claim that they are all genuine

17. Abrams and Fiorina, "Leaning Independents."

TABLE 6.1. **Do Any of the Parties Represent Your Views?**

	2004 CSES	*2008 CSES*	*2015 Polimetrix*
Strong Democrats	80	81	87
Weak Democrats	72	69	46
Independent Democrats	58	53	40
Pure Independents	47	36	11
Independent Republicans	66	49	50
Weak Republicans	83	60	63
Strong Republicans	93	85	93

Source: Comparative Study of Electoral Systems; Polimetrix

TABLE 6.2. **Leaning Independents Vote for Third Parties at Higher Rates Than Weak Partisans Do**

	Strong Democrats	*Weak Democrats*	*Leaning Democrats*	*Independents*	*Leaning Republicans*	*Weak Republicans*	*Strong Republicans*
1968	8	15	19	21	14	8	2
1980	4	8	26	14	13	10	4
1992	4	17	24	36	26	25	11
1996	3	10	19	28	12	11	1
2000	1	1	8	16	8	1	1

Source: ANES Cumulative Data File

independents either. Where the proportion of true independents lies between the low estimate of 10 percent and the high estimate of 40 percent of the eligible electorate is a question to which political science currently has no precise answer. Recent research suggests that independents and partisans differ psychologically.[18] Clearly independents are a heterogeneous category. Some are closet partisans. Some are ideological centrists. Some are cross pressured, preferring one party on some issues but a different party on other issues. Some are unhappy with both parties, and some are, quite simply, clueless. But whatever they are, they are an important component of the electoral instability that characterizes the contemporary era. Their critical contribution to contemporary elections lies in their volatility.

18. This is an area that needs much more research. An important recent contribution is Samara Klar and Yanna Krupnikov, *Independent Politics: How American Disdain for Parties Leads to Political Inaction* (New York: Cambridge University Press, 2016).

Independents and Electoral Instability

Figure 6.3 is a graph of the independent vote in presidential elections. Above the 50 percent line independents voted for the popular vote winner; below the line they voted for the loser. Evidently in most elections the party that carries the independent vote wins the election.[19] The only exceptions are 1960 and 1976—both extremely close elections at a time when the Democrats could theoretically win the election with only Democratic votes—and 2004, when the Bush campaign de-emphasized swing voters, went all out to maximize turnout of the base, and managed to win narrowly.

The picture in House elections is even more striking. As figure 6.4 shows, big swings in the independent vote are associated with big electoral changes. A 20 percentage point shift in the Republican direction contributed to the "Reagan Revolution" in 1980. A similar shift was associated with the Republican takeover of the House in 1994. Then the independents thumped the Republicans in 2006 and turned around and shellacked the Democrats four years later—a massive 35 percentage-point shift in support over a four-year period. These movements illustrate my point about alienating the marginal members of your electoral coalition. Each of the overreaches discussed in chapter 5 is followed by a significant loss of independent support in the next election.

What about the Rising American Electorate?

Although I emphasize the critical role of independents as the marginal members of electoral majorities, others place greater emphasis on specific demographic categories as the marginal voters who contribute to our shifting majorities. Often called the "rising American electorate," RAE for short, the argument is that pro-Democratic demographics are increasing while pro-Republican demographics are declining, and that pro-Democratic demographic groups are more likely to turn out in presidential elections than in congressional

19. Although Trump lost the popular vote in 2016, he won the election and won a plurality of independents.

FIGURE 6.3. **Presidential Winners Usually Are Those Who Carry the Independents**

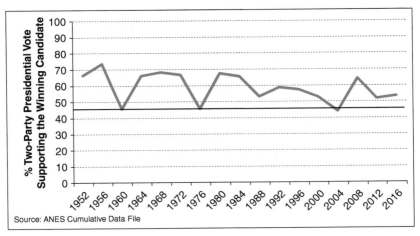

Source: ANES Cumulative Data File

FIGURE 6.4. **Independents Register Big Swings in House Elections**

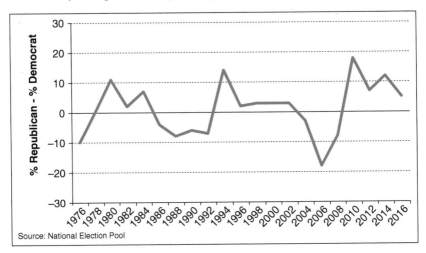

Source: National Election Pool

elections. John Judis and Ruy Teixeira often are credited with first advancing the argument.[20] The RAE includes ethnic minorities, especially Latinos, unmarried women, college-educated professionals, and young people. By implication the declining electorate consists of whites, married people, the less well educated, and older people

20. See John Judis and Ruy Teixeira, *The Emerging Democratic Majority* (New York: Scribner, 2002).

(perhaps not coincidentally the Trump coalition). The demographic trends are undeniable, and there is no question that *other things being equal,* they tend to work in a pro-Democratic direction. But recent elections have not been kind to the thesis, as Judis himself noted in a 2015 article.[21] Gains in the RAE have been offset by losses in the white working and middle classes. It should come as no surprise that after hearing Democratic leaders repeatedly trumpet that their coalition of ethnic minorities, unmarried women, and young people will soon overwhelm the party of married, middle-aged, middle-class whites, increasing numbers of the latter decide that they have no future in a society governed by the new Democratic majority.[22] It may not be much of an exaggeration to say that enthusiastic proponents of the RAE thesis contributed to the success of Donald Trump's campaign. I will have more to say on this in chapter 10.

Demography is important, but—contrary to the old proverb—it is not destiny, at least not in politics. Political parties are composed of goal-oriented individuals who recognize demographic changes and react to them. Thus far, the emphasis has been on Democrats who clearly tailor the party's appeal to take advantage of favorable demographic trends. But political parties do not stay stupid forever, although they may stay stupid for a long time. It is safe to assume that Republicans (eventually) will act to offset unfavorable demographic trends. Thus, the italicized *other things being equal* clause generally will not hold over the long run.

The British Labour Party lost four consecutive elections in the eighteen years between 1979 and 1997, an impressive record roughly

---

21. John Judis, "The Emerging Republican Advantage," *National Journal,* January 30, 2015, www.nationaljournal.com/magazine/the-emerging-republican -advantage-20150130.

22. Particularly white men. As Rosenthal comments about the 2016 Democratic platform, "The platform has many economic references to women and people of color—such as equal pay, expanding Social Security for widows and women who exited the workforce to care for children or family, of housing foreclosures, of access to housing. The platform seeks to 'nurture the next generation of scientists, engineers and entrepreneurs, especially women and people of color.' The platform mentions whites only in the context of their greater wealth, lower arrest rates and lower job losses." Howard Rosenthal, "Why Do White Men Love Donald Trump So Much?" *Washington Post,* September 8, 2016, www.washingtonpost.com/news/monkey -cage/wp/2016/09/08/why-do-white-men-love-donald-trump-so-much/.

comparable to the Democrats, who lost five out of six presidential elections in the twenty-four years between 1968 and 1992. But Tony Blair and his allies and Bill Clinton and his eventually managed to reorient their parties.[23] At some point those who espouse platforms that are demonstrated electoral losers will be succeeded or pushed aside by a new cohort that espouses policies that are more electorally salable.[24] Given the history of the Democrats in the 1970s and 1980s, the Republicans could be in for several more presidential election thumpin's before they wise up, but there is no reason why Latinos, young people, professionals, and unmarried women should be lost to them for decades.

What about the two-electorate variant of the rising American electorate thesis? This is the argument that the presidential electorate has, and will continue to have, a pro-Democratic cast but that the midterm electorate is more Republican because of the lower turnout of groups that make up the RAE. While it is true that the presidential electorate is more Democratic leaning than the midterm electorate *given the present alignment of the parties,* I do not think that this is the major factor in the electoral instability of recent decades. The argument does not explain how the Republicans can win the presidential election but lose the midterm badly as in 2004–6. Moreover, consider that a midterm electorate that was 79 percent white thumped the Republicans in 2006, while a midterm electorate that was only 75 percent white shellacked the Democrats in 2010.[25] Other things being equal, demographics alone would have predicted

23. As noted in the first chapter, the only Democratic presidential victory in that stretch was Jimmy Carter's one-point win over the unelected incumbent who succeeded a president who resigned in disgrace.

24. The election of Jeremy Corbyn as leader of the British Labour Party reminds us that the process can work in reverse as well. Labour appears to have become stupid again. Alex Massie, "The Labour Party's Two Word Suicide Note," *The Daily Beast,* September 12, 2015, www.thedailybeast.com/articles/2015/09/12/labour-s-two-word-suicide-note.html.

25. Similarly, Harry Enten points out that the 2014 midterm and 2008 presidential electorates were very similar demographically, but the Republican share of the popular vote was 13 percentage points *higher* in the midterm. Harry Enten, "Voters Were Just as Diverse in 2014 as They Were in 2008," FiveThirtyEight, July 16, 2015, http://fivethirtyeight.com/datalab/voters-were-just-as-diverse-in-2014-as-they-were-in-2008/.

the opposite, but other things are rarely equal in politics. Seth Hill, Michael Herron, and Jeffrey Lewis calculate that 78 percent of the nation's counties registered a higher vote for Barack Obama in 2008 than for John Kerry in 2004, with most of the exceptions located in the South.[26] Any minor improvement in pro-Democratic demographics in those four years obviously pales in comparison to the negative impacts on the Republicans of the housing crisis and unpopular wars. Even more noteworthy, the slight improvement in pro-Democratic demographics between 2006 and 2010 was evidently overwhelmed by the vast differences in enthusiasm between Democratic and Republican voters in the two elections, a difference that favored the Democrats in 2006 and the Republicans in 2010.[27] So, rather than stake their parties' futures over differences of a percentage point or two in demographic categories, party leaders would do better to do what they can to help an administration govern competently and restrain the temptation to overreach.[28]

26. Seth J. Hill, Michael C. Herron, and Jeffrey B. Lewis, "Economic Crisis, Iraq, and Race: A Study of the 2008 Presidential Election," *Election Law Journal* 9, no. 1 (2010): 41–62.

27. Seth J. Hill, "A Behavioral Measure of the Enthusiasm Gap in American Elections," *Electoral Studies* 36 (2014): 28–38.

28. Moreover, some recent analyses indicate that demographic differences between voters and nonvoters may be systematically exaggerated because people who overreport voting (i.e., say that they voted when they didn't) look more like actual voters than actual nonvoters. Stephen Ansolabehere and Eitan Hersh, "Who *Really* Votes?" in *Facing the Challenge of Democracy: Explorations in the Analysis of Public Opinion and Political Participation*, ed. Paul Sniderman and Benjamin Highton (Princeton, NJ: Princeton University Press, 2011), 267–91.

CHAPTER 7

The (Re)Nationalization of Congressional Elections

*Partisan ideological realignment has not eliminated national
tides in elections. It has, however reduced their magnitude.*
—Alan I. Abramowitz

The 2006, 2010, and 2014 congressional elections were not kind to
the preceding claim. As the political parties sorted, electoral patterns
changed, but in a manner that accentuated rather than dampened
the likelihood of national tides. The outcomes of presidential, congressional, and even state legislative elections now move in tandem
in a way that was rare in the mid- to late twentieth century, not
just in the so-called wave elections, but in elections more generally.
Political scientists commonly describe this development as nationalization. I write re-nationalization in the title of this chapter because
contemporary elections have returned to a pattern that was common
in earlier periods of American history.[1] When elections are nationalized, people vote for the party, not the person. Candidates of the
party at different levels of government win and lose together. Their
fate is collective.

Alan I. Abramowitz, *The Disappearing Center: Engaged Citizens, Polarization, and
American Democracy* (New Haven, CT: Yale University Press, 2010), 110.

   1. Much of the data on recent congressional elections recall patterns that prevailed from the mid-nineteenth century until the Progressive Era in the early twentieth century. Thus, current developments are more of a return to prior patterns than
something new in our history.

"All Politics Is Local" (No More)

Late twentieth-century political observers generally accepted this aphorism, credited to Democratic Speaker of the House Thomas P. "Tip" O'Neill of Massachusetts, who served in Congress from 1952 to 1987. In retrospect, the period in which O'Neill served might be viewed as the golden age of the individual member of Congress.[2] Party leadership was decentralized with committee and subcommittee chairs operating relatively independently of the party floor leadership. Members could pursue their policy interests relatively unconstrained by the positions of the leadership or party caucus.[3] Party discipline was weak, enabling members to adopt whatever political coloring best suited their districts. Democratic representatives and senators could take the conservative side of issues, especially in the South, and Republicans could take the liberal side, especially in the northeast. Bipartisanship and cross-party coalitions were not at all uncommon.[4] At the presidential level Democrats could fracture as the party did in 1968 or lose in landslides as in 1972 and 1984, but voters would split their tickets and return Democratic majorities to Congress. Members had learned to exploit every advantage their incumbency offered and to build personal reputations that insulated them from the national tides evident in the presidential voting.[5]

2. The allusion is to the golden age of the MP (Member of Parliament) in eighteenth-century Britain before the development of the modern responsible party system characterized by centralized party leadership and strong party discipline. See Lewis Namier, *The Structure of Politics at the Accession of George III* (London: Macmillan, 1957).

3. I use the modifier "relatively" in these sentences to recognize that there were limits on member independence, of course. For example, a member could not vote against his party's nominee for speaker. And in the aftermath of the 1964 elections, the Democratic caucus stripped the seniority of two members who had endorsed Republican Barry Goldwater for president.

4. For a good survey of how Congress operated during this period, see Kenneth Shepsle, "The Changing Textbook Congress," in *Can the Government Govern?* ed. John Chubb and Paul Peterson (Washington, DC: Brookings, 1989), 238–67.

5. The literature on these subjects is massive. For a review as the period drew to a close see Morris Fiorina and Timothy Prinz, "Legislative Incumbency and Insulation," *Encyclopedia of the American Legislative System*, ed. Joel H. Silbey (New York: Charles Scribner's Sons, 1994), 513–27. For the most up-to-date survey

Throughout this period, Republicans had talked about their goal of nationalizing congressional elections, by which they meant getting people to vote for congressional candidates at the same levels that they voted for Republican presidential candidates. This would have resulted in Republican House majorities in big presidential years like 1972 and 1980–84.[6] But voters seemed content to behave in accord with "all politics is local"—until 1994.

The Republican wave in 1994 shocked not only pundits but even academic experts on congressional elections. Republican gains were expected, to be sure, but most analysts expected two dozen or so seats on the outside. Most of us dismissed as fanciful Newt Gingrich's prediction that the Republicans would take the House.[7] But when the electoral dust settled, Republicans had netted fifty-four seats in the House and ten in the Senate to take control of both chambers for the first time since the election of 1952. When political scientists looked back over the period, they saw that growing nationalization had been under way for some time, but the signs had not been appreciated.[8]

Elections in the Era of Incumbency and Insulation

Political scientist Walter Dean Burnham first pointed out that the declining correlation between presidential and congressional voting lessened the responsiveness of the political system.[9] That is, as incumbents insulated themselves from electoral tides, the capacity of voters to hold the government as a whole accountable weakened.

of congressional elections, see Gary C. Jacobson and Jamie L. Carson, *The Politics of Congressional Elections*, 9th ed. (Lanham, MD: Rowman & Littlefield, 2015).

6. Continued Democratic congressional strength in the South would have made it difficult to win a House majority in a narrow presidential election. See Stephen Ansolabehere, David Brady, and Morris Fiorina, "The Vanishing Marginals and Electoral Responsiveness" *British Journal of Political Science* 22, no. 1 (January 1992): 21–38.

7. "He's blowing smoke," as I put it to a *Congressional Quarterly* reporter at the time. Wrong.

8. See the essays in David W. Brady, John F. Cogan, and Morris P. Fiorina, eds., *Continuity and Change in House Elections* (Stanford, CA: Stanford University Press and Hoover Institution Press, 2000).

9. Walter Dean Burnham, "Insulation and Responsiveness in Congressional Elections," *Political Science Quarterly* 90, no. 3 (Autumn 1975): 411–35.

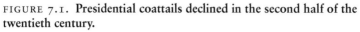

FIGURE 7.1. Presidential coattails declined in the second half of the twentieth century.

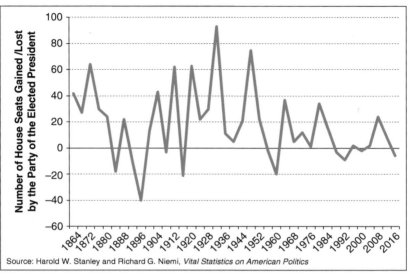

Source: Harold W. Stanley and Richard G. Niemi, *Vital Statistics on American Politics*

In contrast to elections in the late nineteenth century, presidential coattails had all but disappeared by the 1980s (figure 7.1). Thus, fewer members of Congress felt indebted to the president for their elections. Moreover, midterm seat losses in the modern era were pale reflections of those that occurred in the late nineteenth century (figure 7.2). With most of their fates independent of his, members of the president's party had less incentive to help an administration of their party, especially if it entailed any political cost to them. The unproductive relationship between President Jimmy Carter and the large Democratic majorities in Congress epitomized this state of affairs.

The dissociation between the presidential and congressional electoral arenas probably was both a cause and a consequence of the rapid growth in the advantage of incumbency in the second half of the twentieth century. This terminology referred to a "personal vote," the additional support that incumbents could expect compared to what any generic nonincumbent member of their party running in their district in a given election could expect.[10] Scholars

10. Bruce Cain, John Ferejohn, and Morris Fiorina, *The Personal Vote: Constituency Service and Electoral Independence* (Cambridge, MA: Harvard University Press, 1987).

FIGURE 7.2. Midterm seat losses by the party of the president declined in the second half of the twentieth century.

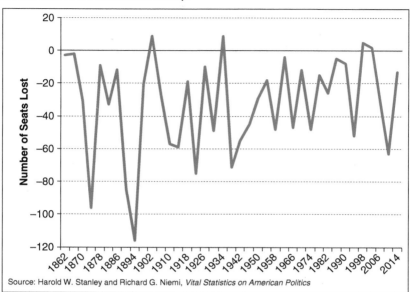

Source: Harold W. Stanley and Richard G. Niemi, *Vital Statistics on American Politics*

identified numerous advantages of incumbency: the growth in non-partisan, nonideological constituency service as the federal role in society and the economy expanded, the decline in high-quality challengers as local party organizations withered and became too weak to recruit and fund strong candidates, and, later, the widening campaign funding advantage incumbents enjoyed. Various measures of the incumbency advantage appear in the literature, but the one with the firmest statistical basis is that of Andrew Gelman and Gary King.[11] As figure 7.3 shows, from the mid-1950s to the late 1990s the estimated advantage fluctuated between 6 and 12 percentage points until beginning a downward trend in the new century.[12]

Figure 7.4 provides what is perhaps the most striking illustration of the growing dissociation between the presidential and electoral

11. Andrew Gelman and Gary King, "Estimating Incumbency Advantage without Bias," *American Journal of Political Science* 34 (1990): 1142–64.

12. For a recent comprehensive analysis of the decline in the incumbency advantage, see Gary Jacobson, "It's Nothing Personal: The Decline of the Incumbency Advantage in US House Elections," *Journal of Politics* 77, no. 3 (July 2015): 861–73.

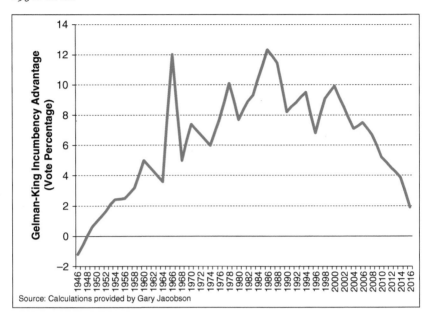

FIGURE 7.3. The incumbency advantage in House elections has declined to 1950s levels.

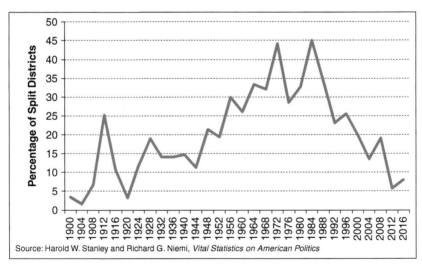

FIGURE 7.4. Split presidential and House majorities in congressional districts today are the lowest in a century.

arenas: the growth in the proportion of congressional districts that cast their votes for the presidential candidate of one party while electing a member of the other party to the House of Representatives. In the late nineteenth century when straight-ticket voting was prevalent, such split district majorities were rare, but they jumped after 1920 and increased rapidly after World War II, culminating in elections like 1972 and 1984 when nearly half the districts in the country split their decisions. This development and its reversal in recent elections had important incentive effects. Suppose that after President Reagan's reelection in 1984, Speaker O'Neill had decided to follow the kind of oppositional strategy that congressional Republicans adopted during the Obama presidency. Had he announced his strategy to the members of the Democratic caucus, they likely would have rejected it. In 1985, 114 Democratic representatives held districts carried by Reagan. They might well have said, "Wait a minute, Tip. I have to be careful—Reagan won my district. I can't just oppose everything he proposes." Contrast that situation with 2013 when only sixteen House Republicans came from districts that voted to reelect Obama in 2012. An overwhelming majority of the Republican conference saw little electoral danger in opposing Obama's every proposal. After the 2016 elections, only twelve Democrats represented districts that voted for Trump. Very few Democrats will have any electoral incentive to support him.

The decline in split outcomes reflects the decline in split-ticket voting shown in figure 7.5. During the height of the incumbency era, a quarter to a third of voters split their ballots between the presidential and House levels. Since 1980 that figure has dropped in every election but one. By 2016 it had declined to less than half the 1984 figure.

For a number of reasons, Senate elections are more difficult for political scientists to study. Only thirty-three or thirty-four states hold them every two years, making statistical analysis iffy. Moreover, it is not the same third of the Senate that runs every two years, and the third of states that holds elections in a presidential year next holds them in an off year, and vice-versa. For all these reasons, political scientists tend to focus on the 435 House elections held every two years. But patterns analogous to those discussed have appeared

FIGURE 7.5. Split ticket (president/House) voting has declined.

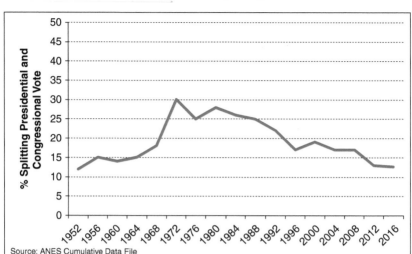

Source: ANES Cumulative Data File

in Senate elections as well, despite the noisier data. As figure 7.6 shows, the number of states that elected one senator from each party rose sharply in the same period as split outcomes in the presidential and House arenas surged, peaking in 1978 when twenty-six of the fifty states were represented in Washington by one senator from each party.[13] This number dropped in half by 2002 but then began to rise again. I know of no research that explains this recent development. But despite the unexplained recent trend, it is clear that states today show more consistency in their Senate voting than they did several decades ago.[14]

13. Thomas L. Brunell and Bernard Grofman, "Explaining Divided US Senate Delegations, 1788–1996: A Realignment Approach," *American Political Science Review* 92, no. 2 (June 1998): 391–99.

14. Special elections for the House have some of the same characteristics as Senate elections—there aren't many of them and they are held in very different electoral contexts. Thus, it is interesting that a statistically significant effect of presidential approval shows up in special election results beginning with the 2002 election. That is, special elections have become more nationalized. H. Gibbs Knotts and Jordan M. Ragusa, "The Nationalization of Special Elections for the U.S. House of Representatives," *Journal of Elections, Public Opinion and Parties* 26, no. 1 (2016): 22–39.

FIGURE 7.6. Split-party Senate delegations have declined in recent decades.

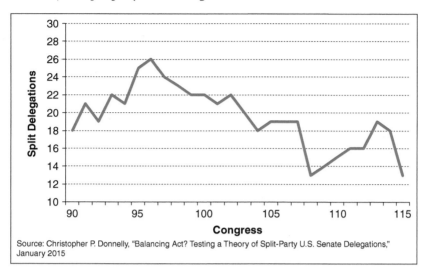

Source: Christopher P. Donnelly, "Balancing Act? Testing a Theory of Split-Party U.S. Senate Delegations," January 2015

A very striking demonstration of rising nationalization appears in figure 7.7. Suppose you wanted to predict the outcome of a midterm election in a specific district. Suppose further that you had two pieces of information: (1) the Democratic presidential candidate's vote in that district two years earlier and (2) the Democratic congressional candidate's vote in that district two years earlier. Almost everyone would guess that the second piece of information is the more important of the two, especially since in the vast majority of the districts one of the candidates—the incumbent—is the same candidate who ran two years prior. Congressional election researchers typically treat the presidential vote as capturing the national forces at work in an election—the state of the economy, domestic tranquility or lack thereof, peace and war, and so forth, while the congressional vote captures the local, more individual, more personal factors at work. Statistically speaking, the local component of the vote was more important until the turn of the new century, although the relative strength of the national component had been increasing.[15]

15. This analysis was originally conducted by David Brady, Robert D'Onofrio, and Morris Fiorina, "The Nationalization of Electoral Forces Revisited," in Brady,

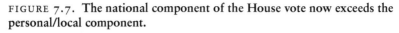

FIGURE 7.7. The national component of the House vote now exceeds the personal/local component.

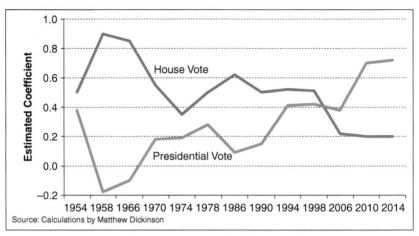

In 2006, however, the lines crossed and the national component has continued to be more important. Today one can better predict the winner's vote in a congressional district using the district's previous presidential vote than its previous House vote.

Finally, although there is little research on state level elections, there are indications that the growing nationalization of national elections has extended downward to the state level as well. Gubernatorial outcomes increasingly track presidential results—David Byler reports a simple analysis of the relationship between the presidential vote in a state and the number of legislative seats won.[16] The relationship has fluctuated considerably since World War II. But after falling to a low and statistically insignificant level in 1988, it has steadily risen since. Moreover, recall the discussion in the first chapter about the hun-

Cogan, and Fiorina, *Continuity and Change*. It has been updated over the years by Arjun Wilkins and Matthew Dickinson.

16. Kyle Kondik and Geoffrey Skelley, "My Old Kentucky Home: Could Matt Bevin Soon Be in the Governor's Mansion?" *Sabato's Crystal Ball*, July 16, 2015, www.centerforpolitics.org/crystalball/articles/my-old-kentucky-home-could-matt-bevins-soon-be-the-governors-mansion/; David Byler, "2016 Presidential Election Could Decide State Legislative Races," *Real Clear Politics*, January 14, 2015, www.realclearpolitics.com/articles/2015/01/14/presidential_election_could_decide_state_legislative_races.html.

dreds of legislative seats lost in the midterm waves of 2006, 2010, and 2014. In recent decades, state elections too seem to be showing increasing evidence of nationalization.

Within the political science community there is general agreement that party sorting, which has produced more internally homogeneous parties, underlies the movements shown in the figures presented above. But in my view a number of observers have erroneously located the cause almost entirely in party sorting in the *electorate*. For example, Gary Jacobson writes that the incumbency advantage "has fallen in near lockstep with a rise in party loyalty and straight-ticket voting, a consequence of the widening and increasingly coherent partisan divisions in the American electorate."[17] Abramowitz agrees: "The decline in ticket-splitting can be traced directly to increasing partisan-ideological consistency within the electorate."[18] To some extent that is surely the case, but such conclusions overlook the increasing partisan-ideological consistency among the *candidates*. Fifty years ago a New Jersey Democrat and a New Mexico Democrat faced different primary electorates. Today both cater to coalitions of public sector workers, racial and ethnic minorities, and liberal cause groups like environmental and pro-choice organizations. Similarly, fifty years ago Ohio and Oregon Republicans depended on different primary electorates. Today both cater to business and professional organizations and conservative cause groups like taxpayers and pro-gun and pro-life groups. This growing homogenization of each party's candidates has been reinforced by developments in campaign finance. Individual contributions increasingly come from ideologically committed donors who hail from specific geographic areas—Texas for Republicans, Manhattan and Hollywood for Democrats.[19] And while anonymity prevents similar research for contributions to

17. Jacobson, "It's Nothing Personal," 861–62.

18. Abramowitz, *Disappearing Center*, 96.

19. James G. Gimpel, Frances E. Lee, and Shanna Pearson-Merkowitz, "The Check Is in the Mail: Interdistrict Funding Flows in Congressional Elections," *American Journal of Political Science* 52, no. 2 (April 2008): 373–94. See also Michael J. Barber, "Representing the Preferences of Donors, Partisans, and Voters in the US Senate," special issue, *Public Opinion Quarterly* 80 (March 2016): 225–49.

independent committees and other recipients of "dark money," the same is probably true for campaign funds that come through those avenues. No matter what state or district you come from, if you need contributions from Texas oil interests or Hollywood liberals, you are going to lean in their direction.[20] Recent research suggests that these trends may extend to congressional primary elections as well.[21]

Now, if Democratic presidential and House candidates are nearly all liberals endorsed and supported by the same liberal groups and organizations, and Republican presidential and House candidates are nearly all conservatives endorsed and supported by conservative organizations and groups, one major reason to split your ticket has disappeared.[22] The simple fact is that we don't know how many voters would split their tickets if they were offered chances to vote for conservative Democratic or liberal Republican House candidates because the parties offer them few such choices anymore. Consider that in the 2012 elections in West Virginia, Mitt Romney shellacked Barack Obama by a margin of 26.8 percentage points at the same time that Democratic senator Joe Manchin thumped his Republican opponent by a margin of 24 percentage points. If one assumes that everyone who voted for Obama also voted for Manchin, which seems reasonable, the implication is that 25 percent of West Virginians split

20. Tina Daunt, "Obama, Hollywood Huddle to Take Back Senate, House," *The Hill*, April 6, 2016, http://thehill.com/blogs/ballot-box/house-races/275386-obama -hollywood-huddle-to-take-back-senate-house.

21. "Primary challengers, particularly ideological primary challengers, are raising more money, and they are raising much of that money from donors who do not reside in their states or districts." Robert G. Boatright, *Getting Primaried: The Changing Politics of Congressional Primary Challenges* (Ann ArborI: University of Michigan Press, 2013), 137.

22. Readers familiar with my earlier "policy-balancing" hypothesis will understandably ask how the decline in split-ticket voting relates to the balancing hypothesis. While researchers reported some cross-sectional support for balancing, temporally speaking, as the parties diverged, more balancing (split-ticket voting) should have occurred. The fact that it declined indicates either that the balancing hypothesis is wrong or (I would prefer to think) that its effect has been overwhelmed by other factors. See Morris Fiorina, *Divided Government*, chap. 5 (New York: Macmillan, 1992). But see Robert S. Erikson, "Congressional Elections in Presidential Years: Presidential Coattails and Strategic Voting," *Legislative Studies Quarterly* 41, no. 3 (August 2016): 551–74. Erikson's analysis indicates that balancing occurs but is dominated by coattails.

their tickets, voting for Romney and Manchin. Are West Virginians unique in their willingness to ticket-split, or are they just unusual in having the opportunity to vote for a pro-life, pro-gun Democrat?

Similarly, noting that self-identified liberals increasingly vote for Democratic congressional candidates and self-identified conservatives for Republicans, *New York Times* columnist Charles Blow opines, "We have retreated to our respective political corners and armed ourselves in an ideological standoff over the very meaning of America."[23] Such a conclusion is not justified. Liberal and conservative voters may not have changed at all. Compared to a couple of decades ago, in how many House districts today does a liberal voter have a liberal Republican candidate she could vote for, and in how many districts does a conservative voter have a conservative Democratic candidate he could vote for? Commentators have blithely equated the *lack of opportunity* to make the kind of choices made in the past with *unwillingness* to make the kind of choices made in the past. As I discussed in chapter 3, ordinary voters—even some strong partisans—are still much less well sorted than high-level members of the political class. Thus, I believe that the increased similarity of partisan candidates is an important part of the explanation for the decline in ticket-splitting along with the not-so-increased similarity of partisan voters.[24] Only the appearance of candidates like Donald Trump whose positions cut across the standard party platforms can let us determine whether electoral stability results from stable voters or similar candidates. Speaking purely as an electoral analyst, I would say that the data generated by nominations of nonstandard candidates like Senator Bernie Sanders (I-VT), Trump, and third-party candidates would enhance our understanding of the contemporary electorate.

23. Charles M. Blow, "The Great American Cleaving," *New York Times*, November 5, 2010, www.nytimes.com/2010/11/06/opinion/06blow.html?ref=charlesmblow.

24. An additional factor underlying the decline in split-ticket voting may well be that, with the close party divide, voters realize that they are actually voting for an entire party, not just for individuals. For example, the seats of liberal Republicans like Chris Shays of Connecticut (defeated) and Marge Roukema of New Jersey (retired) became untenable not because they were personally unpopular but because voters in their districts understood that they would be part of a congressional majority they disliked.

Are More Nationalized Elections Good or Bad?

This question is related to the one asked at the conclusion of chapter 4. In contrast to the elections of the late twentieth century when Democratic members of Congress could regularly win despite the travails of their presidential candidates, the electoral fates of candidates at different levels are now intertwined. When combined with the tendency to overreach discussed in chapter 5, the result *contra* Abramowitz can be wave elections like those of 2006, 2010, and 2014 that drastically change governing arrangements over a short period.

Here again there are arguments on both sides. On the plus side, more members of each party are held collectively responsible than previously, giving them more incentive to focus on policies that advance the interests of the country as a whole and less incentive to focus on, say, how many pork-barrel projects they can get for their districts. On the negative side, the disruption of government control gives parties very little time to pass and implement their programs. Some decades ago I argued for more collective responsibility on the part of the parties; whether it has gone too far is now the question.[25]

Interestingly, the American electorate shows mixed feelings about the current state of affairs. The Pew Research Center regularly queries voters about their satisfaction with the election result. As table 7.1 reports, the voters' collective minds have shown a change across the most recent wave elections. Solid majorities were happy about the thrashings of the Clinton Democrats in 1994 and the Bush Republicans in 2006. But only minorities registered satisfaction with the two more recent waves. It is almost as if voters are collectively saying, "This hurts us as much as it hurts you, but given your overreach, we have to do it."

25. Morris Fiorina, "The Decline of Collective Responsibility in American Politics," *Daedalus* 109 (Summer 1980): 25–45. Cf. Morris P. Fiorina, with Samuel J. Abrams, *Disconnect: The Breakdown of Representation in American Politics,* chap. 7 (Norman: University of Oklahoma Press, 2009).

TABLE 7.1. **Popular Reaction to Wave Elections**

Feel Happy About	%
1994 Republican Victory	57
2006 Democratic Victory	60
2010 Republican Victory	48
2014 Republican Victory	48

Source: Pew Research Center

CHAPTER 8

Is the US Experience Exceptional?

The American experience of increasing polarization is untypical: most other countries witnessed constant or declining levels of polarization. In recent years, American levels of polarization are particularly high in comparative perspective.
—Philip Rehm and Timothy Reilly

Attempts to explain American political developments naturally begin with a focus on factors present and operating in the United States. But it is generally prudent to consider the experiences of other advanced democracies as well. If similar developments in other countries are evident and similar factors are present, that reinforces confidence in our explanations. But if similar developments are (are not) occurring in other countries in the absence (or presence) of factors thought to be causal in the United States, that raises the likelihood that our explanations are too country specific and other, more general explanatory forces are at work.

Given the attention paid to the subject of political polarization in the United States, it is not surprising that political scientists in other countries have closely examined their politics to see if comparable developments are present. The findings reported in their studies are both puzzling and provocative, for they describe the opposite of American developments. As in the United States, Western European electorates in the aggregate have changed little or not at all in recent decades. But at the higher reaches of their political parties, the opposite of what we have seen in the United States has happened: the

Quotation from Philip Rehm and Timothy Reilly, "United We Stand: Constituency Homogeneity and Comparative Party Polarization," *Electoral Studies* 29 (2010): 48.

major parties have *depolarized*. Whether causally or not, however, that depolarization has been accompanied by the rise of populist parties that are roiling the political waters.

Depolarization in Western European Democracies

Several studies conducted in Great Britain illustrate the general pattern. The Tories have softened their platform considerably since the days of Margaret Thatcher, to the point that some argue they now more closely resemble the American Democrats than the Republicans.[1] Meanwhile, under the leadership of Tony Blair, the Labour Party transitioned from the militant, union-dominated party that Thatcher vanquished to a more garden-variety center-left party.[2] James Adams, Jane Green, and Caitlin Milazzo wrote in 2012, "In contrast to American elites' policy polarization, British politics over the past 20 years has witnessed dramatic depolarization, that is, policy convergence, between the elites of the two dominant political parties, Labour and the Conservatives."[3] Like their counterparts in the United States, the British public recognizes what has occurred at the elite level. The British Election Study includes four categories of issues. Within each cluster the British public saw a dramatic drop in the distance between the positions of the Conservative and Labour Parties between 1987 and 2001 (figure 8.1).

Did the British public depolarize in tandem with elite depolarization? As in the United States, the evidence for a connection between public opinion and elite positioning is largely negative: in the aggregate public opinion in Britain has changed very little. Adams, Green,

1. Jim Messina, "Why the GOP Can't Get No Satisfaction," *Real Clear Politics,* May 17, 2015, www.realclearpolitics.com/2015/05/17/why_the_gop_can039t_get _no_satisfaction_357195.html.

2. In the years following Blair's prime ministership, Ed Miliband led Labour back to its old ways with seriously negative consequences in the 2015 general election. And as noted in the previous chapter, with the election of Jeremy Corbyn as their leader, Labourites seem determined to keep digging.

3. James Adams, Jane Green, and Caitlin Milazzo, "Has the British Public Depolarized along With Political Elites? An American Perspective on British Public Opinion," *Comparative Political Studies* 45, no. 4 (April 2012): 507–30.

FIGURE 8.1. Perceived differences between the Labour and Conservative Parties have declined.

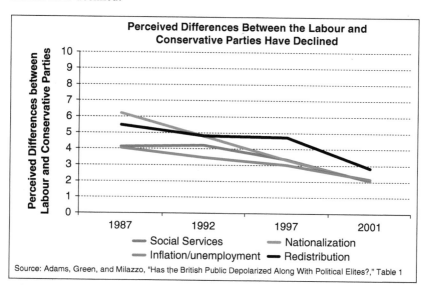

Source: Adams, Green, and Milazzo, "Has the British Public Depolarized Along With Political Elites?," Table 1

and Milazzo examine the frequency of extreme responses on the issues and the standard deviation of responses (both of which should decline if the public were depolarizing) and report that "during the time period when the British public perceived dramatic policy convergence between Labour and Conservative elites on all four of these policy dimensions, the public itself depolarized significantly on only one dimension, inflation/unemployment."[4]

Significantly, Adams, Green, and Milazzo report that as British elites depolarized, party de-sorting has occurred. As graphed in figure 8.2, "The mean distance between Labour and Conservative partisans decreased on each policy scale. In addition, on three of the four scales this mass partisan convergence was dramatic, with the policy gap between Conservative and Labour identifiers diminishing by roughly 50%."[5] There was no significant decline in attitude consistency, however. In the United States, as party elites sorted

4. Ibid., 515–16.
5. Ibid., 519.

FIGURE 8.2. Actual differences between Labour and Conservative partisans have declined.

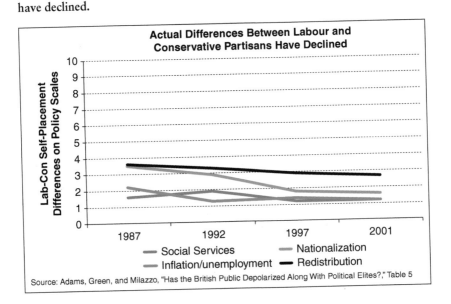

Actual Differences Between Labour and Conservative Partisans Have Declined

Source: Adams, Green, and Milazzo, "Has the British Public Depolarized Along With Political Elites?," Table 5

and polarized, attitude consistency in the public increased. In Great Britain, as party elites depolarized, voters de-sorted, but attitude consistency in the public did not decrease.

In a more detailed follow-up study, Adams, Green, and Milazzo report that the patterns noted above are "moderately" more pronounced among the more educated, affluent, and politically informed, but are apparent even among those who do not fall into those categories.[6] All in all, the changes in Britain are the mirror image of those we have described in the United States: as elites depolarized, the public de-sorted, with the patterns more pronounced among the more politically informed and involved.

Since 2013 Germany has been governed by a grand coalition of the Social Democrats and Christian Democrats. (American readers should try to imagine the Democrats and Republicans splitting the congressional leadership posts and committee chairs, dividing up the

6. James Adams, Jane Green, and Caitlin Milazzo, "Who Moves? Elite and Mass-level Depolarization in Britain, 1987–2001," *Electoral Studies* 31, no. 4 (December 2012): 643–55.

cabinet departments and regulatory agencies, agreeing to alternate Supreme Court appointments, etc.) Simon Munzert and Paul Bauer ask whether German public opinion has tracked the dramatic depolarization of the parties that has occurred in Germany.[7] Again the answer is no.

Their study is modeled on Delia Baldassari and Andrew Gelman's study of US public opinion and focuses primarily on attitude consistency.[8] Thus, it is more a study of party sorting than of polarization, as discussed in chapters 2 and 3.[9] The authors examine twenty-four survey items from the biennial German ALLBUS survey categorized into four policy domains: gender, moral, distribution, and immigration. They report a general decrease in attitude consistency both within and between the issue domains, which they consider "strong indicators of public opinion depolarization."[10] The gender domain is the exception, where consistency among those with lower levels of education has increased, leading to an overall increase in attitude consistency among items like female employment quotas and child care issues. The authors suggest that gender is "one of the few remaining cleavages" between the Left and Right.[11]

In a subsidiary analysis, the German researchers calculate the standard deviations of responses to the issue items. While the overall trend is one of declining standard deviations—depolarization—the trends are not statistically significant. Again, movement on gender issues runs counter to the prevailing trends but not significantly so.

According to James Adams, Catherine De Vries, and Debra Leiter, "During the 1980s and the 1990s, the elites of the two largest Dutch

7. Simon Munzert and Paul C. Bauer, "Political Depolarization in German Public Opinion, 1980–2010," *Political Science Research and Methods* 1, no. 1 (June 2013): 67–89.

8. Delia Baldassarri and Andrew Gelman, "Partisans without Constraint: Political Polarization and Trends in American Public Opinion," *American Journal of Sociology* 114, no. 2 (September 2008).

9. As in the American literature, the concept of "polarization" is used in different ways by European researchers and often conflated with sorting.

10. Ibid., 77.

11. Ibid., 79.

FIGURE 8.3. Standard deviations of Dutch self-placements on policy scales have declined.

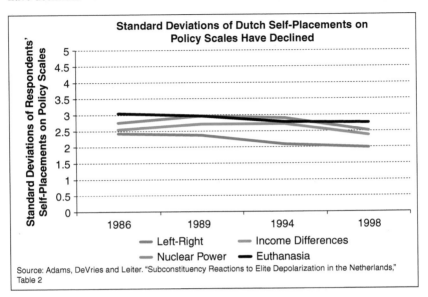

Source: Adams, DeVries and Leiter. "Subconstituency Reactions to Elite Depolarization in the Netherlands," Table 2

parties converged dramatically in debates on income redistribution, nuclear power, and the overall Left-Right dimension."[12] Again, the Dutch public clearly recognized the convergence—the perceived gap between the positions of the two major parties on the issues declined significantly during the period studied. The researchers calculated three measures that have been used to study polarization. First is the standard deviation of public opinion on the issues. Figure 8.3 shows that the standard deviations of public opinion have declined—less polarization in the sense of attitude extremity.

As in the British and German studies, the researchers also calculated trends in consistency of attitudes, finding again that issue consistency generally has decreased as party elites depolarized (figure 8.4). And finally, as party elites depolarized, the Dutch public de-sorted: the policy distance between adherents of the two major parties lessened over the period studied (figure 8.5). The researchers

12. James Adams, Catherine E. De Vries, and Debra Leiter, "Subconstituency Reactions to Elite Depolarization in the Netherlands: An Analysis of the Dutch Public's Policy Beliefs and Partisan Loyalties, 1986–98," *British Journal of Political Science* 42, no. 1 (January 2012): 81.

FIGURE 8.4. Correlations between Dutch self-placements on issues have generally declined.

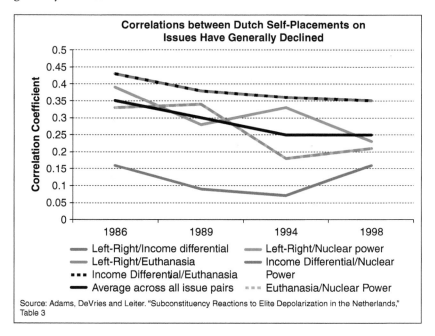

FIGURE 8.5. Partisan differences in Dutch self-placements on policy scales have declined.

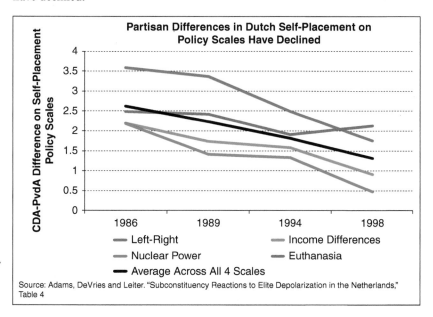

conclude that the Dutch public clearly depolarized as Dutch party elites did. Moreover, these trends extended throughout the population ("subconstituencies") and were not limited to the more educated and more involved stratum of the public.

In an ambitious cross-national study, Rehm and Reilly compare polarization in the United States with that in eight other member nations of the Organisation for Economic Co-operation and Development, incorporating in their measure of party polarization considerations of party size and internal homogeneity.[13] As quoted at the beginning of this chapter , they conclude that "the American experience of increasing polarization is untypical: most other countries witnessed constant or declining levels of polarization. In recent years, American levels of polarization are particularly high in comparative perspective, at least according to expert and mass-level perception scores of party positions."[14]

Although I have not found systematic studies in other countries,[15] informal communications and media reports suggest trends similar to those discussed above. Italian colleagues report that their major parties are much closer than a generation ago—not to mention that the entire party system is more fractured. In France, the Hollande socialist government adopted more centrist pro-business policies and the 2017 presidential election suggests that it may have converged itself out of existence. According to one Bloomberg commentator, all over Europe the mainstream parties have converged "into a kind of colorless sludge."[16]

So, the comparative literature identifies another example of American exceptionalism. Party politics in the United States appears to be following a path opposite to the one followed by the parties in other developed democracies. A generation ago the conventional wisdom held that the platforms ("manifestos") of European parties

13. Rehm and Reilly, "United We Stand," 40–53.

14. Ibid., 48.

15. Of course, this may be more a reflection of the limitations of a mono-English scholar not knowing all the places to look, rather than the absence of other studies.

16. Leonid Bershidsky, "Syriza, Le Pen and the Power of Big Ideas," Bloomberg, January 26, 2015, www.bloombergview.com/articles/2015-01-26/syriza-le-pen-and -the-power-of-big-ideas.

were much more divergent than those of the American parties. Sports allusions were common. Scholars quipped that the Europeans played varsity politics while the Americans played intramural, or that American politics was played entirely between the forty-yard lines while Europeans used the entire field. No more. How do we account for such a reversal in politics within the course of a mere generation?

Lessons from the Comparative Findings?

Puzzles and contradictions are great stimuli for social science research. What explains the opposing trajectories of elite polarization in Europe and the United States? Start with the most obvious possibilities. The United States is one of a minority of world democracies that utilize the single-member, simple-plurality electoral system, sometimes called "majoritarian" for short. (As noted in chapter 5, this electoral system "manufactures" majorities.) In contrast, most of the European democracies use some variant of proportional representation.[17] But Great Britain is an even purer example of a majoritarian electoral system. The pattern of elite decentralization there resembles that in the proportional systems of the continent; hence, the electoral system alone does not seem to be the determining factor.[18]

Multiple parties—a correlate of the electoral system—is a more likely possibility. Rarely do parties other than the Democrats and Republicans get more than a trivial percentage of the popular vote in US presidential elections.[19] But even in Great Britain, a third

17. The French electoral system is most similar to that in the United States. France has an independently elected president, and members of the National Assembly are elected from single-member districts by plurality vote. Germany uses a hybrid system where half the members of the Bundestag are elected from single-member districts and the other half from party lists. But the number taken from the lists is determined in such a way that the overall seat distribution is proportional to the popular vote.

18. A majority of the House of Commons is essentially the entire government. There is neither an independent executive nor a coequal upper chamber as in the United States.

19. Generally the total vote for all "other" parties is less than 5 percent. Major recent exceptions are George Wallace, the American Independent Party candidate, who got almost 14 percent of the vote in 1968, and Ross Perot, the Reform Party candidate, who got about 19 percent in 1992.

party, now the Liberal Democrats, has been contesting elections for a century.[20] Regional parties, especially the Scottish Nationalist Party, have surged, and a new UK Independence Party appeared on the scene in the 1990s. One obvious question is whether there is a relationship between the presence of these other parties and the convergence of Labour and the Conservatives.

The experience of continental democracies raises the same question. In Germany, the Christian Democrats and Social Democrats dominated post-World War II politics, but a small Free Democratic Party often held the balance of power.[21] A "green" party currently holds about 10 percent of the seats. Elsewhere in Europe, multiple parties and coalition governments are the rule (table 8.1). So perhaps there is a relationship between the number of parties contesting elections and the likelihood of convergence between the two major parties—the more parties, the more convergence. Interestingly, however, a long-standing argument in the comparative politics literature is that the more parties in a country, the *more* polarized it will be.[22] Recent experience seems at least partially inconsistent with this generalization. Temporally, as the number of contending parties expanded in European countries, the major parties became less polarized. And in the cross section, the greater number of parties in European countries seems to be associated with less polarization than in the two-party United States. Clearly we need some serious thinking about the mechanism(s) that might produce a relationship—positive or negative—between the number of parties and the degree of polarization. The present state of research does not support generalizations.

There is at least one positive takeaway from the experiences of European democracies, however. If despite their variety of electoral systems and governmental structures, all their parties were polarizing like those in the United States, it would suggest the operation

20. Through various incarnations, alliances, and mergers, this is the Liberals, the Social Democrats, and now the Liberal Democrats. The party was almost wiped out in the 2015 British general election.

21. However, in the 2013 German elections the Free Democrats failed to win seats in the Bundestag for the first time since the party's founding after World War II.

22. Giovanni Sartori, *Parties and Party Systems: A Framework for Analysis*, vol. 1 (New York: Cambridge University Press, 1976), 316–17.

of large-scale forces that affect all countries. This in turn would imply that there is little possibility of decreasing party polarization in the United States. But the fact that the major parties in other countries are following a different path—depolarizing, rather than polarizing—indicates that polarization in the United States is more contingent and perhaps not an inevitable feature of politics in the contemporary world.

Party Convergence and the Rise of Far-Right Parties in Europe

In addition to the depolarization of the major parties in Europe, an important political development is the rise of "far right" (i.e., anti-immigrant) parties in Europe.[23] Some researchers suggest the existence of a link between the appearance of such parties and the convergence of major parties which began in the early to mid-1980s. In a number of countries, the far-right parties now play a significant role in elections. Marine Le Pen's National Front finished second in the polling for the April French presidential election. UKIP in Britain received almost 13 percent of the popular vote in the 2015 elections. In April 2016, an anti-immigrant Freedom Party won the first round of the presidential election in Austria with more than one-third of the vote, then lost the runoff by less than 1 percent.[24] Table 8.1 lists a sample of such parties in Western European democracies. Adams, De Vries, and Leiter note that, subsequent to their 1986–98 analysis, Dutch elites and voters began to polarize on a new issue: immigration. The authors suggest that convergence on the old Left-Right cleavage encouraged political entrepreneurs to exploit new cleavage lines. More anecdotal reports cite the move to the center by leftist

23. The terminology is a bit confusing for Americans since some of these parties (e.g., the National Front in France) offer economic policies that are clearly left-wing in the American context. There is historical precedent in the United States, however. Populist parties often combined racist and xenophobic appeals with attacks on economic elites—railroad corporations, the trusts, Wall Street banks, and so on. One can hear an echo in the rhetoric of Donald Trump.

24. Zack Beauchamp, "A Party Founded by Nazis Just Lost the Austrian Election—Barely," *Vox*, May 23, 2016, www.vox.com/2016/5/23/11745038/austrian -election-2016-results-freedom-party. The Austrian Supreme Court ordered a do-over because of election irregularities, but the far-right party lost again.

TABLE 8.1. Recent Vote for Right-Wing Populist Parties in Western
European Democracies

Party	Vote*
Swiss People's Party	26.6
Freedom Party of Austria	20.5
New Flemish Alliance	20.3
Progress Party (Norway)	16.3
National Front (France)	13.6
Sweden Democrats	12.9
United Kingdom Independence Party	12.6
Danish People's Party	12.3
Party for Freedom (Netherlands)	10.1

*Popular vote in most recent national election

Source: Aisch, Gregor; Pearce, Adam; Rousseau, Bryant. "How Far Is Europe Swinging to the Right?" *New York Times*, July 5, 2016. http://valgresultat.no/?type=st&år =2013

parties in a time of economic difficulty, leaving the hard-pressed working class vulnerable to appeals by anti-immigrant politicians.[25]

There are some careful academic studies of the rise of such right-wing populist parties, but most of them are dated and at any rate they do not yield a clear picture. On the one hand, an extensive statistical analysis of far-right voting in sixteen Western European countries in the 1990s found no relationship between support for such parties and the amount of policy "space" left open by the positioning of the mainstream parties.[26] The data were from elections in 1994–97, however, so the study was limited in what it could say about the dynamics of far-right party support in more recent decades. The same is true for a subsequent study of seven continental European countries from 1984 to 2001 that reports support for right-wing populist parties decreases with the proportionality of the electoral system—the more proportional the system, the lower the support. Other findings are somewhat puzzling. The smaller the policy space to the right of the most right-wing mainstream party, the *greater* the

25. Steven Erlanger, "As Europe's Political Landscape Shifts, Two-Party System Fades," *New York Times*, April 7, 2015, www.nytimes.com/2015/04/08/world /europe/as-european-voting-fragments-days-of-single-party-rule-fade.html.

26. Marcel Lubbers, Merove Gijsberts, and Peer Scheepers, "Extreme Right-wing Voting in Western Europe," *European Journal of Political Research* 41, no. 3 (May 2002): 345–78.

support for far-right parties, but the larger the distance between the mainstream parties, the *greater* the support for far-right parties.[27] As the authors note, there are arguments in the comparative literature for why each of these variables might increase or decrease support for the far right. It is impossible for a study like this to sort them out; it can only identify net effects.[28]

Arim Abedi studied the relationships between party system characteristics and support for antiestablishment parties of all ideological stripes.[29] His analysis covered sixteen European countries over the periods 1945–74 and 1982–93. He found that convergence of the main establishment parties is associated with support for antiestablishment parties both across countries at a single point in time and—more weakly—within countries over time. Overall polarization of the party system adds to the effect when the establishment parties are close together.

Despite my hopes, this foray into the comparative literature does not suggest any clear lessons for analyses of party polarization in the United States. While scholars have advanced a number of hypotheses about the relationships among party polarization, the proportionality of the electoral system, and the (related) number and types of parties,

27. Austria, Belgium, Denmark, France, Germany, Italy, and Norway. Kai Arzheimer and Elisabeth Carter, "Political Opportunity Structures and Right-wing Extremist Party Success," *European Journal of Political Research* 45, no. 3 (May 2006): 419–43.

28. For example, some scholars argue that the more centrist the position taken by the more right-wing of the mainstream parties the larger the policy space left open for a far-right party to exploit. Mark Kayser and Arndt Leininger, "A Far-Right Party Just Won Seats in Three German State Parliaments. Here's Why," *Washington Post,* March 22, 2016, www.washingtonpost.com/news/monkey-cage/wp/2016/03/22/a -far-right-party-just-won-seats-in-three-german-state-parliaments-heres-why/. Other scholars suggest that the more extreme the position taken by the more right-wing mainstream party, the less extreme and more legitimate the far-right party's position looks. If both factors are roughly as important (or neither is important), there will be no statistical relationship between the size of the open policy space and the appearance of far-right parties. Herbert Kitschelt and A. J. McGann, *The Radical Right in Western Europe: A Comparative Analysis* (Ann Arbor: University of Michigan Press, 1995). Cf. Piero Ignazi, "The Crisis of Parties and the Rise of New Political Parties," *Party Politics* 2 (1996): 549–66.

29. Arim Abedi, "Challenges to Established Parties: The Effects of Party System Features on the Electoral Fortunes of Anti-Political-Establishment Parties," *European Journal of Political Research* 41, no. 4 (June 2002): 551–83.

the findings of empirical analyses to date yield an unclear picture. As Lorenzo De Sio notes, current developments in Western democracies challenge "existing theories of party competition—as none of the existing theoretical frameworks is able to convincingly describe and explain the competitive dynamics of these recent years."[30]

The Resurgence of Populism—Brexit, Trump, and ?

As noted in the previous section, social science research generally trails real-world developments, a source of frustration for those caught up in those developments. After a time research can shed light on unfolding events, but often not soon enough to be useful to people who are dealing with them. Probably the most important political development of the past decade is the resurgence of populism in the electorates of Western democracies. Scholars define the term somewhat differently[31] and there are myriad differences in the experiences of countries, but there is no denying the similarities between the success of the Trump candidacy in the United States and the growing strength of nationalist, anti-immigrant parties in Britain, France, Germany, Austria, Sweden, the Netherlands, and other Western democracies. Brexit in the United Kingdom and the threat of exits from the European Union by elements in France, Spain, Italy, and other countries are another manifestation of this rising populist tide. In the 2017 elections, the French party system essentially collapsed while Italy appears to be in the process of realignment as issues of globalization and immigration crosscut the traditional Left-Right divide.

Research thus far has described the kinds of people most receptive to populist appeals. Surveys indicate that they tend to be older and male, natives rather than newcomers (i.e., white in the United States, ethnic German and French, etc., in Europe), and have lower educational levels. Contextually, populist appeals seem stronger in areas populated by people with such characteristics, especially where

30. Leonard De Sio, *The Return of Politics* (forthcoming).

31. Jan-Werner Müller, *What Is Populism?* (Philadelphia: University of Pennsylvania Press, 2016).

economic growth is slow. Interestingly, Trump supporters are not themselves especially disadvantaged economically, but they are pessimistic about their economic futures and those of their children. For example, in an Economist/YouGov panel, Trump supporters report more anger about political developments than nonsupporters, and anger in turn correlates with economic pessimism.

Commentaries on the populist revival attribute it to various causal factors. Those who are least sympathetic see it largely as a manifestation of widespread racism and xenophobia.[32] White men, particularly those with less education and with skills that are not in demand in the new economy, express their frustration by lashing out at newer arrivals of different skin color and religions. As Hillary Clinton commented, "You know, to just be grossly generalistic, you could put half of Trump's supporters into what I call the 'basket of deplorables.' Right? The racist, sexist, homophobic, xenophobic, Islamophobic—you name it."[33] More than a few commentators thought that, if anything, she was being generous in attributing this motivation to only half of Trump's supporters.[34] For political elites on both the Left and Right, this view has the considerable merit of placing the blame for the rise of a purportedly antidemocratic movement on the moral failings of ordinary citizens, while leaving the more enlightened layers of society blameless.

Certainly, it would be naïve to deny that there is a significant element of ethnocentrism and racism in the populist revival. But the important question is: How much? There seems little doubt that in continental Europe the arrival of people of different color and

32. E.g., Sanford Schram, "It's Racism, Stupid: The Populist Challenge Going Forward," *Public Seminar,* August 16, 2016, www.publicseminar.org/2016/08/its -racism-stupid-the-populist-challenge-going-forward/.

33. Dan Balz, "Clinton's 'Deplorables' Remark Sums Up a Deplorable Election Season," *Washington Post,* September 10, 2016, www.washingtonpost.com/politics /clintons-deplorables-remark-sums-up-a-deplorable-election-season/2016/09/10 /78977694-777b-11e6-be4f-3f42f2e5a49e_story.html.

34. Ta-Nehisi Coates, "Hillary Clinton Was Politically Incorrect, but She Wasn't Wrong about Trump's Supporters," *The Atlantic,* September 10, 2016, www.the atlantic.com/politics/archive/2016/09/basket-of-deplorables/499493/; Jamelle Bouie, "Do Half of Trump's Supporters Really Belong in a 'Basket of Deplorables'?" *Slate,* September 11, 2016, www.slate.com/articles/news_and_politics/politics/2016/09 /trump_s_basket_of_deplorables_hillary_clinton_was_right.html.

religions has fanned the populist flames; but in England, home of UKIP and Brexit, much of the resentment focuses on Poles and other Eastern Europeans who are both white and Christian. And in the United States, the Sanders branch of the populist tendency stands in contrast to the Trump branch. Sanders supporters were more heavily male, but not less well educated, than Clinton supporters, and while charges of sexism were common, no one to my knowledge labeled the Sandernistas as racists.

Those who are more sympathetic to the populist resurgence view it as in significant part a reflection of the failure of elites.[35] "The list is familiar to you by now: 9/11. Iraq. Katrina. Congressional corruption. Financial meltdown. Bank bailouts. Failed stimulus. A health care mess. Stagnant wages. Rising distrust. Diminished hopes. Sixteen years of promises from Republicans and Democrats alike that failed to live up to what people wanted. This distrust was earned."[36] All over the Western world economic experts have failed to develop policies that pulled their countries out of the Great Recession. Historically, political upheaval travels with economic stagnation.[37] In the United States, we can add a decade and a half of wars that consume lives and resources and appear to have no end. Add the inexcusable bailouts of the financial sector and it is plausible to argue that the resurgence of populism in the United States reflects a stew of resentment of the "establishment."[38] There is something for

35. William A. Galston, "The Populist Revolt against Failure," *Wall Street Journal,* August 30, 2016, http://www.wsj.com/articles/the-populist-revolt-against -failure-1472598368.

36. Ben Domenech, "Blame the Elites for the Trump Phenomenon," *The Federalist,* September 14, 2016, http://thefederalist.com/2016/09/14/blame-the-elites-for -the-trump-phenomenon/.

37. Dalibor Rohac, "It's Still the Economy Stupid," *Foreign Policy,* September 16, 2016, http://foreignpolicy.com/2016/09/16/its-still-the-economy-stupid-populism -trump-syriza/; John B. Judis, "All the Rage," *New Republic,* September 19, 2016, https://newrepublic.com/article/136327/all-rage-sanders-trump-populism?utm _source=New+Republic&utm_campaign=b1e08addcd-Daily_Newsletter_9_19_169 _19_2016&utm_medium=email&utm_term=0_c4adoaba7e-b1e08addcd -59578357.

38. Not just in the United States, of course. As Nigel Farage, former leader of UKIP, commented about Brexit, "It was the first victory against an international political elite who have led us into an endless series of foreign wars and seen politics effectively

almost all Americans to resent—politicians and plutocrats, public- and private-sector bureaucracies, cultural elites and financial elites, and, of course, the media.[39] I return to this subject in chapter 11.

Some European scholars take a similar position about developments in their countries: "These parties and their voters should not, then, be labelled as arrogant insiders attacking downtrodden outsiders like immigrants, workers, and minorities. Instead, the right-wingers are more justly portrayed as outsiders and underdogs, raising their anger and frustration against the insiders: the media elite and the leftists and the artists."[40]

Most social scientists fall into a middle category of "it's complicated." No doubt there is some validity in both of the two preceding explanations. If world economies were growing at a rate of 4 percent per year, I very much doubt that the political conversation would take the form it currently does. We tend to talk about prejudice as a fixed characteristic of individuals, but it likely varies somewhat with people's satisfaction with their own lives. In good times, they are less prejudiced and more tolerant. In bad times, they grow understandably frustrated and become more likely to seek targets to blame for their difficulties. Unfortunately, few economists are predicting a return of widespread prosperity anytime soon.

purchased by the big banks and the multinationals." Nigel Farage, "Donald Trump Calls Himself 'Mr. Brexit.' Here's Why He's Right," *Washington Post*, September 6, 2016, www.washingtonpost.com/posteverything/wp/2016/09/06/nigel-farage-don-ald-trump-calls-himself-mr-brexit-heres-why-hes-right/?utm_term=.c047d0c0835c.

39. Glenn Reynolds, "The Suicide of Expertise," *USA Today*, March 20, 2017, www.usatoday.com/story/opinion/2017/03/20/americans-reject-experts-failure -history-glenn-reynolds-column/99381952/#.

40. Goran Adamson, *Populist Parties and the Failure of the Political Elites* (Bern: Peter Lang, 2016), www.peterlang.com/view/9783653966107/xhtml/hints.xhtml.

CHAPTER 9

A Historical Perspective

These were not pleasant days. . . Men were not nice in their treatment of each other.
—Thomas B. Reed, Speaker of the House,
1889–91, 1895–99

In chapter 1, I noted that some analysts view the current decade as a return to the divided government era of the late twentieth century— only in reverse. In their view, since the 2010 elections the country has had a Democratic presidential majority and a Republican congressional majority—the opposite of the earlier pattern. Given that we are living in the current period and do not yet have the benefit of hindsight, generalizations must be tentative. But in my view the current period more closely resembles the late nineteenth-century pre-McKinley era. The four elections between 2004 and 2010 resulted in four different patterns of institutional control; the six elections between 2004 and 2014 resulted in five different patterns. The major historical precedent for such instability of institutional control came during the so-called Period of No Decision or Era of Stalemate in the late nineteenth century when the five elections held between 1886 and 1894 produced five different patterns of institutional majorities.[1]

This chapter draws on several earlier writings: Morris Fiorina, *Divided Government* (New York: Macmillan, 1992) and Morris Fiorina, "America's Missing Moderates," *The American Interest* 8, no. 4 (March/April 2013), www.the-american-interest .com/2013/02/12/americas-missing-moderates-hiding-in-plain-sight/.

1. The elections of 1840–48 also produced five consecutive changes in control patterns, although the Free Soil candidacy of former president Martin Van Buren prevented what likely would have been a unified Democratic government in 1848.

TABLE 9.1. **The Era of No Decision: 1874–1894**

	President	House	Senate
1874	R	D	R
1876	D/R*	D	R
1878	R	D	D
1880	R	R	T**
1882	R	D	R
1884	D	D	R
1886	D	D	R
1888	D/R*	R	R
1890	R	D	R
1892	D	D	D
1894	D	R	R

*Popular vote winner lost the Electoral Vote

**Tie

Table 9.1 lists the election outcomes for this period when tenuous majorities were the rule for two decades.[2]

The Panic of 1873 combined with the return of Southern Democrats to the Congress resulted in Democratic control of the House for the first time since the onset of the Civil War. For the next twenty years national elections were very closely fought. The Republicans had an edge in presidential elections, but in the five presidential elections held during this period only once did a candidate receive a majority of the popular vote.[3] The other four winners received less than 50 percent (the remaining votes went to third parties like the Greenback, Prohibition, and Populist Parties that contested elections during the period). Moreover, twice (Samuel Tilden in 1876 and Grover Cleveland in 1888), the winner of the popular vote lost the presidency in the Electoral College, something that did not happen again until the 2000 election. Democrats typically controlled the House and Republicans generally controlled the Senate. The latter

2. One could make a case that the Era of No Decision actually began with the appearance of the Republican Party in 1856. Often forgotten today is that Abraham Lincoln received a bit less than 40 percent of the popular vote in the 1860 election. Unified Republican control from 1860 to 1872 was due in part to Democratic states seceding from the Union.

3. Ironically, it was Samuel Tilden in 1876, who lost to Rutherford B. Hayes after a negotiated political settlement gave Hayes a majority in the Electoral College.

was accomplished in part by strategically admitting new Republican-leaning states to the Union.[4] In all, one party enjoyed control of all three elective institutions for only four years of the twenty-year period, and each episode of unified control lasted only two years.

As discussed in an earlier work, periods of divided government in American history tend to occur in times of chronic societal strain.[5] Historical parallels are always tempting and sometimes misleading, but one does not have to work very hard to draw parallels between the late nineteenth century and contemporary times. In the chaotic post–Civil War period the parties in Congress became more cohesive and more distinct—they sorted.[6] Brady calculates that in the 1896 House elections, for example, 86 percent of the victorious Republicans came from industrial districts whereas 60 percent of the victorious Democrats came from agricultural districts.[7] Thus, each party contained a strong majority of members with common interests—interests that were in conflict with the dominant interest of the other party.[8] A consideration of socioeconomic developments in this earlier period of majority instability shows at least five similarities with the contemporary period.

1. Economic Transformation In the last quarter of the nineteenth century the United States experienced the Industrial Revolution—the country transitioned from an agricultural to an industrial economy with all the attendant dislocations. By 1885 America surpassed Britain as the world leader in industrial output. Today, of course, the United States is undergoing another economic transformation, from an industrial

4. These Western states had small populations so did not much affect the party balance in the House, but they each had two senators. See Barry Weingast and Charles Stewart III, "Stacking the Senate, Changing the Nation: Republican Rotten Boroughs, Statehood Politics, and American Political Development," *Studies in American Political Development* 6, no. 2 (October 1992): 223–71.

5. Fiorina, *Divided Government*, 8.

6. Keith T. Poole and Howard Rosenthal, *Ideology & Congress*, chap. 4 (New Brunswick, NJ: Transaction Publishers, 2007).

7. David Brady, *Congressional Voting in a Partisan Era: A Study of the McKinley Houses and a Comparison to the Modern House of Representatives*, chap. 3 (Lawrence: University Press of Kansas, 1973).

8. Whether the electorate was similarly well sorted (or polarized) is unknown in times preceding the development of scientific survey research.

economy to one variously described as post-industrial, communications, service, informational, or whatnot—but an economy clearly different from the manufacturing economy that prevailed for most of the twentieth century. Capitalism fosters creative destruction, but there is no guarantee that those who experience the destruction will be compensated by the creation. There were many winners from this earlier economic transformation but also losers and certainly significant dislocations. The same is true today.

2. Globalization Although not always linear, globalization is an ongoing process, not something that suddenly happened in recent decades. The late nineteenth century was a period of economic globalization. Members of Congress from the Midwest condemned the railroads in the debates about railroad regulation, complaining that their constituents could outcompete the Russians and Ukrainians in the European grain markets if only railroad abuses could be curbed. The rapidly industrializing United States was a prime opportunity for foreign investment. British finance helped build the American railroad system (probably several times over, given the financial chicanery and frequent bankruptcies). And investment opportunities abounded in steel and other industrial sectors. Globalization then was viewed in more positive terms—as an opportunity for economic growth. But in common with globalization today, it brought with it rapid and significant social and economic change.

3. Population Movements As the United States industrialized, Americans left the farms and moved to the cities to work in the new manufacturing enterprises. They exchanged a hard rural life for the miserable conditions of the cities and industrial workplaces.[9] In the second half of the twentieth century, the United States witnessed several major population movements. As late as 1950, the stereotypical African American was a sharecropper in a Southern cotton field. By the 1970s the stereotype had changed to a Northern tenement dweller. The movement of African Americans from South to North

9. Upton Sinclair, *The Jungle* (New York: Doubleday, 1906).

was the greatest internal migration in American history.[10] At about the same time, whites were leaving the Frostbelt and moving to the Sunbelt, altering the Southern and Southwestern economies and the geographic balance of political power. Population movements generate social problems, create tensions between old and new residents, and change the political balance.

4. Immigration Beginning in the 1880s, immigration surged as millions left Europe to work in America's mines and factories. The open door closed in the 1920s and remained closed until it reopened in the 1960s, after which a new surge of immigration began that has continued to the present. The debate today is characterized by a great deal of historical amnesia, but anyone who has studied the earlier period will recognize that the issues and conflicts generated by the current wave of immigration are strikingly similar to those of a century and more ago.

5. Inequality The Era of No Decision is more commonly known as the Gilded Age. It was a time when robber barons amassed great fortunes, legitimate and otherwise. Coupled with the development of a mass working class, the general socioeconomic equality described by Tocqueville gave way to great disparities in wealth between the owners and investors in the new industrial economy and those who labored in their enterprises. Today, economic inequality is back on the political agenda in a serious way for the first time since the New Deal. Related to this development is the return of crony capitalism to Gilded Age levels.[11]

10. Nicholas Lemann, *The Promised Land: The Great Black Migration and How It Changed America* (New York: Vintage Books, 1991).

11. To anyone who has followed the news about fraudulent home mortgage assessments and securities ratings, obscene bonuses, Goldman-Sachs, AIG, Tim Geithner, Jack Lew, Eric Holder, "too big to fail," "too big to jail," and numerous other aspects of the 2008–9 crash and its aftermath, the discussion of corruption in the late nineteenth century will seem familiar. For a survey of the earlier period see Jay Cost, *A Republic No More: Big Government and the Rise of American Political Corruption*, chap. 5 (New York: Encounter Books, 2015). There is a huge literature on the contemporary period, inter alia, Michael Lewis, *The Big Short: Inside the*

Social and economic changes like these create numerous social and economic problems. They disrupt old electoral coalitions and suggest new possibilities to ambitious political entrepreneurs.[12] When changes are major, rapid, and cumulative as described above, their effects are all the more pronounced. Very likely, the electoral instability of the current era reflects the new issues and problems created by the socioeconomic changes of the past half century. In fact, electoral instability probably bears a complex cause-and-effect relationship with the existence of serious socioeconomic problems.

Notice that "great presidents" do not seem to govern during periods of unstable party control. Rutherford B. Hayes, Chester Arthur, and Benjamin Harrison do not lead any historian's ranking, nor do Franklin Pierce and James Buchanan from the pre–Civil War divided government period when the country was being torn apart by the forces of sectionalism and slavery. Lincoln's election in 1860, however, inaugurated fourteen years of unified Republican government, as did McKinley's in 1896. Franklin D. Roosevelt's 1932 victory did the same for the Democrats. Electoral stability may increase the likelihood that successive administrations of the same party can successfully meet the challenges of their time; conversely, electoral instability may prevent them from doing so. Thus, electoral instability may be both cause and consequence of societal problems. The tensions that fracture existing electoral coalitions encourage political entrepreneurs to explore new opportunities, contributing to instability. New problems and issues create opportunities to construct new majorities.

The late nineteenth-century era of electoral instability ended when the Democratic Party was captured by a populist insurgency led by William Jennings Bryan. The party adopted an antiestablishment populist platform and its Republican opponents moved to co-opt

---

Doomsday Machine (New York: Norton, 2010); Matt Taibbi, "Eric Holder, Wall Street Double Agent, Comes in from the Cold," *Rolling Stone,* July 8, 2015, www .rollingstone.com/politics/news/eric-holder-wall-street-double-agent-comes-in-from -the-cold-20150708.

12. For a discussion of how socioeconomic change contributed to electoral change in the late twentieth century, see Morris Fiorina, with Samuel Abrams, *Disconnect: The Breakdown of Representation in American Politics,* chaps. 5–6, (Norman: University of Oklahoma Press, 2009).

elements of the Democratic coalition with an alternative vision of a prosperous industrial future. The result was a thoroughgoing defeat for the Democrats. Importantly, the Republican majority delivered on its promises, at least well enough to hold its coalition together for most of three decades. I suspect that if the current era is to end, it will end similarly—when one party wins a decisive victory, restrains the temptation to overreach, delivers a satisfactory performance, and holds its majority together for a decade or more. The critical question is if and when that will happen.[13]

The troubling difference between these two periods more than a century apart is that our times are arguably more dangerous than those in the late nineteenth century. Then Britannia still ruled the waves. The United States could free ride in international affairs as the rest of the free world free rides on America today. And while terrorism—domestic and international—was not uncommon a century ago, weapons of mass destruction were not the threat they are today.[14] In economics, the country was growing rapidly during the Era of Indecision—how to dispose of the federal budget surplus was a major political issue (seriously). In contrast, slow growth characterizes the economy today. The United States could afford twenty years of political chaos in the late nineteenth century before a new majority emerged. It remains to be seen whether we can do so today.[15]

13. This is probably the best-case scenario. In an earlier period of electoral instability, 1840–1860, eleven elections resulted in seven different patterns of institutional control. That period ended, of course, with the collapse of the party system in the 1860 elections followed by the Civil War.

14. In my experience one of the consequences of the transformation of history teaching in American schools is that students are generally unaware of the frequency of nonracial violence in the United States. See Hugh Davis Graham and Ted Robert Gurr, *The History of Violence in America* (New York: Bantam, 1969), especially chaps. 1, 2, 4, 5, 8, 15, and 16, and the appendix.

15. Nearly forty years if we start the Era of No Decision in 1856. See Fiorina, *Divided Government*, and Fiorina, "America's Missing Moderates: Hiding in Plain Sight," *The American Interest* 8 (no. 4).

CHAPTER 10

The 2016 Presidential Election—An Abundance of Controversies

Even by the colorful standards of presidential primaries, the 2016 election cycle has been filled with jaw-dropping, head-scratching moments.

—Eric Bradner

While the world celebrates and commiserates a Donald Trump presidency, one thing is clear: this will go down as the most acrimonious presidential campaign of all.

—Rachel Revesz

Controversial presidential elections are nothing new in American electoral history, 2016 being the latest, but certainly not the first. Despite much apocalyptic commentary, however, the implications of the 2016 election seem less dire than those of some elections held in earlier eras. The four-candidate 1860 election started the country on the path to civil war and the disputed election of 1876 threatened to reignite that conflict. In more recent times, the strong showing of a racist third party in 1968 coupled with political assassinations and civil disorders on a scale not seen since the labor violence of the early twentieth century led some contemporary observers to believe

Quotations are from Eric Bradner, "13 Jaw-dropping Moments of the 2016 Campaign," CNN, August 10, 2015, www.cnn.com/2015/08/09/politics/2016-campaign-surprise-moments-donald-trump/; and Rachael Revesz, "How the 2016 Presidential Election Was Won: The Timeline, Controversies and Seats that Led to the White House," *The Independent*, November 9, 2016, www.independent.co.uk/news/world/americas/us-elections/presidential-election-2016-results-timeline-controversies-quotes-seats-maps-polls-quotes-a7398606.html.

that the country was "coming apart."[1] The 2000 Florida electoral vote contest raged for more than two months, threatening a constitutional crisis and deeply dividing partisan activists on both sides. Still, even allowing for the fact that secession and revolution are not seriously on the table, for the sheer number and breadth of the controversies that accompanied it, the 2016 election does seem out of the ordinary.

Parties have nominated flawed candidates before—Republican Barry Goldwater in 1964 and Democrat George McGovern in 1972, for example—but at least since the advent of scientific survey research, no major party has nominated a candidate so wanting in the eyes of the electorate, let alone both doing so simultaneously. Charges of ethnocentrism and racism are as American as apple pie, but in their prevalence and virulence in 2016 (with misogyny added to the toxic mix) they were reminiscent of 1928, if not the late nineteenth century.[2] "Biased media" is a complaint common to all elections, but the retreat from objectivity by the mainstream media in 2016 struck many observers as a significant break with modern journalistic practices.[3] The increasingly visible role of social media like Twitter threatened to further diminish the importance of the legacy media. Swing voters, largely missing in action in recent elections, suddenly reappeared in 2016.[4] Possible foreign intervention in the election was a new development (at least insofar as the United States was the intervenee rather than the intervener), as was FBI involvement (but possibly only because earlier instances did not become public). Meanwhile journalists scrambled to read up on "populism,"

1. William L. O'Neill, *Coming Apart: An Informal History of America in the 1960s* (New York: Quadrangle, 1973).

2. In 1928, the Democratic candidate was Catholic Al Smith of New York. Religious, ethnic, and urban-rural divisions dominated the election. As noted in chapter 4, much of the politics of the late nineteenth century revolved around ethnocultural divisions.

3. See the debate sparked by Jim Rutenberg, "Trump Is Testing the Norms of Objectivity in Journalism," *New York Times,* August 7, 2016, www.nytimes.com /2016/08/08/business/balance-fairness-and-a-proudly-provocative-presidential -candidate.html?_r=0.

4. Nate Silver, "The Invisible Undecided Voter," *FiveThirtyEight,* January 23, 2017, fivethirtyeight.com/features/the-invisible-undecided-voter/.

which had not played such a significant role in American elections since the 1960s. "Class," long ago displaced by discussions of race, ethnicity, gender, and sexual orientation in college course syllabi, enjoyed an academic as well as political revival (so did "authoritarianism," another oldie but goodie).[5] All of this was overlaid on a split decision where Hillary Clinton won a clear popular vote plurality and Donald Trump a clear electoral vote majority. The impact of this troubling outcome was probably exacerbated by the sheer shock of a Trump victory when the various polls and "models" assured the political universe that Clinton was a surefire winner; you could take it to the bank.

This chapter and the next review some of the aforementioned developments. Such a review is necessarily modest and incomplete given that in these postelection months the ratio of opinion to research is highly skewed toward the former.

Some Perspective

In the aftermath of every election, commentators vie to explain its meaning. Winners rejoice and losers lament, both often arguing that the key to the outcome was some specific factor supporting their point of view. In the aftermath of the 2016 election, sentiments like these were common among disappointed Clinton supporters:

> For anyone who voted for Donald Trump, **bald-faced racism** and sexism were not the deal-breakers they should have been. Hatred of women was on the ballot in November, and it won (emphasis in original)[6]

> Donald Trump has won the presidency, despite an unprecedented level of unfitness and in defiance of nearly every prediction and

5. Amanda Taub, "The Rise of American Authoritarianism," www.vox.com/2016/3/1/11127424/trump-authoritarianism; cf. Wendy Rahn and Eric Oliver, "Trump's Voters Aren't Authoritarians, New Research Says. So What Are They?" *Washington Post*, March 9, 2016, https://www.washingtonpost.com/news/monkey-cage/wp/2016/03/09/trumps-voters-arent-authoritarians-new-research-says-so-what-are-they/.

6. Christina Cauterucci, "In 2016, America Was Forced to Face the Reality of Sexual Assault," *Slate*, December 28, 2016, www.slate.com/blogs/xx_factor/2016/12/28/_2016_was_the_year_america_learned_what_sexual_assault_looks_like.html.

poll. And he's done this not despite but [*sic*] because he expressed unfiltered disdain toward racial and religious minorities in the country.[7]

As I discuss in greater detail in the next chapter, many disappointed Clinton supporters made such claims and no doubt many more agreed with them. But imagine an alternative universe in which the Clinton campaign followed Bill Clinton's advice to devote more attention and resources to the Rust Belt states, with the result that Hillary Clinton gained 39,000 more votes distributed in such a way that she carried Pennsylvania, Michigan, and Wisconsin (which Trump won by a bit less than 78,000). This would have given her a comfortable Electoral College majority along with a clear popular vote plurality. Then, in all likelihood, the day-after story line in the media would have been, "Americans reject racism and sexism!"

The larger meaning of a presidential election should not hinge on the distribution of .0006 of the vote in three states. Failing to appreciate that fact led to a widespread loss of perspective among election commentators in the aftermath of the 2016 elections. In a majoritarian electoral system like ours, small changes in the vote can have enormous consequences for party control of our governing institutions and the policies they produce.[8] Turning the sentence around, consequential changes in control of our institutions produced by an election do not imply that the electorate underwent any kind of sea change, which seems to be the assumption made by many of those disappointed by the 2016 outcome. If the US electoral system were a variation of a proportional representation system as in most parliamentary democracies, then *ceteris paribus,* the verdict among the

---

7. Jenee Desmond-Harris, "Trump's Win Is a Reminder of the Incredible, Unbeatable Power of Racism," *Vox,* November 9, 2016, www.vox.com/policy-and-politics/2016/11/9/13571676/trump-win-racism-power.

8. Conversely, large changes in the vote can have minimal consequences for institutional control and policy change. Ronald Reagan gained 8 percentage points in the popular vote between 1980 and 1984, but the large Democratic majority in the House diminished by only sixteen seats and the narrow Republican majority in the Senate fell by one.

commentariat would have been that 2016 was a status quo election that produced no significant change from 2012.[9]

So, while there is no discounting the potential consequences of Trump's victory, in itself it provides little basis for concluding that the election reflected some sort of massive shift in the values and beliefs of the American public. As in all elections, the vote reflected a combination of long-term conditions in the country and short-term factors associated with the candidates and the campaigns. In the case of 2016, a substantial portion of the electorate had become increasingly dissatisfied with long-term developments. One candidate (Trump) was positioned to capitalize on this dissatisfaction and the other one (Clinton) was not. Overlaid on these long-term considerations were short-term factors, most importantly, the two candidates.

The Flight 93 Election[10]

As emphasized in chapters 1 and 7, voters can choose only between the alternatives the political parties offer them. If both parties nominate unacceptable candidates, voters will elect an unacceptable candidate.[11]

The media tend to emphasize candidate personality characteristics. Is the candidate authentic, warm, modest, sincere, trustworthy, and moral, or their opposites? In general, research indicates that candidate personality characteristics are overrated as influences on the vote. In 1980, for example, voters thought that Jimmy Carter was a peach of a guy personally and Ronald Reagan a somewhat scary prospect, but that did not stop them from replacing what many viewed as a failed president with a risky alternative.[12] To a greater

9. Parliamentary systems have no equivalent to our midterm elections.

10. Publius Decius Mus, "The Flight 93 Election," *CRB*, September 5, 2016, www.claremont.org/crb/basicpage/the-flight-93-election/.

11. Political scientists of a certain vintage will recognize the allusion to V. O. Key Jr., the great mid-twentieth-century political scientist who wrote, "If the people can choose only from among rascals, they are certain to choose a rascal." *The Responsible Electorate* (New York: Vintage, 1966), 3.

12. Morris Fiorina, "You're Likeable Enough, Mitt," *New York Times,* June 7, 2012, https://campaignstops.blogs.nytimes.com/2012/06/07/youre-likeable-enough

degree than usual, campaign coverage in 2016 revolved around the personas of the two candidates, especially Trump's. Indeed, some Democratic critics of the Clinton campaign complained that it had too little substance and focused too much on driving home the notion that Trump was a horrible human being.[13] And while I recognize the deep admiration for Clinton among her ardent supporters, the data clearly indicate that a substantial portion of the American electorate viewed the election as something akin to the movie *Alien vs. Predator.* Rightfully or wrongfully, the simple fact is that the American public saw both candidates as deeply flawed. According to Gallup, "Donald Trump and Hillary Clinton head into the final hours of the 2016 presidential campaign with the worst election-eve images of any major-party presidential candidates Gallup has measured back to 1956."[14] Figure 10.1 graphs Gallup's candidate "Scalometer," which asks voters to rate the candidates positively or negatively on a 1-5 scale.

Before Trump, the most negatively rated Republican candidate was Goldwater in 1964 with a 47-point unfavorable rating. Trump obliterated this long-standing record by 16 points. Before Clinton, the most negatively rated Democratic candidate was McGovern in 1972 with a 41-point unfavorable rating. Not to be outdone, Clinton nearly matched Trump's record-shattering performance by topping McGovern's negatives by 14 points.[15]

-mitt/. More generally, research finds that voters prioritize candidate qualities that are relevant to governing rather than characteristics that determine whom they'd rather have a beer with. See David B. Holian and Charles L. Prysby, *Candidate Character Traits in Presidential Elections* (New York: Routledge, 2015).

13. A Wesleyan University study of campaign ads reported that the Clinton campaign was imbalanced in just this way. Kyle Olson, "Study: Hillary Campaign Most Negative, Least Substantive," *The American Mirror,* March 9, 2017, www.the americanmirror.com/study-hillary-campaign-negative-least-substantive/.

14. Lydia Saad, "Trump and Clinton Finish with Historically Poor Images," Gallup, November 8, 2016, www.gallup.com/poll/197231/trump-clinton-finish-historically -poor-images.aspx.

15. On average, candidates appear to be evaluated more negatively beginning in the 1980s. A possible explanation is that because the Gallup measure captures policy and performance evaluations as well as personal qualities, it would trend downward after the process of party sorting begins, as partisans expressed increasingly negative evaluations of the other party. See chapters 2 and 3.

FIGURE 10.1. Unfavorable Ratings of Major Party Presidential Nominees: 1956–2016

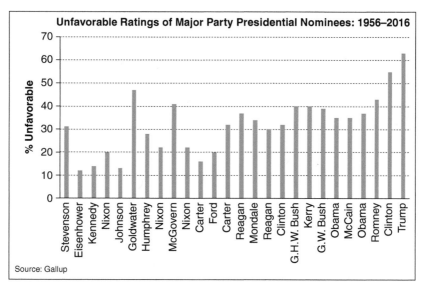

Of course, voters can harbor positive or negative feelings about a candidate for reasons other than their personas—namely, the candidate's records, the positions they advocate, the groups who endorse them, and other considerations. Various polls provide more specific measures of candidates' personal characteristics, although they do not provide the longtime series of Gallup and ANES measures. Table 10.1 compares personal ratings of the 2016 candidates. The top panel reports ratings for all adults from the Economist/YouGov survey and the bottom panel only for voters from the exit polls, but the figures are very similar. For many Clinton supporters, her long record of public service was a major reason to support her, but only half the electorate believed that she was qualified to serve as president and had the right temperament to serve. A possible reason for discounting her record is that nearly two-thirds of those who voted considered her dishonest and untrustworthy. Not even one-third of voters believed she was sincere in what she said—Trump's strongest point. Whether the reason was a quarter-century long Republican campaign of character assassination and trumped-up scandals (as

TABLE 10.1. **Americans Voted for Trump in Spite of . . .**

Economist/YouGov (all adults)		
	Trump	*Clinton*
Qualified	34	49
Honest and Trustworthy	31	24
Says what s/he believes	53	29
Like a lot	16	17
Dislike	47	53
Exit polls (voters only)	*Trump*	*Clinton*
Qualified	38	52
Honest and Trustworthy	33	36
Right Temperament	35	55
Bring Needed Change	83	14

Democrats claimed) or the just desserts from a quarter century of skating on the boundary between the ethical and unethical (as Republicans claimed) is not the issue. Whatever the causes, the negative numbers were the issue.

The figures for Trump are striking in their implications. Only about a third of the electorate considered him qualified to serve, to have the right temperament to serve, and to be honest and trustworthy. Only 16 percent of the voters liked him a lot and nearly half disliked him (Clinton's figures were slightly worse). Yet Trump received 46 percent of the popular vote. Rather than an enthusiastic endorsement of Trump's controversial comments and positions, the conclusion must be that a significant number of Americans cast their vote for him *in spite of* their negative views of him. As noted repeatedly in previous chapters, a vote for a candidate does not imply enthusiastic support, only that the voter thinks that candidate is preferable to the alternative. Why was Trump preferable for voters who considered him unqualified to serve? A strong hint from the exit polls comes from the reasons voters gave for their decisions. By a significant margin they chose change over empathy, experience, and judgment, and on that dimension Trump led Clinton—the candidate of continuity—by a margin of 6 to1. Numerous liberal commentators embraced this interpretation, often expressing it in vivid prose. For Thomas Frank, "She was exactly the wrong candidate for this

angry, populist moment. An insider when the country was scream-
ing for an outsider. A technocrat who offered fine-tuning when the
country wanted to take a sledge-hammer to the machine."[16] And former MSNBC commentator Krystal Ball wrote, "Voters were offered
a choice between a possibility of catastrophe in Trump and a guarantee of mediocrity in Clinton. Clearly, they picked the high-risk bet
that they felt at least gave them some chance to escape the certain
economic doom that they feel in their current lives."[17]

The implication that many if not most votes for Trump did not
reflect enthusiasm for him as much as negative judgments about
Clinton received clear support in various polls. Throughout the campaign, only about 40 percent of Trump supporters said that they
were voting for Trump rather than against Clinton.[18] According to
Harry Enten, "No candidate since 1980 has had a lower percentage of voters say they plan to cast a vote *for* their candidate. That
includes candidates whose campaigns were viewed as disastrous,
including Jimmy Carter in 1980, Michael Dukakis in 1988 and Bob
Dole in 1996."[19] Clinton did not fare much better. In the exit polls,
57 percent of Americans said they would have negative feelings if
Trump won, but 53 percent said the same about Clinton.

Other things being equal, one would have expected an average Democrat to crush a historically flawed candidate like Trump.
Instead, Clinton's margin over Trump was lower than Obama's
margin over Romney in thirty-seven states. In my view, explanations of why the Democrats lost the presidency in 2016 focus too
much on Trump and not enough on Clinton. Earlier in the summer

16. Thomas Frank, "Donald Trump Is Moving to the White House, and Liberals
Put Him There," *The Guardian,* November 9, 2016, https://www.theguardian.com
/commentisfree/2016/nov/09/donald-trump-white-house-hillary-clinton-liberals.

17. Krystal Ball, "The Democratic Party Deserved to Die," *Huffington Post,*
November 10, 2016, www.huffingtonpost.com/entry/the-democratic-party-deserves
-to-die_us_58236ad5e4b0aac62488cde5.

18. "Diminished Enthusiasm Dogs Trump: Clinton Gains in Affirmative Support,"
ABC News, October 24, 2016, www.langerresearch.com/wp-content/uploads/1184a
22016ElectionTrackingNo.2.pdf.

19. "Clinton Voters Aren't Just Voting against Trump," *FiveThirtyEight,* October 25, 2016, fivethirtyeight.com/features/clinton-voters-arent-just-voting-against
-trump/.

of 2016, when Republican acquaintances expressed the hope that the FBI would recommend an indictment of Hillary Clinton, I cautioned them to be careful what they wished for, suggesting that this would be the worst possible outcome for Republicans. The likely last-minute replacement on the ticket would be Joe Biden, and in all likelihood he would win the election and with it the Senate. Biden is largely scandal free, a pauper by senatorial standards, and his background and record appeal to precisely the segment of the electorate that defected from Obama to Trump. Some believe the same is true for Bernie Sanders as well, although that is a harder case to make given some of his economic views.

The Split between the Electoral College and the Popular Vote

For the second time in sixteen years, the popular vote leader did not win an Electoral College majority. When this happened in 2000, many political analysts expected much more of a negative popular reaction than the limited one that ensued. Most Americans who were not locked into the two partisan camps seemed to accept the sports analogies that were offered: in the World Series and the NBA play-offs the winner is determined by games won, not the most runs or points. In the 1960 World Series, for example, the New York Yankees outscored the Pittsburgh Pirates 55 to 27, but the Pirates won the series four games to three, and no one questioned the outcome. The same analogies were offered in 2016 after Clinton supporters railed that she had legitimately won the election but lost in an undemocratic vestige of an eighteenth-century political compromise.

I am of two minds about such analogies. When the topic is the legitimacy of elections and the governments they determine, such analogies are inapt. Elections are the way democracies determine a legitimate government. The political equality embodied in majority rule is the most fundamental component of a democratic form of government. So if the rules of the electoral game crown a candidate who gets fewer votes than an opponent, that violates political equality and undercuts the legitimacy of the winner. I see no way around that conclusion.

As a description of the way to play the electoral game, however, sports analogies are apt. Many Clinton supporters claim that she would now be president had the election been based on the popular vote. Probably they are correct, but we can never know for sure, because one cannot assume the popular vote would have been the same absent the Electoral College: the candidates would have conducted different campaigns. From the standpoint of the Trump campaign it mattered not at all whether he lost California by 270 votes or by the 4,270,000 that he actually did. The 4-million-plus vote margin that Clinton racked up in California was irrelevant under the Electoral College rules. Reports indicate that the Trump campaign set aside the states certain to go either Republican or Democratic and concentrated on the sub-election occurring in the thirteen battleground states.[20] Trump won that sub-election—by about 800,000 votes.[21] Had the outcome been determined by popular vote, however, Trump would have made more of an effort in friendly areas of states like California and New York, and Clinton in friendly areas of deep red states. How it all would have netted out is the kind of counterfactual that sparks interesting discussions but is probably beyond resolution with data.

The Polls and Models

In the immediate aftermath of the election, a number of columns concluded that "the polls blew it."[22] But as Clinton's popular vote plurality mounted, analysts realized that the polls had performed pretty well. Most of the major national polls pegged Clinton's lead at 2–4 percentage points, and she ultimately won the popular vote by about 2 points. So, the polls slightly overestimated Clinton's lead,

20. John Judis, "On the Eve of Disruption: Final Thoughts on the 2016 Election," *TPM*, December 18, 2016, talkingpointsmemo.com/edblog/--100887.

21. 2016 National Popular Voter Tracker, undated, https://docs.google.com /spreadsheets/d/133Eb4qQmOxNvtesw2hdVnso73R68EZx4SfCnP4IGQf8 /edit#gid=19.

22. Michelle Jamrisko and Terrence Dopp, "Failed Polls in 2016 Call into Question a Profession's Precepts," Bloomberg, November 8, 2016, https://www .bloomberg.com/politics/articles/2016-11-09/failed-polls-in-2016-call-into-question -a-profession-s-precepts; Andrew Mercer, Claude Deane, and Kyley McGenney, "Why 2016 Election Polls Missed Their Mark," Pew Research Center, November 9, 2016, www.pewresearch.org/fact-tank/2016/11/09/why-2016-election-polls-missed -their-mark/.

but that overestimate is actually a bit smaller than the underestimate of Obama's 2012 vote.[23] A bigger problem was the exaggerated certainty that various polls and models gave to a Clinton win. Although criticized earlier for giving Trump as *high* a probability of winning as 30 percent, Nate Silver at 538 turned out to be closer to the mark than *HuffPost*'s 98 percent and Sam Wang's 99 percent predicted probabilities of a Clinton victory.[24]

The state polls, on the other hand, revealed some problems. On average, they tended to underestimate Trump's support, particularly in the states he ultimately carried—including, critically, Pennsylvania, Michigan, and Wisconsin, where 4–6 point poll advantages for Clinton the week before the election evaporated on Election Day.[25] The polling disparities were correlated with the state's proportion of voters without college degrees.[26] The polls may have under-sampled white noncollege voters, underestimated their likelihood of voting, or both.

A great deal of ink and airtime was devoted to predictive models during the campaign. There are two kinds of election models, although they overlap a bit.[27] The first type, discussed above, are

23. Sean Trende, "It Wasn't the Polls That Missed, It Was the Pundits," *Real Clear Politics,* November 12, 2016, www.realclearpolitics.com/articles/2016/11/12/it_wasnt_the_polls_that_missed_it_was_the_pundits_132333.html.

24. "Who Will Win the Presidency?" *FiveThirtyEight,* November 8, 2016, https://projects.fivethirtyeight.com/2016-election-forecast/#plus; "Forecast," *Huffington Post,* November 8, 2016, http://elections.huffingtonpost.com/2016/forecast/president; "Is 99% a Reasonable Probability?" Princeton Election Consortium, November 6, 2016, http://election.princeton.edu/2016/11/06/is-99-a-reasonable-probability/. I have not delved into the guts of these models, but any methodology that generates an election prediction in the range of 98–99 percent strikes me as prima facie problematic.

25. Dhrumil Metta, "How Much the Polls Missed by in Every State," *FiveThirty Eight,* December 2, 2016, fivethirtyeight.com/features/how-much-the-polls-missed-by-in-every-state/; David Weigel, "State Pollsters, Pummeled by 2016, Analyze What Went Wrong," *Washington Post,* December 30,2016, https://www.washingtonpost.com/news/post-politics/wp/2016/12/30/state-pollsters-pummeled-by-2016-analyze-what-went-wrong/?utm_term=.e4e8d652d728.

26. Nate Silver, "Pollsters Probably Didn't Talk to Enough White Voters without College Degrees," *FiveThirtyEight,* December 1, 2016, fivethirtyeight.com/features/pollsters-probably-didnt-talk-to-enough-white-voters-without-college-degrees/.

27. Actually, three, but models of the third type—formal or mathematical—are too abstract to make empirical predictions about an election.

poll based, although they aggregate, evaluate, simulate, standardize, and in other ways try to extract more accurate information from the universe of polls. The second type consists of political science forecasting models that get less media attention, probably in part because they omit the subjects most dear to the hearts of journalists—the candidates and campaigns. The political science models are generally based on the so-called fundamentals—chiefly peace and war and the state of the economy, which are viewed as factors that set the election context and determine the kinds of campaigns that can be conducted.[28] For the most part these models do not include the candidates; the latter are implicitly assumed to account for only a little variation on the margins.[29] A few of these models incorporate some poll data, just as the 538 polls plus model includes some aspects of the fundamentals. But for the most part these models implicitly assume that the election is often determined before the campaign formally begins or in some cases even before the candidates are nominated. Table 10.2 summarizes the principal forecast models for 2016.

Most of the models predicted a narrow Democratic edge in the two-party vote, although two models went the other way.[30] None of them calculated the same degree of confidence as the polling models did. In this situation, the most reasonable interpretation is that the fundamentals indicated a fifty-fifty election that would be determined by the marginal effects of the candidates and campaigns. Thus, the verdict is that they performed decently, although Brady and Parker

28. Lynn Vavreck, *The Message Matters* (Princeton: Princeton University Press, 2009).

29. It's not that the campaigns and candidates are irrelevant, but the assumption is that both candidates fall within a range of acceptability and that both campaigns will have access to roughly equal resources and expertise. Thus, the candidates and campaigns generally offset, leaving the election to reflect mostly the underlying fundamentals.

30. Abramowitz predicted a lower Clinton vote because his "time for a change" model includes a variable for an incumbent party that has held office for two terms. Despite the prediction of his model, Abramowitz expressed doubt about the forecast because he viewed Trump as outside the bounds of acceptability. Alan I. Abramowitz, "Will Time for Change Mean Time for Trump?" *PS: Political Science & Politics* 49 (October 2016): 659–60.

TABLE 10.2. 2016 Election Forecasting Models

Forecast	Predicted Two-Party Popular Vote for Clinton	Certainty of Popular Vote Plurality
Erikson & Wlezien (economic indicators/polls)	52	82%
Lockerbie (economic expectations/ 1st term)	50.4	62%
Lewis-Beck & Tien (approval/growth)	51.1	83%
Campbell (convention/growth)	51.2	75%
Abramowitz (approval/growth/ 1st term)	48.6	66%
Norpoth (primaries)	47.5	87%

Source: James Campbell. "Forecasting the 2016 American National Elections." *PS: Political Science & Politics* 49 (2016): 652.

report that the accuracy of some of the best known economic models has been declining since 1992.[31]

Swing Voters

Analysts define swing voters in various ways.[32] At its broadest the concept excludes only those who are sure to turn out and sure to vote for one of the parties and not the other, leaving as swing voters everyone who is uncertain about whom they will vote for and/ or whether they will vote at all. The conventional wisdom is that the proportion of swing voters in the American electorate has greatly declined, but in chapter 1 and various earlier writings I have argued that swing voters are made, not born.[33] To reiterate, today's sorted parties nominate candidates who look similar to the ones they nominated in previous elections, so most voters will probably vote the

31. David Brady and Brett Parker, *Now Is the Winter of Our Discontent: The 2016 U.S. Presidential Election* (Basingstoke, UK: Palgrave Macmillan, forthcoming).

32. William G. Mayer, ed., *The Swing Voter in American Politics* (Washington, DC: Brookings, 2008).

33. Morris P. Fiorina, "If I Could Hold a Seminar for Political Journalists . . ." *The Forum* 10, no. 4: 2–4, https://www.degruyter.com/downloadpdf/j/for.2012.10 .issue-4/forum-2013-0011/forum-2013-0011.xml.

same as they did in previous elections. Rather than being less willing to move between parties than voters in earlier decades, contemporary voters may simply have less reason to do so. The three members of the Democratic sequence of Gore, Kerry, and Obama from 2000 to 2008 looked a lot more similar to each other than did the members of the Humphrey, McGovern, and Carter sequence of 1968–72. On the Republican side, Bush, McCain, and Romney in 2004–12 looked considerably more similar to each other than the sequence of Eisenhower, Nixon, and Goldwater in 1956–64. Other things being equal, party sorting at the candidate level should produce less voter swinging in contemporary elections than in the late twentieth century even if voters were just as willing to swing now as they were then.

As argued in chapter 4, however, to the dismay of the Republican thought establishment, Trump broke the mold of recent Republican nominees. He demonstrated the appeal of a de-sorter in the primaries. By the time the general election campaign was under way, he was a full-scale disrupter, in Silicon Valley jargon.[34] This qualitative impression is consistent with the quantitative data about swing voters in 2016. Numerous commentators noted the large increases in the number of voters who indicated they were undecided, intended to vote for third-party candidates, or claimed that they would vote but not for president. An Economist/YouGov survey in July and August 2016 found 31 percent of voters distributed roughly evenly across those three categories. In contrast, most commentators put the numbers of such voters in the lower single digits in 2012.[35] Some analysts correctly cautioned that the large number of voters potentially in play meant that the 2016 election had more underlying volatility than other recent elections. Preliminary analyses suggest

34. Peggy Noonan, "Trump Tries to Build a 'Different Party,'" *Wall Street Journal*, January 26, 2017, www.wsj.com/articles/trump-tries-to-build-a-different-party-1485 478386; Edward G. Carmines, Michael J. Ensley, and Michael W. Wagner, "Ideological Heterogeneity and the Rise of Donald Trump," *The Forum* 14, no. 4, https://www.degruyter.com/view/j/for.2016.14.issue-4/for-2016-0036/for-2016-0036.xml?format=INT.

35. The 2016 figures are cited in Brady and Parker, *The Winter of Our Discontent*, 29. On 2012, see Reid J. Epstein, "The Disappearing Undecided Voter," *Politico*, undated, www.politico.com/news/stories/0812/79504_Page3.html.

that late deciders were slightly more likely to go to Trump than to Clinton and that those who changed their minds late in the campaign also did so.[36] The numbers were not large, but they may have eroded Clinton's margin in key areas. Polls also found Republicans registering gains in the generic congressional vote in the last week of the campaign, suggesting a general movement in the Republican direction.[37]

The Media

On several subjects, the weight of social science research conflicts with what is widely believed in popular, journalistic, and political circles. Two prominent—and related—examples are the ability of the mass media to shape public opinion and the impact of campaign events. Surveys show that Americans believe the media are very powerful—hence the concern about bias in the media—and that people less sophisticated than they are (that is, most of those on the other side) are easily manipulated by slanted news and sophisticated ads. Naturally, people who work for the media or make their livings producing political ads believe that the media are very important. But as communications scholar Diana Mutz observes, scholarly research does not support such claims of major media influence; there is an "enormous chasm" between the beliefs held by journalists (and the typical voter) about the effects of campaign media and the findings of political communications scholars. "Public perceptions of the power of media in elections, and the academic evidence of its influence, could not be further apart."[38]

36. Dan Hopkins, "Voters Really Did Switch to Trump at the Last Minute," *FiveThirtyEight*, December 20, 2016, fivethirtyeight.com/features/voters-really-did -switch-to-trump-at-the-last-minute/.

37. The generic vote item reads, "This November, do you plan to vote for a Democratic or a Republican candidate in your congressional district?" Harry Enten, "Senate Update: The Generic Ballot Is Hurting Democrats' Chances," *FiveThirtyEight*, November 7, 2016, fivethirtyeight.com/features/senate-update-the -generic-ballot-is-hurting-democrats-chances/.

38. Diana Mutz, "The Great Divide: Campaign Media in the American Mind," *Daedalus* 141, no. 4: 83–87.

If ever there were an election designed to pit the popular belief of major media influence against the scholarly consensus of minor influence, 2016 was it. The legacy media were almost unanimous in opposing Trump. For many of them their editorial positions spilled over onto the news pages, with the apparent approval of their editors.[39] The tone of their op-ed and other editorial efforts seemed to grow more frantic as Clinton failed to pull away from Trump in the polls. Some newspapers endorsed a Democrat for the first time in memory or history.[40] After every embarrassing revelation or outrageous comment, the media chorus would pronounce the end of the Trump campaign, and still he marched on to win. Thomas Frank asked, "How did the journalist's crusade fail? The fourth estate came together in an unprecedented professional consensus."[41]

As the next chapter will discuss, a plausible hypothesis is that a strong current of antielitism was running in the 2016 election and those associated with the national media are viewed as card-carrying members of the elite. Along with other institutions, trust in the media has declined precipitously in recent decades (figure 10.2). Why should voters be influenced by people they distrust? Did the media's recent record merit trust? Columnist Matt Bai expressed this sentiment in an acerbic passage:

> But Trump had figured out that no one really believed the elite media anymore— the same media that said Iraq was an existential threat, that the banks had to be saved, that Obama would transform our dysfunctional politics. The same media that nightly featured a cavalcade of smug morons whose only qualification to opine on TV was an almost pathological shamelessness.

39. Rutenberg, "Trump Is Testing the Norms."

40. Hannah Levintova, "This Newspaper Just Endorsed Its First Democrat for President in Almost a Century," *Mother Jones,* September 23, 2016, www.motherjones .com/politics/2016/09/donald-trump-just-forced-yet-another-newspaper-endorse -democrat-first-time-almost-c; Rebecca Shapiro, "For the First Time In Its 126-Year History, This Newspaper Endorsed a Democrat," *Huffington Post,* September 28, 2016, www.huffingtonpost.com/entry/arizona-republic-hillary-clinton-endorsement _us_57eb284fe4b024a52d2b7437.

41. Frank, "Donald Trump Is Moving to the White House."

Bai added,

> Because this is what he [Trump] learned from his first-ever cam-
> paign experience—that if you pit yourself against powerful agen-
> cies or politicians or a corrupt media, people now will believe
> almost anything. Or maybe they won't really care what you're
> saying, as long as it's infuriating to the so-called experts.[42]

FIGURE 10.2. **Trust in Media Hits New Lows**

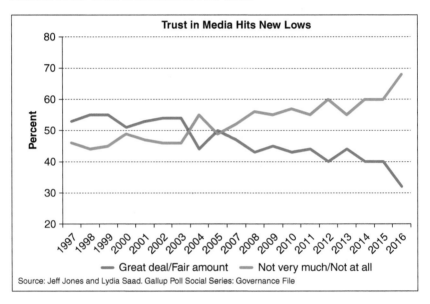

Thomas Frank's answer to why the "journalists' crusade" failed
is similar: "They [the media] chose insulting the other side over try-
ing to understand what motivated them. They transformed opinion
writing into a vehicle for high moral boasting. What could possibly
have gone wrong with such an approach?"[43]

I suspect future research will find that there is considerable support
for such arguments. Media opposition to Trump may have backfired.
The more unbalanced the opposition to Trump became, the more

42. Matt Bai, "The Moment That Made Trump Possible," *Yahoo! News*, December 15, 2016, https://www.yahoo.com/news/the-moment-that-made-trump-possible
-100008601.html.

43. Frank, "Donald Trump Is Moving to the White House."

some voters were tempted to strike back at people and institutions they resented.[44] The point here is not whether Trump deserved unbalanced treatment, but whether in the eyes of some voters the media had overdone it. The next chapter returns to this subject.

The obvious objection to the preceding line of argument is that the media *were* more important than ever in 2016, but they were different media. The era of the *New York Times* and *Washington Post,* the broadcast TV channels, and even the cable channels has passed; the information world belongs now to Twitter, Facebook, and their ilk. With his background in popular entertainment, Trump exploited the rapidly evolving media environment while the Clinton campaign was spending millions of dollars on ads—"so twentieth-century," as our grandchildren might say. Numerous analyses document that Trump received billions of dollars in free media during the primary and general election campaigns, considerably offsetting the huge funding advantage enjoyed by the Clinton campaign.[45] Trump was an inveterate Twitterer and many of his tweets were amplified by media coverage (even if much of the latter was largely negative in tone).[46] There are claims that Trump's son-in-law, Jared Kushner, ran a highly sophisticated analytics and social media operation that flew under the radar of the mainstream media and the Clinton campaign, an operation that helped to explain the better than expected showing for Trump in critical areas.[47] Journalists and politicos focused on traditional metrics—the money spent, the field offices opened, and

44. After the election, I talked to an editor from a major national newspaper who related that his paper had invited Trump voters to e-mail their reasons for supporting Trump. One of the most common responses was some version of "I wanted to see your heads explode."

45. Nicholas Confessore and Karen Yourish, "$2 Billion Worth of Free Media for Donald Trump," *New York Times,* March 15, 2016, www.nytimes.com/2016/03/16 /upshot/measuring-donald-trumps-mammoth-advantage-in-free-media.html?_r=0; Jason Le Miere, "Did the Media Help Donald Trump Win? $5 Billion in Free Advertising Given to President-Elect," *International Business Times,* November 9, 2016, www.ibtimes.com/did-media-help-donald-trump-win-5-billion-free-advertising -given-president-elect-2444115.

46. Why aren't such posts called "twits" rather than "tweets"? The former term seems more accurate.

47. Stephen Bertoni, "Exclusive Interview: How Jared Kushner Won Trump the White House," *Forbes,* December 20, 2016, www.forbes.com/sites/stevenbertoni/2016

the workers deployed by the Clinton campaign—but they had no way of evaluating the impact of Trump's tweets, Facebook presence, Reddit groups, and so on, if they were even aware of most of these activities.

Communications scholars are diligently examining these questions as I write. But until data prove otherwise, I remain skeptical of the Twitter effect at least. Political journalists need to realize that nearly everyone they talk to is abnormal—abnormally interested, abnormally well informed, and abnormally opinionated. Relatively few normal people live in the Twitterverse that political journalists and other members of the chattering class inhabit. According to a Pew Research Center study conducted just as the 2016 primary season got under way, 16 percent of US adults claimed to be on Twitter, but only 9 percent reported getting news from Twitter.[48] In another study, Allcott and Gentzkow report that in 2016 only 14 percent of the public relied on social media as their most important source of news. Moreover, as discussed in chapter 2, most Americans have an expansive concept of what is "news."[49] In the Pew study noted above, the "news" included sports, science and technology, local weather and traffic, entertainment, crime, people and events in your community, and health and medicine. In sum, only a small fraction of the small minority of Americans with Twitter accounts follows what we call "hard news."

The Trump campaign claimed 20 million Twitter followers, a claim difficult to fact-check because Twitter audiences are difficult

---

/11/22/exclusive-interview-how-jared-kushner-won-trump-the-white -house/#23e54fea2f50.

48. Jeffrey Gottfried and Elisa Shearer, "News Use Across Social Media Platforms 2016," Pew Research Center, May 26, 2016, www.journalism.org/2016/05/26/news -use-across-social-media-platforms-2016/201, noting that 67 percent of adults use Facebook, but only 44 percent said it was a source of news. A study one year earlier found that 55 percent of adults said they get news from neither Facebook nor Twitter. Amy Mitchell and Dana Page, "The Evolving Role of News on Twitter and Facebook," Pew Research Center, July 14, 2015, www.journalism.org/files/2015/07 /Twitter-and-News-Survey-Report-FINAL2.pdf.

49. Hunt Allcott and Matthew Gentzkow, "Social Media and Fake News in the 2016 Election," working paper, January 18, 2017, https://web.stanford.edu /~gentzkow/research/fakenews.pdf.

TABLE 10.3. **Millions of Twitter Followers**

	Millions of Twitter Followers
Katy Perry	95.4
Justin Bieber	91.3
Barack Obama	80.7
Britney Spears	50
Kim Kardashian	49.6
CNN Breaking News	45.4
LeBron James	34.1
New York Times	33
ESPN	30.5
Bruno Mars	27.7
NBA	24.1
Pitbull	23.3
Kourtney Kardashian	21.7
NASA	21.2
Salman Kahn	20.5
Zayn	20.7
Donald Trump	16.9

to measure with any degree of accuracy. One analyst calculates that after adjusting for accounts that are inactive, zombies, or held by foreigners, the number of (American) Trump followers is probably closer to 4 million.[50] Moreover, most Twitter followers do not see what is tweeted.[51] But even taking highly inflated numbers as given, one early 2017 report put Trump's followers (17 million) as a small fraction of those who follow Katy Perry (95 million) or Kim Kardashian (49 million), LeBron James (34 million), Pitbull (who?) (23 million), and even Zayn (who?) (21 million).[52]

50. Rob Salkowitz, "Trump's 20 Million Twitter Followers Get Smaller under the Microscope," *Forbes*, January 17, 2017, www.forbes.com/sites/robsalkowitz/2017 /01/17/trumps-20-million-twitter-followers-get-smaller-under-the-microscope /#6084f458675b.

51. Danny Sullivan, "Just Like Facebook, Twitter's New Impression Stats Suggest Few Followers See What's Tweeted," *Marketing Land*, July 1, 2014, http://marketing land.com/facebook-twitter-impressions-90878.

52. "Twitter: Most Followed," *Friend or Follow*, http://friendorfollow.com/twitter /most-followers/.

Comey, Russians, Hollywood Access, Fake News, Etc.

Scholarly research and popular beliefs also conflict on a second subject: the importance of campaign events that receive so much coverage in the traditional media. Journalists tend to view campaigns like an athletic contest where a single excellent or disastrous play is a "game changer" that will shift momentum and ultimately be the turning point in determining the winner.[53] Once again, political scientists tend to be skeptical. Careful empirical research finds little evidence for such game changers.[54] Campaign effects tend to be small and transitory, in part because few people are paying much attention to them.

In 2016, this difference in popular and scholarly perspective emerged immediately after it became apparent that Trump would be president. Clinton supporters blamed the Comey letter, Wikileaks, Russian interference, and fake news, among other things. In a very close election, almost everything matters, of course, but one cannot pick and choose the events that went against your side and ignore those events and developments that went against the other side.[55] Determining whether campaign events mattered is particularly difficult in this case. The real question is whether they swung Michigan, Wisconsin, and Pennsylvania into Trump's camp. Moreover, there is a tendency for partisans to "come home" during the course of the campaign. Thus, Trump's numbers were expected to improve simply because his support among Republicans had more room to grow than did Clinton's among Democrats. Preliminary evidence is conflicting. Some see evidence of a "Comey effect" in state and national polls and early voting numbers.[56] Others see no close correspondence

53. John Heilemann and Mark Halperin, *Game Change* (New York: Harper-Collins, 2010).

54. John Sides and Lynn Vavreck, *The Gamble* (Princeton: Princeton University Press, 2013).

55. After the election, journalist Carl Cannon identified thirty-one reasons why Trump won. "How Donald Trump Won," *Real Clear Politics*, November 10, 2016, www.realclearpolitics.com/articles/2016/11/10/how_donald_trump_won_132321 .html.

56. Sean McElwee, Matt McDermott, and Will Jordan, "4 Pieces of Evidence Showing FBI Director James Comey Cost Clinton the Election," *Vox*, Janu-

between poll trends and major campaign developments: Clinton's numbers were rising while the Wikileaks releases were at their peak, and Trump's numbers had begun to rise before the Comey letter was released.[57] Yglesias argues that the problem faced by the Clinton campaign was real news, not fake news.[58]

Scholars are marshalling every bit of data they can get their hands on to study the questions arising from the 2016 campaign. Whether they can provide definitive answers remains to be seen. Consistent with past research, the first comprehensive study reports minimal campaign effects. After an intensive analysis of three different data-bases, Allcott and Gentzkow conclude that "even the most widely circulated fake news stories were seen by only a small fraction of Americans." Considering the counterfactual that fake news caused Hillary Clinton to lose Pennsylvania, Michigan, and Wisconsin, they calculate, "For fake news to have changed the election outcome, one fake news article would need to be 36 times as persuasive as one political ad."[59] Based on previous scholarly research, my expectation would be that campaign events in 2016 had little or no net effect on the outcome, subject to the aforementioned caveat that in such a close election everything mattered if everything else but that one thing is held constant. That is not to say that events like the Russian connection may not have important consequences—investigations are ongoing as I write—but only that the record of past research suggests that such campaign events had little effect on the election itself.

ary 11, 2017, www.vox.com/the-big-idea/2017/1/11/14215930/comey-email-election -clinton-campaign; Nate Silver, "How Much Did Comey Hurt Clinton's Chances?" *FiveThirty Eight,* November 6, 2016, https://fivethirtyeight.com/features/how-much -did-comey-hurt-clintons-chances/.

57. Harry Enten, "How Much Did Wikileaks Hurt Hillary Clinton?" *FiveThirty Eight,* November 6, 2016, fivethirtyeight.com/features/wikileaks-hillary-clinton/.

58. Matthew Yglesias, "Fake News Is a Convenient Scapegoat, but the Big 2016 Problem Was the Real News," *Vox,* December 5, 2015, www.vox.com/policy-and -politics/2016/12/15/13955108/fake-news-2016.

59. Allcott and Gentzkow, "Social Media and Fake News in the 2016 Elections."

The 2016 Presidential Election— Identities, Class, and Culture

The most qualified candidate in a generation was defeated by the least qualified of all time. That is what misogyny looks like, and, like all bigotries, it will end up dragging us all down.

—Hadley Freeman

2016 Was the Year White Liberals Realized How Unjust, Racist, and Sexist America Is.

—L. V. Anderson, *Slate*

These are good people, man! These aren't racists, these aren't sexists.

—Joe Biden

You have to accept that millions of people who voted for Barack Obama, some of them once, some of them twice, changed their minds this time. They're not racist. They twice voted for a man whose middle name is Hussein.

—Michael Moore

Quotations are from, in order: Hadley Freeman, "I've Heard Enough of the White Male Rage Narrative," *The Guardian*, November 10, 2016, https://www.theguardian .com/commentisfree/2016/nov/10/misogyny-us-election-voters; L. V. Anderson, "2016 Was the Year White Liberals Realized How Unjust, Racist, and Sexist America Is," *XX Factor* (blog), *Slate*, December 29, 2016, www.slate.com/blogs/xx_factor /2016/12/29/_2016_was_the_year_white_liberals_learned_about_disillusionment .html; Joe Biden, "White Working Class Not Racist, Sexist," interview with Jake Tapper, CNN, December 11, 2016, www.cnn.com/videos/tv/2016/12/11/sotu-biden -eaten-alive.cnn; and James Barrett, "Michael Moore Slaps Down Attempts to Smear Trump Voters as 'Racist,'" *Daily Wire*, November 12, 2016, www.dailywire.com/news /10742/michael-moore-slaps-down-attempts-smear-trump-james-barrett. It should be noted that Michael Moore was all over the map on this issue.

Nigel Farage in Great Britain, Donald Trump in the United States, Geert Wilders in Holland, Marine Le Pen in France—all would have represented fringe positions in the politics of their countries a decade or so ago. Not today. Although different in important respects, it is difficult to deny that recent elections reflect a general populist impulse now energizing the electorates of the Western democracies. Chapter 8 noted that explanations of the resurgence of populism fall into two general categories. One category condemns the populist impulse, considering it at best the scapegoating of ethnic and racial minorities in an era of economic difficulty and at worst as a xenophobic reaction to immigration and the resulting diversification of previously white societies. A second category recognizes real economic grievances held by certain sectors of native populations that are at least partly attributable to immigration, globalization, and other social and economic transformations. This second explanation tends to include an antiestablishment or antielite impulse that blames political and economic elites for not preventing economic difficulties, or at least alleviating them after the fact. And, everywhere, especially in the United States, the target list of the populist impulse has broadened to include cultural elites: the cosmopolitan denizens of our saltwater cities who now find themselves viewed as the opposition by many of those who reside in less urban and more peripheral parts of the country.

Some Basics

Hillary Clinton won the popular vote by a margin of almost 2.9 million votes, coming within 100,000 votes of Barack Obama's 2012 total. Trump received about 2 million votes more than Mitt Romney did in 2012. In percentage terms, Clinton won 48.5 percent of the vote to Trump's 46.4 percent. Turnout across the nation was about 60 percent of 232 million eligible Americans, a bit higher than in 2012 (58.6 percent).[1] Clinton's margin over Trump was lower than Obama's margin over Romney in thirty-seven states, however.

---

1. "2012 November General Election Turnout Rates," United States Election Project, www.electproject.org/2012g.

In particular, Trump improved on Romney's performance across the north-central United States, roughly from Pennsylvania to the Dakotas, flipping the battleground states of Ohio, Iowa, Wisconsin, Michigan, and Pennsylvania (plus Florida in the South). In the aggregate, 2016 voting statistics do not look very different from the 2012 statistics, so—as emphasized in the previous chapter—there is no sea change in voting that needs to be explained. But in a majoritarian system like ours, small changes on the margins can have major consequences.[2] Turnout and/or vote choices changed enough for Donald Trump to breach the "blue wall" that many pundits thought all but guaranteed Electoral College majorities for the Democrats.[3] Why?

Racism and Ethnocentrism

As quotations scattered through this chapter and the previous one indicate, for many disappointed supporters of Hillary Clinton the answer is all too clear: Trump's election represented a victory for racism, sexism, and deep-seated resentment of liberal social trends. Are some Americans bigots, misogynists, and/or homophobes? Of course. So are some Britons, French, Dutch, Germans—even Scandinavians.[4] But were these motivations more powerful in the 2016 voting than in other recent elections? There is no way to answer that question in this chapter. For four decades social scientists have debated the prevalence and power of racism with no apparent consensus, and no amount of studies employing contested measures seems likely to settle the debate.[5] But the claim that racism played a larger role in

2. For further discussion of aggregate similarities in the 2012 and 2016 voting, see David Brady and Brett Parker, *Now Is the Winter of our Discontent: The 2016 U.S. Presidential Election* (Basingstoke, UK: Palgrave Macmillan, forthcoming).

3. Ronald Brownstein, "Is Donald Trump Outflanking Hillary Clinton?" *The Atlantic*, November 2, 2016, www.theatlantic.com/amp/article/506306/.

4. "Populists in Europe (3/8): Danish Ethnocentrism," May 15, 2014, *La Redaction*, http://en.myeurop.info/2014/05/15/populists-europe-danish-ethnocentrism-13847.

5. The debate has multiple dimensions, starting with how to define racism and then to measure it. For critical discussions of two of the most commonly used measures, see Jesse Singal, "Psychology's Favorite Tool for Measuring Racism Isn't Up to the Job," *New York* magazine, January 11, 2017, http://nymag.com/scienceofus/2017/01/psychologys-racism-measuring-tool-isnt-up-to-the-job.html?mid=twitter_scienceofus; and Edward G. Carmines, Paul M. Sniderman, and

the 2016 election than in other recent elections must deal with several pieces of unsupportive data.

First, at the time of the election a clear majority of Americans approved of the performance of a black Democratic president; millions fewer of them voted for a white Democratic presidential candidate. Second, according to the exit polls, whites did not surge to the polls in unusually large numbers. If anything, Trump did ever so slightly *worse* among white voters than Romney did in 2012. Moreover, as noted in chapter 10, the Clinton campaign underperformed in many areas that gave majorities to Obama four and eight years ago. Of 676 counties that twice voted for Obama, almost a third (209) voted for Trump in 2016. On average, these counties were more than 80 percent white. Of course, such observations are subject to the standard ecological inference objection—we do not know *which* county residents voted and for whom they voted. With aggregate data alone, there is a logical possibility that white racists who had not voted in 2012 turned out in 2016, while white nonracists who voted in 2012 stayed home in 2016. If those flows were to offset, that would leave the net white vote for Trump more racist but about the same size as that for Romney. Such an argument seems tortured. But more important, the data shown in table 11.1 provide little support for it. In the Economist/YouGov panel, whites who did not vote in 2012 disproportionately supported Trump if they voted in 2016, but Clinton held scarcely two-thirds of white 2012 Obama voters, as one out of eight switched to Trump in 2016 and one out of five claimed they didn't vote.[6] Trump's gains from that defecting group were eight times larger than those from the 2012 white nonvoters who turned out to vote for him in 2016: white defection contributed far more to Clinton's loss than did a surge in white turnout.[7]

Beth C. Easter, 2011, "On the Meaning, Measurement, and Implications of Racial Resentment," *Annals of the American Academy of Political and Social Science* 634, no. 1 (March 2011): 98–116.

6. Only 4 percent of whites who voted for Romney in 2012 switched to Clinton in 2016. Early release ANES figures are consistent with the Economist/YouGov figures.

7. Early reports suggest that turnout increased among rural voters in some key states. So in, say, Michigan, where Clinton lost by less than 11,000 votes, turnout could have made the difference, *other things being equal.* Failure of minorities to turn out at Obama-election levels also could have made the difference, as could

TABLE 11.1. **How 2012 Voters Voted in 2016 (whites only)**

	Clinton	Trump	Other	DNV	n
Obama	64%	13	3	19	1233
Romney	3	78	4	15	897
Other	12	41	28	19	96
DNV	4	10	1	84	339

Source: Economist/YouGov Panel

All in all, those who believe racism propelled Trump's ascension to the presidency need to construct an argument that explains how racism would lead millions of whites who voted for and approved of a black president to desert a white Democrat.[8]

What about Hispanics? Given Trump's numerous ethnocentric comments, many commentators expected a doubly negative effect—outraged Hispanics would surge to the polls and vote even more Democratic than usual. Surprisingly, the evidence is conflicting. Following the election there was a vigorous debate about how Hispanics voted. The exit polls reported that Trump captured 28 percent of the Latino vote.[9] If this figure is accurate, Clinton's margin among Latinos was slightly *smaller* than Obama's in 2012. The Latino polling firm, Latino Decisions, vigorously disputed this finding, critiquing the methodology of the exit polls and concluding from their own polls that Trump received only 21 percent of the Latino vote in 2016.[10] The exit polls and Latino Decisions reported

---

defections among white Obama voters. Also, to repeat a point made earlier, a shift of a few thousand votes near the 50 percent line can produce major consequences without indicating a major shift in popular sentiment.

8. Despite the misleading title, one very preliminary analysis using a widely used measure of racism reported that Trump voters scored slightly *lower* on the scale than Romney voters. Thomas Wood, "Racism Motivated Trump Voters More Than Authoritarianism," *Washington Post,* April 17, 2017, https://www.washingtonpost.com/news/monkey-cage/wp/2017/04/17/racism-motivated-trump-voters-more-than-authoritarianism-or-income-inequality/.

9. Jens Manuel Krogstad and Mark Hugo Lopez, "Hillary Clinton Won Latino Vote but Fell Below 2012 Support for Obama," Pew Research Center, November 29, 2016, www.pewresearch.org/fact-tank/2016/11/29/hillary-clinton-wins-latino-vote-but-falls-below-2012-support-for-obama/.

10. Gabriel Sanchez and Matt A. Barreto, "In Record Numbers, Latinos Voted Overwhelmingly against Trump. We Did the Research," *Washington Post,* November 11,

nearly identical results in 2012, however, when both were presumably using the same methodologies as in 2016, so it is unclear why they would disagree in 2016 but not in 2012. A Washington Post/ABC News tracking poll conducted November 3–6 reported a figure (25 percent) halfway between the exit polls and Latino Decisions, as did the Economist/YouGov poll. Still other analyses support the exit poll figures, concluding that Trump did marginally better with Latinos than did Romney.[11]

Polling minority groups is difficult, as the previous conflicting studies suggest, so the exact Latino vote in 2016 will never be known. But at a minimum, and surprisingly, the aspersions Trump cast on Latinos during the campaign did not seem to put him at a significantly bigger disadvantage among that demographic than other Republicans since George W. Bush experienced.[12] Any additional negative associations attached to Trump appear to have been partially offset by other considerations among Latinos.

Gender

If it is difficult to make a convincing case that racism and ethnocentrism played an unusually prominent role in the 2016 voting, sexism provides an obvious alternative explanation.[13] Some analysts conclude that gender bias was an important component of support for Trump.[14] Nearly all polls reported that a majority of

2016, https://www.washingtonpost.com/news/monkey-cage/wp/2016/11/11/in-record-numbers-latinos-voted-overwhelmingly-against-trump-we-did-the-research/.

11. Harry Enten, "Trump Probably Did Better with Latino Voters Than Romney Did," *FiveThirtyEight,* November 18, 2016, https://fivethirtyeight.com/features/trump-probably-did-better-with-latino-voters-than-romney-did/.

12. For a useful compilation of polling on Latino voting going back to 1960, see Alvaro Corral, David L. Leal, and Joe Tafoya, "Introduction: The 2008 Primary and General Election Campaign," in *Latinos and the 2008 Elections: Can You Hear Us Now?* ed. David L. Leal, Rodolfo de la Garza, and Louis DeSipio (forthcoming).

13. In common usage, misogyny is the stronger term, implying hatred of women. Sexism is less hostile, even at times perhaps "benevolent." Peter Glick and Susan T. Fiske, "The Ambivalent Sexism Inventory: Differentiating Hostile and Benevolent Sexism," *Journal of Personality and Social Psychology* 70, no. 3 (1996): 491–512.

14. Carly Wayne, Nicholas Valentino, and Marzia Oceno, "How Sexism Drives Support for Donald Trump," *Washington Post,* October 23, 2016, https://www

women intended to vote for Clinton whereas a majority of men generally supported Trump, and the gender gap among actual voters in the exit polls was 14 percent. But as Burden, Crawford, and DeCrescenzo caution, "this disparity between the sexes is larger than gaps observed in previous elections, but not by much. It is only three points larger than the gap in 2012 and just two points larger than it was in 2000."[15] Moreover, *women*'s support for Clinton was slightly *lower* than their support for Obama in both 2008 and 2012 (men were lower still). Table 11.2 lists the figures for various subgroups of men and women in the Economist/YouGov panel. Black and Latino women voted very heavily for Clinton, a bit more than black and Latino men. White women also voted more heavily for Clinton than men did. Such figures are consistent with the existence of sexism, but they are fairly typical of recent elections and not significantly larger, which we would expect if sexism were an especially important factor in 2016. Moreover, a majority of white women voted for Trump. Does it make sense to conclude that a majority of white women are sexist? Some commentators say yes—women are victims of false consciousness, as Marxists used to say.[16]

An alternative view is that most women have multiple identities, some of which are more important than their identities as feminists. The popular stereotype (probably promoted more by critics than sympathizers) holds that identification as a feminist is most prevalent among single, white women who are college educated, working full time, and economically secure.[17] Conversely, feminist identity would

---

.washingtonpost.com/news/monkey-cage/wp/2016/10/23/how-sexism-drives-support-for-donald-trump/.

15. Barry C. Burden, Evan Crawford, and Michael G. DeCrescenzo, "The Unexceptional Gender Gap of 2016," *De Gruyter* 14, no. 4 (December 2016), https://www.degruyter.com/downloadpdf/j/for.2016.14.issue-4/for-2016-0039/for-2016-0039.pdf.

16. In a letter to the editor, a leader of a liberal women's group wrote condescendingly, "I still find it shocking that women could excuse a presidential candidate whose own demeaning and offensive recorded words were not sufficient to prevent them from voting for him. It must be a reflection of very low self-esteem." Marcia Herman, "Paths for Feminism after the Election," *New York Times*, January 9, 2017.

17. Surprisingly, there does not seem to be an extensive descriptive literature on who adopts the feminist identity. Rating "feminists" higher on the ANES feeling thermometer is significantly associated with being female, of course, and also

TABLE 11.2. The Gender Gap in 2016

	Clinton	Trump
Black Women	90%	3
Black Men	83	13
Latino Women	70	23
Latino Men	62	26
White Women	42	51
White Men	31	60

Source: Economist/YouGov Panel

rank lower among married white women with children (especially male children), without college degrees, whose lives are economically stressed and/or insecure. As Tina Brown writes, "The angry white working class men who voted in such strength for Trump do not live in an emotional vacuum. They are loved by white working class women—their wives, daughters, sisters and mothers, who participate in their remaindered pain."[18]

Political science studies are not unanimous, but some solid empirical research concludes that sexism is not a major factor when female candidates run for election.[19] And, as discussed in chapter 10, in the case of Hillary Clinton sexism must compete with other explanations for voting against her, most prominently the perception that she was an untrustworthy, inauthentic candidate. As political scientist Jennifer Lawless commented, "People have vehement reactions to her in one direction or another, and have for 20 years. So I've

college educated, especially postgraduate education, unmarried, especially never married, and age (over fifty). Although statistically significant, these relationships are substantively weak. Melody Rodriguez, "Women United: Feminist Identification as Measured by ANES Data," unpublished seminar paper, Stanford University.

18. In a further comment that caused considerable outrage, Brown adds, "There are more tired wives who want to be Melania sitting by the pool in designer sunglasses than there are women who want to pursue a PhD in earnest self-improvement. And there are more young women who see the smartness and modernity of Ivanka as the ultimate polished specimen of blonde branded content they want to buy." Many comments on Brown's article were "removed by a moderator because it didn't abide by our community standards." Tina Brown, "My Beef over Hillary Clinton's Loss Is with Liberal Feminists, Young and Old," The Guardian, November 13, 2016, https://www.theguardian.com/commentisfree/2016/nov/12/hillary-clinton-liberal-feminists.

19. Danny Hayes and Jennifer Lawless, Women on the Run: Gender, Media, and Political Campaigns in a Polarized Era (New York: Cambridge University Press, 2016).

often said that if people are fundamentally opposed to her, I'm not convinced that it's sexism; it could be 'Clinton-ism.'"[20]

How can we account for the apparent absence of strong and unambiguous evidence for an increased racial, ethnic, and gender dimension in the 2016 voting, when so many commentators view these as important—if not the most important—explanations of the 2016 voting? Earlier chapters, especially chapter 5, provide part of the answer. The priorities of the political class and normal voters differ considerably. Surveys show that issues of race, gender, and sexual orientation are more important for the former than the latter, especially among educated, affluent liberals.[21] Moreover, liberal activists are quick to see racism and sexism at work (e.g., "dog whistles") where less politically involved people see more innocent explanations. Mainstream journalists and media commentators are part of the political class and so tend to share these tendencies.

What Happened to the RAE?

Chapter 6 discussed what political commentators variously refer to as the rising American electorate, the new American majority, or the coalition of the ascendant—the notion that demographic trends are inexorably moving the country in a Democratic direction.[22] Such trends suggested that the "Obama coalition" would only grow larger in the coming decades. Most importantly, projections from birth rates indicated that the country would become majority-minority by 2044; Latinos in particular would become an increasingly large proportion of the electorate.[23] Additionally, declining

20. Linda Feldmann, "Hillary Clinton's Challenge: Sexism or 'Clinton-ism'?" *Christian Science Monitor,* September 30, 2015, www.csmonitor.com/USA/Politics/2015/0930/Hillary-Clinton-s-challenge-Sexism-or-Clinton-ism.

21. Variously referred to as "limousine liberals" or "gentry liberals" in recognition of their prioritization of nonmaterial issues. Joel Kotkin and Fred Siegel, "The Gentry Liberals," *Los Angeles Times,* December 2, 2007, http://articles.latimes.com/2007/dec/02/opinion/op-kotkin2.

22. Ronald Brownstein, "The Clinton Conundrum," *The Atlantic,* April 17, 2015, https://www.theatlantic.com/politics/archive/2015/04/the-clinton-conundrum/431949/.

23. US Census Bureau. Using a narrower definition, the Pew Research Center pushes the date of a majority-minority country further out to 2055.

marriage rates suggested that the number of single, working women would increase and rising educational levels indicated that the voting power of socially liberal young college graduates would grow. To some Democrats these trends suggested that majority party status was inevitable. The only question was: How soon?

I noted possible problems with the RAE thesis in chapter 6. First, it depended on two critical *ceteris paribus* assumptions. The first was that the groups rising in number would maintain or even strengthen their Democratic allegiances. But over the span of decades a group's political allegiances can change. Catholics, for example, were heavily Democratic before 1968, less so afterward. As a group's cultural or economic positions change, its political positions follow. Moreover, the parties can reorient their platforms. If demographic trends are working against a party—Republican in this case—one should expect that eventually the party will change its platform to meet the challenge. Of course, given Donald Trump's position on immigration and his remarks about women, there is no indication as yet that such a Republican reorientation is under way.

A second assumption was that emphasis on the RAE would not cause a loss of support among whites who came to see the Democratic Party as representing the interests of other racial and ethnic groups at the expense of whites. The 2016 voting may have demonstrated the fragility of this assumption. As David Dayen comments, "Democrats comforted themselves with the emergence of a new majority of women, Latinos, African-Americans, Asian-Americans, gays and lesbians, immigrants, and Muslims. . . . placing such a big bet on so fragile a coalition looks to have been unwise. It left behind people who voted twice for Obama in the process."[24]

More recently, demographers have pointed out a more fundamental problem: census figures exaggerate the most important demographic trend underlying the RAE thesis—the growth in minorities. The definition used by the US Census Bureau maximizes the number of minority group members by classifying anyone who does not have

---

24. David Dayen, "The 'Deplorables' Got the Last Laugh," *New Republic*, November 9, 2016, https://newrepublic.com/article/138615/deplorables-got-last-laugh.

two Anglo-white parents as a minority.[25] But interracial and inter-ethnic marriage rates have risen sharply and are expected to con-tinue to do so. Research to date indicates that some of the children of such marriages will identify as white, and few of them consider their mixed-race heritage a disadvantage.[26] So the future proportion of Americans who identify as minority rather than white is lower than common calculations indicate. Consequently, how much the increasing diversity of the country will produce increasing support for the Democrats is even more uncertain than the first two assump-tions suggest.[27]

Class Conflict: The Revolt of the Masses?[28]

No election in recent decades has seen so much attention paid to the "working class." Accelerating with the splintering of the Democratic Party in the mid- to late 1960s, the importance of social class as an electoral cleavage slipped behind cleavages based on race and ethnic-ity, religion, gender, and sexual orientation.[29] But for many commen-tators—on both sides of the political spectrum—the 2016 election witnessed a revolt of the masses. *New York Times* columnist Frank Bruni writes, "The arc of this election has been one of disillusion-ment, bending toward disarray. Trump's initial window of oppor-tunity was so many Americans' belief that Washington, Wall Street and the media had been irredeemably corrupted by self-interested

---

25. Richard Alba, "The Likely Persistence of a White Majority," *American Prospect*, January 11, 2016, http://prospect.org/article/likely-persistence-white-majority-0.

26. "Multiracial in America," Pew Research Center, June 11, 2015, www.pew socialtrends.org/2015/06/11/multiracial-in-america/.

27. For the most comprehensive study of mixed-race Americans, see Lauren Davenport, *Politics beyond Black and White: Multiracial Identity and Attitudes in America* (New York: Cambridge University Press, forthcoming).

28. José Ortega y Gasset, *The Revolt of the Masses* (New York: W. W. Norton, 1932).

29. Despite popular perceptions, the importance of income as an electoral cleavage did not decrease during this period. If anything, it increased. See Morris P. Fiorina, with Samuel J. Abrams and Jeremy C. Pope, *Culture War? The Myth of a Polarized America* (Harlow, UK: Longman, 2010), 135–38.

elites."[30] On the other side of the political spectrum, *Wall Street Journal* columnist Peggy Noonan writes about those whom she calls the "protected":

> The protected make public policy. The unprotected live in it. The unprotected are starting to push back, powerfully. . . . [The protected] are figures in government, politics and media. They live in nice neighborhoods, safe ones. Their families function, their kids go to good schools, they've got some money. All of these things tend to isolate them, or provide buffers.[31]

Antielitism has a long history in the United States, of course, more so than in some European countries like Britain where the "upper" classes historically had been accorded "deference." Chapter 9 discussed the contemporary recurrence of a number of the social and economic dislocations the United States experienced in the late nineteenth-century populist era. Antielitism then focused on economic elites—the trusts, the moneyed interests, those who (in presidential candidate William Jennings Bryan's words) "would crucify mankind on a cross of gold." And it was only a short move from there to an attack on the politicians who were controlled by the economic elites.

In the contemporary era, the crash of 2008 precipitated the Great Recession. Irresponsible and even fraudulent financial practices were all too apparent, but economic elites responsible for them paid only a token price. Then Treasury secretary Tim Geithner may be correct in asserting that the bailouts were necessary to save the economy, but it was not necessary for him to pressure AIG to pay off Goldman Sachs 100 cents on the dollar, then to pressure Attorney General Eric Holder to quash criminal indictments in the HSBC case.[32] The bail-

30. Frank Bruni, "Why This Election Terrifies Me," *New York Times*, November 5, 2016, https://www.nytimes.com/2016/11/06/opinion/sunday/why-this-election-terrifies-me.html?_r=0.

31. Peggy Noonan, "Trump and the Rise of the Unprotected," *Wall Street Journal,* February 25, 2016, https://www.wsj.com/articles/trump-and-the-rise-of-the-unprotected-1456448550.

32. Michael Corkery, "AIG Bailout Keeps Dogging Tim Geithner," *Deal Journal* (blog), *Wall Street Journal*, January 7, 2010, http://blogs.wsj.com/deals/2010/01

outs and resulting deficits contributed to the rise of the tea party and then the Democratic Party's electoral debacle in 2010.

The status quo election of 2012 may have suggested that the populist moment had passed, but the 2016 campaigns suggest otherwise. Popular resentment seemed to shift its focus away from economic elites and more in the direction of political elites who had failed to control or even abetted the actions of economic elites. Bernie Sanders and Trump attacked outsourcing, free trade agreements, tax provisions, and other economic policies supported by both parties that hurt some Americans. Sanders charged that the Democratic Party had become too dependent on Wall Street for financing, with resultant inattention to the economic distress experienced by many Americans. The establishments in both parties attempted to squelch the Sanders and Trump insurgencies—successfully in the case of Sanders, failing completely in the case of Trump—but in both cases reinforcing the grievances of their supporters and adding to the perception that party leaders were allied to a corrupt status quo. Some commentators, including *Washington Post* writer Marc Fisher, see this as the fertile soil in which Trumpism grew:

> Trump ran against the elites and won. . . . He defined the election as a people's uprising against all the institutions that had let them down and sneered at them—the politicians and the parties, the Washington establishment, the news media, Hollywood, academia, all of the affluent, highly educated sectors of society that had done well during the time when middle-class families were losing their bearings.
>
> . . .
>
> All he had to do, he said, was connect directly to the pains, fears and frustrations of a nation that had been smacked around by globalization, terrorism, rapid demographic change, and a technological revolution that enriched and enraptured the kids with

/07/aig-bailout-keeps-dogging-tim-geithner/; William K. Black, "The Second Great Betrayal: Obama and Cameron Decide That Banks Are above the Law," *New Economic Perspectives,* December 17, 2012, http://neweconomicperspectives.org/2012 /12/the-second-great-betrayal-obama-and-cameron-decide-that-banks-are-above -the-law.html.

the stratospheric SAT scores, but left millions of Americans watching their jobs fall victim to the latest apps, overseas outsourcing, robots, and a stunning shift in the nature of commerce and community.[33]

As such charges indicate, the notion of "elites" today has broadened to include cultural elites—people who work in academia, the professions, the entertainment industry, the media, and the higher levels of government, most of whom have advanced educations, if not always exceptional incomes. This appears to be something relatively new, perhaps because the cultural elite a century ago likely would have been a subset of the small economic elite. Most Americans then engaged in manual rather than mental labor and very few went to college—few Americans even graduated from high school, let alone college.[34]

The first indications of a backlash against cultural elites became apparent in the 1960s with the third-party candidacy of George Wallace. The economy was fine and for a time only got better as the Vietnam War ramped up, but racial disorders and the rise of the counterculture made the "pointy headed intellectuals" who excused them a target.[35] So were anarchists, a "catch-all term that could mean students, liberals, the press, militants, etc., depending on the occasion." In an eerie foreshadowing of Trump's rhetoric, Wallace threatened, "I want to say that anarchists—and I am talking about newsmen sometimes—I want to say—I want to make that announcement to you because we regard that the people of this country are sick and tired of, and they are gonna get rid of you— anarchists."[36]

33. Marc Fisher, "How Donald Trump Broke the Old Rules of Politics—and Won the White House," *Washington Post,* November 9, 2016, https://www.washington post.com/politics/how-donald-trump-broke-the-old-rules-of-politics--and-won-the -white-house/2016/11/09/f3190498-a5e1-11e6-8fc0-7be8f848c492_story.html.

34. US Census Bureau, "A Century of Change: America, 1900–1999," https:// msu.edu/~bsilver/pls440century.html.

35. Quotations from Marianne Worthington, "The Campaign Rhetoric of George Wallace in the 1968 Presidential Election," www.ucumberlands.edu/downloads /academics/history/vol4/MarianneWorthington92.html.

36. Ibid.

The spread of mass education (today about 30 percent of the over-twenty-five population has a bachelor's degree) and other social and economic developments have spawned a large upper-middle class whose tastes and lifestyles often differ from those lower on the economic ladder. Although they generally deny it, many of those in the new class feel a degree of condescension or disdain for the middle- and lower-middle-class people who populate the heartland.[37] As Andrew Sullivan writes:

> Much of the newly energized left has come to see the white working class not as allies but primarily as bigots, misogynists, racists, and homophobes, thereby condemning those often at the near-bottom rung of the economy to the bottom rung of the culture as well. . . . They [the white working class] smell the condescension and the broad generalizations about them—all of which would be repellent if directed at racial minorities.[38]

The 2016 election gave such people the opportunity to strike back.[39]

37. Yes, this is a subjective judgment by someone who grew up in the epicenter of Trump country but has been fortunate to live life as one of Noonan's "protecteds." See also Christopher Lasch, *The Revolt of the Elites and the Betrayal of Democracy*, rev. ed. (New York: W. W. Norton, 1996); Christopher Hayes. *Twilight of the Elites: America after Meritocracy* (New York: Broadway, 2012); and Katherine J. Cramer, *The Politics of Resentment: Rural Consciousness in Wisconsin and the Rise of Scott Walker* (Chicago: University of Chicago Press, 2016).

38. Andrew Sullivan, "Democracies End When They Are Too Democratic. And Right Now, America Is a Breeding Ground for Tyranny," *New York* magazine, May 1, 2016, http://nymag.com/daily/intelligencer/2016/04/america-tyranny-donald -trump.html.

39. Another indication of cultural condescension was the spate of articles, many barely rising above the psychobabble level, explaining that loss of social status among white men led them to support Trump. After the election, blogger Glenn Reynolds suggested that the furious reaction to Trump's victory indicated that the shoe had been transferred to the other foot—educated supporters of Clinton now were the ones suffering status anxiety: "Now that Trump has won, people are, in fact, a lot less respectful of the traditional academic and media and political elites. Trump didn't just beat them, after all. He also humiliated them, as they repeatedly assured everyone (and each other) that he had no chance. It's a huge blow to the self-importance of a lot of people. No wonder they're still lashing out." Glenn Reynolds, "New Status Anxiety Fuels Trump Derangement," *USA Today*, January 5, 2017, www.usatoday .com/story/opinion/2017/01/05/gentry-liberals-trump-college-campuses-elite-glenn -reynolds-column/96155458/.

As suggested in chapter 10, the mainstream media's strong opposition to Donald Trump may well have helped him. Much more than in earlier decades, today's media are concentrated in the wealthiest locales in America. New York is not on the list of cities bypassed by the recovery and the Washington, DC, area is recession proof in addition to being wealthy.[40] Why should condemnation of Trump by such fortunate people carry any weight with voters living in Michigan or Pennsylvania?[41] And did Democratic elites really think so little of such Americans to believe that Katy Perry, Beyoncé, and Madonna would sway their votes?[42] *The Atlantic*'s Caitlin Flanagan made an intriguing argument that even the heavily anti-Trump tenor of late-night comedy shows actually helped Trump:

> Though aimed at blue-state sophisticates, these shows are an unintended but powerful form of propaganda for conservatives. When Republicans see these harsh jokes—which echo down through the morning news shows and the chattering day's worth of viral clips, along with those of Jimmy Kimmel, Stephen Colbert, and Seth Meyers—they don't just see a handful of comics mocking them. They see HBO, Comedy Central, TBS, ABC, CBS, and NBC.

40. Jack Shafer and Tucker Doherty, "The Media Bubble Is Worse Than You Think," *Politico*, May/June 2017, www.politico.com/magazine/story/2017/04/25/media-bubble-real-journalism-jobs-east-coast-215048.

41. The elite media seemed to take a surprisingly long time to recognize this. After Trump had been in office nearly a month, Chris Cillizza wrote, "Trump understands something very important: For his supporters, the media represent everything they dislike about American society. The media is composed, to their mind, of Ivy-League-educated coastal elites who look down their noses at the average person, dismissing them and their views as stupid and ill-informed. For people who feel like their voices weren't and aren't heard in politics—or culture more broadly—the media is the perfect scapegoat." Duh! Chris Cillizza, "Donald Trump Delivers a Series of Raw and Personal Attacks on the Media in a News Conference for the Ages," *Washington Post*, February 16, 2017, https://www.washingtonpost.com/news/the-fix/wp/2017/02/16/donald-trump-delivers-a-series-of-raw-and-wild-attacks-on-the-media-in-a-press-conference-for-the-ages/?utm_term=.875b89150fcf.

42. One poll of Ohio voters found that celebrity endorsements could be harmful to candidates' support. Beyonce's endorsement made 20 percent of voters less likely to vote for Clinton and Lena Dunham's endorsement made 12 percent of voters less likely to vote for Clinton. On the other side, Ted Nugent's endorsement made 13 percent of voters less likely to vote for Trump. "The BGSU Poll," Bowling Green State University, www.bgsu.edu/bgsupoll.

In other words, they see exactly what Donald Trump has taught them: that the entire media landscape loathes them, their values, their family, and their religion. It is hardly a reach for them to further imagine that the legitimate news shows on these channels are run by similarly partisan players—nor is it at all illogical. No wonder so many of Trump's followers are inclined to believe only the things that he or his spokespeople tell them directly—everyone else on the tube thinks they're a bunch of trailer-park, Oxy-snorting half-wits who divide their time between retweeting Alex Jones fantasies and ironing their Klan hoods.[43]

People who enjoy elite status tend to lose touch with the interests and concerns of nonelites. Progressive Mike Gecan writes, "Many Dems either don't know how to relate to people with moderate or mixed views or they don't want to. They prefer rock stars and celebrities to bus drivers and food service workers. They like cute sayings and clever picket signs, not long and patient listening sessions with people who have complicated interests, people who might not pass the liberal litmus test."[44] In a similar vein, the rant by former MSNBC commentator Krystal Ball is worth quoting at length:

They said they were facing an economic apocalypse, we offered "retraining" and complained about their white privilege. Is it any wonder we lost? One after another, the dispatches came back from the provinces. The coal mines are gone, the steel mills are closed, the drugs are rampant, the towns are decimated and everywhere you look depression, despair, fear. In the face of Trump's willingness to boldly proclaim without facts or evidence that he would bring the good times back, we offered a tepid gallows logic. Well, those jobs are actually gone for good, we knowingly told them. And we offered a fantastical non-solution. We will retrain you for

43. Caitlin Flanagan, "How Late-Night Comedy Fueled the Rise of Trump," *The Atlantic,* May 2017, https://www.theatlantic.com/magazine/archive/2017/05/how-late-night-comedy-alienated-conservatives-made-liberals-smug-and-fueled-the-rise-of-trump/521472/.

44. Mike Gecan, "How Democrats Are Getting Played," *New York Daily News,* February 2, 2017, www.nydailynews.com/opinion/democrats-played-article-1.2961872. Gecan is codirector of the progressive Industrial Areas Foundation.

good jobs! Never mind that these "good jobs" didn't exist in East
Kentucky or Cleveland. And as a final insult, we lectured a strug-
gling people watching their kids die of drug overdoses about their
white privilege. Can you blame them for calling bullshit? All Trump
could offer was white nationalism as protection against competing
with black and brown people. It wasn't a very compelling case, but
it was vastly superior to a candidate who enthusiastically backed
NAFTA, seems most at ease in a room of Goldman Sachs bankers
and was almost certain to do nothing for these towns other than
maybe setting up a local chapter of Rednecks Who Code.[45]

While recent political commentary suggests the importance of
sentiments like those expressed in the preceding quotations, evidence needed to evaluate them is hard to come by—surveys include
measures of racism and sexism, however imperfect—but to my
knowledge our major databases include few time series measures of
class identity or resentment.[46] Blunt indicators—education, income,
occupation—are the measures most commonly used by those who
study class.

In the aftermath of the election, political commentary emphasized
the divide between the college educated and those with no degrees.
The exit polls reported that college graduates cast a majority for
Clinton, nongraduates a majority for Trump. White college graduates cast a narrow plurality for Trump, however, as female graduates cast a majority for Clinton and men for Trump. The Economist/
YouGov panel study allows a finer breakdown (table 11.3) that
reveals some additional significant nuances. The common observation that among whites only female college graduates cast a majority
for Clinton overlooks an important distinction: Hillary Clinton at

45. Krystal Ball, "The Democratic Party Deserved to Die," *Huffington Post*,
November 10, 2016.

46. The major exception is the "subjective class identification" item that I am
currently analyzing. Recognizing the (hypothesized) reemergence of class cleavages,
the 2016 ANES does include class measures, but the absence of such measures in
past surveys hinders our capacity to understand the contribution of class to the 2016
election. For a good discussion of the myriad issues surrounding the study of class
differences in voting, see Jeffrey M. Stonecash, "The Puzzle of Class in Presidential
Voting," *The Forum* 15 (2017): 29–49.

TABLE 11.3. Class Voting in 2016 (whites only)

	Clinton	Trump	n
Men—High School	15%	80	192
Women—High School	26	69	328
Men Some College	26	63	391
Women Some College	37	53	497
Men College Grad	35	55	348
Women College Grad	46	49	353
Men Post-grad	45	48	235
Women Post-grad	58	36	231

Source: Economist/YouGov Panel

best broke even among white women with only four-year degrees; only among postgraduate women do we find majority support for Clinton. Interestingly, despite the attention focused on less-educated whites, the gender gap if anything is largest among those with postgraduate degrees, where men broke evenly or even slightly for Trump. The sobering reality for the Democratic Party is that it did not just have a problem with white working class men in 2016; it appears to have lost the white middle class—men and women—as well, albeit more narrowly.

A Final Thought

During the campaign, Trump made a number of highly implausible claims: he would build a great wall between the United States and Mexico, which Mexico would pay for; he would deport 11 million illegal immigrants. Such claims were ridiculed by the mainstream media, who jumped to the conclusion that anyone who supported Trump on the basis of his campaign promises must be a gullible yahoo. But I think that Trump-country journalist Salena Zito got it right in one of the most frequently quoted comments of the campaign: "When he makes claims like this, the press takes him literally, but not seriously; his supporters take him seriously, but not literally."[47] Polls showed that voters did not really expect Trump to

47. Salena Zito, "Taking Trump Seriously, not Literally," September 23, 2016, https://www.theatlantic.com/politics/archive/2016/09/trump-makes-his-case-in-pittsburgh/501335/.

carry out his more outlandish promises.[48] Apparently, though, they were not put off by the direction he wanted the country to take.

Such sentiments suggest that political scientists might take another look at a controversial theory—directional voting. Briefly, standard models of electoral competition assume proximity voting—a citizen votes for the candidate closer to her on the issues. The directional voting theory holds that between two candidates on opposite sides of the neutral point (or status quo), citizens vote for a candidate on the same side as they are, even if the candidate's promise far overshoots the voter's own position.[49] A voter on the right (left) prefers any candidate on the right (left) so long as the candidate's position stays within some broad "range of acceptability." While the argument sounds implausible at first, one could motivate it by positing that citizens understand that they are not voting for a dictator. No matter what the president wants to do, his actual achievements in a system of shared powers with checks and balances inevitably will fall short. Hence, voters far more moderate than Trump on immigration, the environment, LGBT issues, and so on might still support him because they estimate that his administration's results will likely move the status quo toward them rather than away from them. Figure 11.1 illustrates the case for immigration. At the extreme left of the dimension there is zero immigration, and undocumented persons are to be rounded up and sent home. At the opposite end of the dimension borders are open and immigrants are eligible for the same government benefits as citizens. Voter V is in the middle. She perceives the policy status quo, SQ, as more liberal than she would prefer. Trump's announced position, T, is much farther away from her on the other side, so a Democrat who endorses the status quo is closer to her. But appreciating all the frictions in the system,

48. In an early-September ABC News/Washington Post poll, 76 percent of respondents said they did not believe Trump would build the wall and make Mexico pay for it. And polls showed that even a majority of Trump voters did not favor deporting all undocumented immigrants.

49. Steven A. Matthews, "A Simple Direction Model of Electoral Competition," *Public Choice* 34 (1979): 141–56; George Rabinowitz and Stuart Elaine Macdonald, "A Directional Theory of Issue Voting," *American Political Science Review* 83, no. 1 (March 1989): 93–121.

FIGURE 11.1 Directional Voting

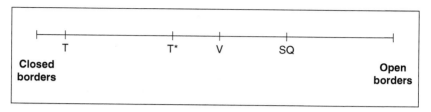

V estimates that Trump could actually move the status quo no farther than T*, which is closer to her than the status quo. Hence she
votes for an extreme candidate even though her own preferences are
much more moderate. Earlier studies report inconclusive empirical
support for the theory, but 2016 may offer a favorable context in
which to revisit it.[50]

50. Jeffrey B. Lewis and Gary King, "No Evidence on Directional vs. Proximity
Voting," *Political Analysis* 8, no. 1 (1999): 21–33.

CHAPTER 12

Where To Now?

Writing a sensible concluding chapter five months after Donald Trump's inauguration is a fool's errand. Thus, this final chapter eschews conclusions; I only offer some observations about the current discontent. Firm conclusions must await the passage of time to make clearer the implications and consequences of the elections.

A Time of Doom and Gloom

"American democracy is doomed." So said Matthew Yglesias a year before the elections.[1]

"America has never been so ripe for tyranny" opined Andrew Sullivan six months before the elections.[2] Sullivan added "America and the Abyss" a few days before the elections.[3]

The day after the elections, David Remnick pronounced the results "An American Tragedy."[4]

1. Matthew Yglesias, "American Democracy Is Doomed," *Vox,* October 8, 2015, accessed July 5, 2017, https://www.vox.com/2015/3/2/8120063/american-democracy -doomed.

2. Andrew Sullivan, "Democracies End When They Are Too Democratic," *New York* magazine, May 1, 2016, accessed July 5, 2017, http://nymag.com/daily/intelligencer /2016/04/america-tyranny-donald-trump.html.

3. Andrew Sullivan, "America and the Abyss," *New York* magazine, November 3, 2016, accessed July 5, 2017, http://nymag.com/daily/intelligencer/2016/11/andrew -sullivan-trump-america-and-the-abyss.html.

4. David Remnick, "An American Tragedy," *New Yorker,* November 9, 2016, accessed July 5, 2017, www.newyorker.com/news/news-desk/an-american-tragedy-2.

In mid-December Robert Kuttner asked "Can American fascism be stopped?"[5]

A few days after the inauguration Dennis Prager pronounced, "America is currently fighting its Second Civil War."[6]

Soon after, David Frum outlined his fears in "How to Build an Autocracy" and Ezra Klein offered advice on "How to Stop an Autocracy."[7]

So, in the judgment of various journalists and politicos the United States is on a fast track to autocracy, fascism, civil war, and ultimately doom. This stream of alarmist commentary shows no signs of abating. Only eight years after an election about "hope and change," many would describe the present mood of the country as one of fear and change.

Although more unnerved by the actions of Donald Trump to date than by those of any other president in my lifetime, I am less pessimistic than commentators like those quoted above. Four reasons underlie my belief that the country is not perched on the brink of the abyss.

First, as noted several times in preceding chapters, in broad outline the 2016 voting was not that different from the voting in 2012. In our electoral system, small changes in the vote can produce major consequences in institutional control and public policies. Knowing that, one cannot assume that an election outcome that is consequential implies that the electorate or some large segment of it intended those consequences. As discussed in chapters 10 and 11, the evidence so far leads me to the preliminary conclusion that the most negative characterizations of the electorate—racist, sexist, fascist—are reflections of disappointment and frustration more than evidence.

5. Robert Kuttner, "The Audacity of Hope," *American Prospect,* December 16, 2016, accessed July 5, 2017, http://prospect.org/article/audacity-hope.

6. Dennis Prager, "America's Second Civil War," *DennisPrager.com,* January 24, 2017, accessed July 5, 2017, www.dennisprager.com/americas-second-civil-war.

7. David Frum, "How to Build an Autocracy," *The Atlantic,* March 2017, accessed July 5, 2017, https://www.theatlantic.com/magazine/archive/2017/03/how-to-build-an-autocracy/513872; Ezra Klein, "How to Stop an Autocracy," *Vox,* February 7, 2017, accessed July 5, 2017, https://www.vox.com/policy-and-politics/2017/2/7/14454370/trump-autocracy-congress-frum.*

Americans who voted for Barack Obama in 2012 did not vote for Donald Trump because their moral character had degenerated over the course of the intervening four years.

Second, after the elections a teacher asked plaintively, "What can I tell my students?" A wise historian answered, "The most important thing you can tell your students, Jessica, is that we have worked through these upheavals before and although the road forward was often rough we managed in the process to enlarge the reach of the American dream."[8] Some may dismiss such sentiments as mere platitudes, but such dismissals reflect ignorance. One of the unfortunate consequences of the demise of survey courses on American history in our schools and universities is the widespread ignorance of the extent of conflict and violence in this country's history. Racial violence is taught, but rarely ethnic violence and labor violence.[9] The disagreement and disorder that characterize politics today are not historically unique. On the contrary, they are of a lower order of intensity even compared to the disruptions of the 1960s. Daniel Kevles's observation reflects historical knowledge, not just hope.

Third, as Francis Fukuyama argues, "America's institutional system is stronger than portrayed."[10] Over the decades, political commentary seems to alternate between fears of an imperial presidency on the one hand and of a president fettered by institutional constraints on the other. Even a Republican Congress, a predominantly

8. Daniel Kevles, "Teaching Trump," *Huffington Post*, November 21, 2016, accessed July 5, 2017, www.huffingtonpost.com/entry/plenty-to-tell-your-students _us_58254fdae4b0852d9ec213ee.

9. However oppressed some immigrants feel today, their reception is worlds more kindly than that accorded to the Irish in the 1840s, the Chinese in the 1880s, and the eastern and southern Europeans at the turn of the twentieth century. To say that the United States is a country of immigrants is not to say that it was ever Mr. Rogers's Neighborhood. Moving to economic discontent, the Occupy and other protests about inequality pale in comparison to the pitched battles strikers fought with the armed forces of the government in the nineteenth and early twentieth centuries. For example, Google "Homestead Strike" "Pullman Strike," "Ludlow Strike," "Battle of Blair Mountain."

10. Francis Fukuyama, "Is American Democracy Strong Enough for Trump?" *Politico*, January 23, 2017, accessed July 5, 2017, www.politico.com/magazine/story /2017/01/donald-trump-american-democracy-214683.

Republican judiciary, and Republican appointees in the bureaucracy will not automatically bow to any president's orders.[11] Our institutions are not as fragile as many fear. They have lasted some two centuries and have frustrated presidents throughout our history. There is no reason to believe they will not continue to do so, particularly as the disarray of the Trump administration mounts.

Fourth, and related to the first, I agree with Robert Merry's observation: "When a man as uncouth and reckless as Trump becomes president by running against the nation's elites, it's a strong signal the elites are the problem."[12] Why pin the blame for Trump on the ordinary citizen? Many of them might reasonably say, "My real income has not increased in forty years through Democratic and Republican administrations and my children face bleak futures, but you ignore our plight and your policies contribute to the demise of our communities. You fight political wars over social and cultural issues that only slivers of the population care about while ignoring the things that affect the daily lives of tens of millions of us. Meanwhile, Republican and Democratic administrations have spent trillions of dollars and destroyed thousands of our soldiers' lives in the longest wars in American history, which you seem to have no idea about how to end and may even intend to extend. What have you experts done for us lately?"

I struggle with how to respond to grievances and questions like these. As discussed in chapter 9, the socioeconomic transformations occurring in the United States and around the world have created problems that call into question old solutions and cut across political coalitions. One might naively think that, in response, a healthy party system would show more creativity, but the parties have not become more creative. The Republicans attempt to hold together an electoral coalition going on four decades old that seems increasingly outdated, while the Democrats can think of little more than identity

---

11. Especially since the Trump administration does not seem to consider staffing the bureaucracy a priority.

12. Robert W. Merry, "Removing Trump Won't Solve America's Crisis," *American Conservative*, May 18, 2017, accessed July 5, 2017, www.theamericanconservative .com/articles/removing-trump-wont-solve-americas-crisis.

politics and demographic change to raise them out of minority status. Small wonder that 40 percent of the American citizenry declines to pledge allegiance to either party.

Can the Status Quo be Destroyed?

In chapter 4, I commented that Trump might play a positive role as a de-sorter, someone with the potential to disrupt the sorted parties that underlie much of our current political discontent and possibly even begin the construction of a new electoral coalition.[13] By taking positions on trade, entitlements, and foreign policy that violate Republican orthodoxy, Trump might drive a wedge between Republican factions. By supporting a big infrastructure program he might drive a wedge between the gentry liberals and the blue-collar factions of the Democrats. Such possibilities seem less likely now given the multiple missteps of the new administration. Thus far Trump arguably has managed to disrupt his own party more than the Democrats, although some of them seem intent on doing it to themselves.[14]

A number of political scientists have proposed an alternative—that Trump is a "disjunctive" president, like Jimmy Carter, the last

13. More recently, see Peggy Noonan, "Trump Tries to Build a 'Different Party,'" *Wall Street Journal*, January 26, 2017, accessed July 5, 2017, https://www.wsj.com /articles/trump-tries-to-build-a-different-party-1485478386.

14. Laura Bassett, "Democratic Party Draws a Line in the Sand on Abortion Rights," *Huffington Post*, April 21, 2017, accessed July 5, 2017, www.huffingtonpost .com/entry/democrats-tom-perez-abortion-rights_us_58fa5fade4b018a9ce5b351d: "Democratic National Committee chairman Tom Perez became the first head of the party to demand ideological purity on abortion rights, promising Friday to support only Democratic candidates who back a woman's right to choose. 'Every Democrat, like every American, should support a woman's right to make her own choices about her body and her health,' Perez said in a statement. 'That is not negotiable and should not change city by city or state by state.'" Also, Clare Foran, "West Virginia's Conservative Democrat Gets a Primary Challenger," *The Atlantic*, May 9, 2017, accessed July 5, 2017, https://www.theatlantic.com/politics/archive/2017/05 /joe-manchin-bernie-sanders-primary-challenge-west-virginia-senate-2018/525918. And Karen Tumulty, "Pelosi: Democratic Candidates Should Not Be Forced to Toe Party Line on Abortion," *Washington Post*, May 2, 2017, accessed July 5, 2017, https://www.washingtonpost.com/politics/pelosi-democratic-candidates-should-not -be-forced-to-toe-party-line-on-abortion/2017/05/02/9cbc9bc6-2f68-11e7-9534 -00e4656c22aa_story.html?utm_term=.7f7c82fab93f.

gasp of a dying political order, whose presidency signals "the end of
the Reagan Era."[15] These arguments build on Stephen Skowronek's
classic work, *The Politics Presidents Make*.[16] For Skowronek, presidential performance is not simply a matter of the president's capaci-
ties and the challenges he faces. Rather, the challenges themselves
depend partly on where the administration falls in "political time."
Andrew Jackson, Abraham Lincoln, Franklin Roosevelt, and Ronald
Reagan were "reconstructive" presidents:

> Presidents stand preeminent in American politics when govern-
> ment has been most thoroughly discredited, and when political
> resistance to the presidency is weakest, presidents tend to remake
> the government wholesale.... By shattering the politics of the past,
> orchestrating the establishment of a new coalition, and enshrining
> their commitments as the restoration of original values, they have
> reset the very terms and conditions of constitutional government
> and politics.[17]

Franklin Pierce, James Buchanan, Herbert Hoover, and Jimmy
Carter presided over the demise of the old orders. They were disjunctive presidents "often singled out as political incompetents," but
such presidents are in an impossible situation:

> To affirm established commitments is to stigmatize oneself as a
> symptom of the nation's problems and the premier symbol of sys-
> temic political failure; to repudiate them is to become isolated from
> one's most natural political allies and to be rendered impotent.[18]

15. Corey Robin, "The Politics Trump Makes," *nplusone*, January 11, 2017,
accessed July 5, 2017, https://nplusonemag.com/online-only/online-only/the-politics
-trump-makes; Julia Azari, "Trump's Presidency Signals the End of the Reagan Era,"
Vox, December 1, 2016, accessed July 5, 2017, https://www.vox.com/mischiefs-of
-faction/2016/12/1/13794680/trump-presidency-reagan-era-end.

16. Stephen Skowronek, *The Politics Presidents Make: Leadership from John
Adams to Bill Clinton* (Cambridge, MA: Harvard University Press, 1993).

17. Ibid., 37, 38.

18. Ibid., 39.

To be sure, this characterization seems to apply more to Hillary Clinton or a typical Republican candidate like Jeb Bush, had he been elected, than to Trump, some of whose characteristics seem more like those of a reconstructive president than a disjunctive one. For example, "These [reconstructrive] presidents set out to retrieve from a far distant, even mythic, past fundamental values that they claimed had been lost in the indulgences of the received order."[19] Sounds like Trump, but in its emphasis on tax cuts and deregulation some principal thrusts of the Trump agenda trace back to the regime constructed by Ronald Reagan in the 1980s. Here as elsewhere, Trump is difficult to pigeonhole.

Looking Ahead to 2018

This book began with a discussion of the tenuous majorities that contend for institutional control of the presidency, Senate, and House of Representatives. The next opportunity for a change in control comes in the 2018 midterm elections. (Even in the unlikely event that the various ongoing investigations turn up conclusive evidence of high crimes and misdemeanors, the presidency would remain under Republican control in the person of Vice President Mike Pence.)

Today Republicans control the Senate fifty-two to forty-eight, so Democrats need a net gain of only three seats to take control. They face an uphill battle, however. Counting independents Bernie Sanders of Vermont and Angus King of Maine, who caucus with the Democrats, the party is defending twenty-five of the thirty-four seats that will be decided. Ten of the twenty-five seats are in states carried by Trump in 2016. Only one Republican will be running in a state carried by Clinton. The Democrats will be challenged to mount an aggressive offense when they have to play defense in so many states.

The House is another story. Democrats need a net gain of twenty-four seats to win control. Given that the Republicans lost thirty seats in the 2006 midterms and the Democrats sixty-three in the 2010

19. Ibid., 37.

midterms, this does not seem like too daunting a task, especially since Republicans represent twenty-three districts that Clinton won and Democrats hold only twelve seats in districts that Trump won. Chapter 5 argues that the inability to maintain institutional control is partly due to overreach—attempting to legislate the priorities and positions of the party base which alienate the marginal voters who supported the party in the preceding election. In that chapter, I noted that the fact that Trump was not a normal Republican might constrain the Republican congressional majorities. For example, one suspects that the fate of Obamacare repeal would have been different had a more garden-variety Republican president not demanded that some of its more popular provisions be retained. Ironically, even failure to accomplish much at all might result in smaller electoral losses than legislative accomplishments widely perceived as overreach. Doing nothing might be less electorally harmful than doing the wrong thing, especially if Republicans can shift some of the blame to the implacable opposition of Democrats and their allies in the media.

The quip that "a week in politics is a long time" often is attributed to former British prime minister Harold Wilson. Whoever said it first, the comment remains apt. The 2018 elections lie nearly eighteen months beyond when this chapter goes to press, so predictions are impossible. The ongoing Washington investigations may turn up evidence that seriously damages the Trump presidency. More likely is that the disarray in the Trump administration will prevent it from doing much beyond what has been accomplished by executive orders thus far. The only thing that seems reasonably clear is that in this era of nationalized elections (chapter 7) the fate of the Republican House majority hinges on the performance of the Trump administration. The major qualification to that statement is the assumption that the Democrats do not actively sabotage their chances. The progressive base is aroused. On the one hand, that is good; it promises resources and high turnout. But the base is a minority faction. To the extent that progressive activists impose litmus tests and push Democratic candidates into issue positions unsalable in their districts,[20] or even

20. Bassett. "Democratic Party Draws a Line in the Sand on Abortion Rights."

run primary opponents against incumbents they see as insufficiently progressive,[21] they undermine the party's chances of winning the kinds of districts they need to achieve majority status. Whether the more pragmatic professionals in the party can harness the energies of the base remains to be seen.[22]

For now, at least, an era of unstable majorities continues.

21. Foran, "West Virginia's Conservative Democrat Gets a Primary Challenger."

22. Tumulty, "Pelosi: Democratic Candidates Should Not Be Forced to Toe Party Line on Abortion."

About the Author

Morris Fiorina is the Wendt Family Professor of Political Science at Stanford University and a senior fellow at the Hoover Institution. He received his undergraduate degree from Allegheny College and his PhD from the University of Rochester; he taught at Caltech and Harvard before coming to Stanford in 1998. Fiorina has published numerous articles and written or edited twelve books, including *Congress--Keystone of the Washington Establishment; Retrospective Voting in American National Elections;* Divided *Government; Culture War? The Myth of a Polarized America* (with Samuel Abrams and Jeremy Pope); and *Disconnect: The Breakdown of Representation in American Politics* (with Samuel Abrams). Fiorina has served on the editorial boards of a dozen journals in political science, political economy, law, and public policy; from 1986 to 1990 served as chairman of the Board of the American National Election Studies. He is an elected member of the American Academy of Arts and Sciences, the American Academy of Political and Social Sciences, and the National Academy of Sciences. In 2006 the Elections, Public Opinion and Voting Behavior Section of the American Political Science Association awarded him the Warren E. Miller Prize for career contributions to the field.

Index